TAPPING THE
SMALL-BUSINESS MARKET

TAPPING THE
SMALL-BUSINESS MARKET

Stuart R. Veale

New York Institute of Finance

Library of Congress Cataloging-in-Publication Data

Veale, Stuart R.
    Tapping the small-business market

    Includes index
    1. Small business—Finance.   2. Brokers.   I. Title.
HG4027.7.V4   1987   332.6'068'8   87-7732
ISBN 0–13–884420–8

This publication is designed to provide accurate and authoritative information in regard to the subject matter covered. It is sold with the understanding that the publisher is not engaged in rendering legal, accounting, or other professional service. If legal advice or other expert assistance is required, the services of a competent professional person should be sought.

From a Declaration of Principles Jointly Adopted by
a Committee of the American Bar Association and a Committee of Publishers and
Associations

New York Institute of Finance
(NYIF Corp.)
70 Pine Street
New York, New York 10270-0003

This book is dedicated to the many financial professionals who have been instrumental in my career. My sincerest gratitude to one and all.

George Goldthorp
W.H. Newbold's & Son Inc.

Robert Byrne
W.H. Newbold's & Son Inc.

Charles Woodworth
Professional Brokerage Services, Inc.

John Maucere
Formerly with Drexel Burnham Lambert, Inc.

Phil Muhlick
Raymond James & Associates, Inc.

Ken Zeisenheim
Raymond James & Associates, Inc.

Steve Putnam
Robert Thomas Securities

Robert Bruce Harris
Robert Thomas Securities

Contents

Chapter 5
Retirement Planning, 65

Chapter 6
Funding Pension Plans, 95

Chapter 7
Nonqualified Deferred Compensation, 111

Preface

Unquestionably, the most difficult part of preparing a book with this title is not what to include, but what to leave out. The range of topics that could be covered is almost limitless in both scope and depth.

This text is therefore a combination of "technical reference" and "marketing guide." Both technical and marketing information is included because, for the broker or financial planner trying to tap the small-business market, having one without the other is of very limited usefulness.

While the book provides a solid background for the practicing broker or planner seeking to work in the small-business marketplace, the educational process required to work in this market is a never ending one. Tax laws, marketing opportunities, and investment products and strategies are all changing constantly, and it is up to the broker or planner to stay current.

Finally, I would like very much to hear your suggestions and comments regarding this text. I will endeavor to include as many of them as possible in subsequent editions. You can write to me at the following address:

Stuart R. Veale
P.O. Box 706
Hoboken, NJ 07030

Acknowledgments

Unless you have written a book, it's very difficult to appreciate the importance of having help and assistance. A book like this is not authored by the lonely writer slaving in the dark over a typewriter. The fact is that putting such a book together requires the input of a number of experts in various areas of expertise. This is especially true in light of our ever changing tax laws.

I would therefore like to thank the following individuals for generously contributing their time and expertise in reviewing sections of this text and making many valuable contributions and corrections:

- Mr. *Ken Zeisenheim* (St. Petersburg, Florida) of Raymond James & Associates for reviewing the chapter on Pension Plan Design.
- Mr. *Winn Kent* of Actuarial Services (Union, New Jersey) for providing me with the actuarial calculations used in the illustration section.
- Mr. *William Knox* of Herold, Haines, Knox, & McGowen (Liberty Corner, New Jersey) for reviewing the chapter on employee stock purchase plans.
- Finally, the *Publisher* for providing me with support, advice, and constant encouragement.

Despite the tremendous amount of assistance that I've received, this text no doubt still contains some factual errors as well as some errors of omission. The responsibility for these errors is mine and mine alone.

TAPPING THE
SMALL-BUSINESS MARKET

Chapter 1

Why Target The Small Business?

If you as a retail broker sat down and made a list of the type of clients you would like to have, you would probably select those with the following characteristics:

- A high net worth.
- A need for a wide variety of financial services.
- A certain amount of aggressiveness.
- Financial sophistication.
- An excellent source of referrals.
- An appreciation of the value of quality service.
- The ability to make quick decisions.
- The ability to derive real benefits and added value from your services.

These characteristics are the same ones that are often found in the successful owners of small to midsize businesses.

High Net Worth

Finding clients who have a high net worth is important because a high net worth usually indicates that surplus funds are available for investments. When you are looking for good clients, it really doesn't matter how much money they earn but how much money they have. A person who earns

$30,000 a year and spends $25,000 is a better client than a person who earns $200,000 and spends $199,000. Successful business owners have high net worths primarily because they have the equity value of their businesses on their personal balance sheets. The equity value of even a small business can easily reach the high six-figure to low seven-figure range. (More on valuing a small business in Chapter 3). Owning this equity gives a business owner much greater borrowing power and buying power than is possessed by a senior executive of a Fortune 500 company who draws the same salary. This is one reason why "business owners" make better prospects and clients than "employees."

Very few people ever become wealthy by working for someone else. Your chances of encountering wealthy people increase dramatically when you concentrate on marketing your services to business owners. Even if you do land an account with a senior executive at a Fortune 500 company, much of that person's net worth is often tied up in company pension plans and savings plans, resulting in the client's having less money available to invest with you. Business owners, on the other hand, generally have access to all their assets, which makes them more desirable clients.

Need For Variety of Services

A small company needs all the financial services that a large company needs, but on a different scale. When you are prospecting the owner of a small business, you are really prospecting three potential accounts: the owner's individual account, the company's account, and the company's pension plan account. All these accounts can be substantial. If you prospect executives who are employees, the most you can usually hope for is to capture their personal business. Table 1-1 illustrates just some of the many financial services that small business owners may need and that many brokerage firms have the resources to offer.

Table 1-1. Financial Services Needed by Small Businesses.

I. PENSION SERVICES
PLAN DESIGN
PLAN ADMINISTRATION
ASSET MANAGEMENT
BROKERAGE SERVICES
EVALUATION OF INVESTMENT PERFORMANCE

II. COMPANY SERVICES
CORPORATE FINANCE

Venture Capital

Private Placements

Equity

Debt

Public Offerings

 Equity

 Debt

Mortgage Lending

Equipment Leasing

Receivable Financing

Consulting Services

CASH MANAGEMENT

Accelerate Receivables

Invest Surpluses

Control Disbursements

Provide Record Keeping

Install Controls

EMPLOYEE BENEFITS

Group Life Insurance

Group Health Insurance

Designing, Installing, Managing, and Administering Employee Savings Plan

Designing, Installing, Managing, and Administering an Employee Stock Purchase Plan

Group Medical Insurance

Group Disability Insurance

CORPORATE TAX PLANNING

RISK MANAGEMENT

Consulting Services

Key Man Insurance

Buy-Back/Buy-Sell Agreements

Property and Casualty Insurance

Liability Insurance

III. PERSONAL INVESTMENT NEEDS
PERSONAL BUDGETING
PERSONAL INVESTMENTS
PERSONAL TAX PLANNING
PERSONAL ESTATE PLANNING
PERSONAL RETIREMENT PLANNING
PERSONAL INSURANCE PLANNING

When you compare the wide range of services you can offer a small business owner relative to the range of services you can offer an employee, another advantage of targeting business owners in your marketing campaign becomes obvious.

Aggressiveness

People who go into business for themselves are, by definition risk takers. The odds against a small business being successful are very high; yet small business owners elect to take the risk. They clearly understand the concept of risk versus reward. They are used to spending money to make money. They understand the businessman's risk that's inherent in every investment. They generally don't have heart attacks if an investment goes sour *provided that the risks of the investment were clearly explained to them before they invested.*

Financial Sophistication

Running even the smallest business successfully requires a certain amount of financial acumen. Many business owners deal with sophisticated financial products and concepts every day in the financing and managing of their own businesses. They are used to writing large checks. They are used to analyzing various financial alternatives. They generally understand how to use leverage, how to compute an internal rate of return, and how to use accelerated depreciation to delay taxes. Any broker who has ever spent an hour trying to get an unsophisticated retail client to understand the concept of *yield to call* will appreciate dealing with clients who possess more financial acumen. Dealing with business owners allows you to spend less time teaching and more time selling.

Source of Referrals

Small business owners know and do business with other small business owners. Small business owners deal with wholesalers, distributors, other service companies, printers and so on. Many of these other companies are also ideal prospects for your services. If you do a good job for one business owner, then getting quality referrals is often part of your reward. In addition, you will often have to work with your client's accountant and attorney. Assuming you work with these people in a professional manner, you may also be able to obtain additional referrals from your clients' other advisors. (More on dealing with spheres of influence in Chapter 2.)

Values Quality Service

Small business owners are busy people; they often work 70 to 80 hours a week. Because they have limited staffs, they often must wear many hats. A small business owner is often his own personnel manager, purchasing manager, plant manager, and sales manager. Because small business owners are so busy, many of them truly appreciate (and are willing to pay top dollar for) top quality service when they can find it.

Makes Decisions Quickly

If you have properly identified your clients' true needs, have developed a realistic and logical plan to meet those needs, and have presented your proposal properly, most business owners will give you a quick decision. Small business owners need to make hundreds of decisions a week and thus they rarely suffer from "analysis paralysis."

Because business owners are so busy, in most cases if they weren't truly interested in your services, they wouldn't take time out of their busy day to talk with you. Therefore, when a business owner asks for information about one of your products or asks you to prepare a proposal, the chances are that the owner is seriously interested and thus you will probably not be "spinning your wheels." Less busy retail prospects have all day to talk and listen to your ideas and proposals, but they often lack either the ability or the willingness to commit money to them.

Real Benefits and Added Value

Most registered representatives would like to be of real value to their clients not only because of the financial rewards but also because of the sense of personal satisfaction that comes from helping clients solve their financial problems. It is hard to provide much added value for a retiree who is looking for a government bond fund. The fund you recommend is probably not much better or worse than the one the firm down the street may recommend, which is in turn not much different from the no-load fund advertised in your client's daily newspaper.

In the corporate market, however, you can make a real difference in the quality of life that your clients enjoy. Consider just how valuable your services really are if you are able to restructure a client's retirement plan so that he can set aside an extra $10,000 a year for 10 years. Assuming the client is in the 33% tax bracket, you will have succeeded in deferring $33,000 in taxes until a later date. (In effect, you will have arranged a no-interest loan from Uncle Sam.) In addition, the interest earned over this 10-year period may easily total another $87,559 (assuming an average 10% return), again completely tax deferred.

Or consider the economic ramifications of designing a deferred compensation plan that allows a client to retain for another five years a key sales rep who has been considering retirement. If over those five years that sales rep increases the company's annual sales volume by $5 million and the company is eventually sold for one times sales, your plan will have grossed your client an additional five "big ones." Compared to being able to provide help on a scale like this, just how important is getting a retail client an extra 1% per year on a $2,000 IRA account?

In the small business market, you can start each day knowing that you can be of tremendous service to both your clients and prospective clients. This knowledge in turn makes working with business owners much more interesting and satisfying than either straight retail or institutional business. Those brokers who seek rewards from their profession beyond the ample financial rewards will find this market to be attractive.

| Chapter 2 | *Prospecting* |
| | *The Small-Business Market* |

Prospecting, as defined in this book, is the art of getting people to provide you with detailed information about their financial needs and objectives so that you can determine how you can be of service and how you can convert them into accounts. Prospecting the corporate market is unquestionably more difficult than prospecting for straight retail business because business owners are generally busier people and are thus difficult to reach. It is very common for business owners to have literally hundreds of bankers, brokers, insurance people, office supplies salespeople, trade people, and the like calling on them.

The fact that business owners are so unreachable has both positive and negative implications for a broker concentrating on this market. Although you will have to expend more effort and creativity in order to reach this market, once you have converted a business owner into an account it becomes even more difficult for the next broker to reach him and try to take the account away (assuming you don't give your client a reason to look for better service).

Prospecting methods can be divided into two categories: traditional and creative. The traditional approaches are those that every broker has used at one time or another: cold calling, direct mail, and seminars. Traditional approaches like these will work only if they are executed both correctly and consistently. Small business owners have received thousands of cold calls, thousands of direct mail pieces, and countless invitations to seminars. For yours to be noticed, they will really have to be something special. If you're going to try the traditional approaches, then you will have to do everything possible to stack the deck in your favor.

Step one in stacking the deck is finding the right list of people to prospect. You primarily want to call on owners of businesses that have been in existence for three years or longer. The reason for this is that most businesses that are going to fail do so in the first three years. Even those businesses that will eventually be successful generally have limited capital for the first three years and thus offer limited opportunity to any broker not specializing in arranging venture capital financing.

The easiest way to build this type of list is to go down to your local city or county clerk's office and copy the names and addresses of business owners from their tax records or occupational licenses. If you have an established book of business, it's often more cost effective to hire someone to do this clerical task for you. Doing this yourself or hiring someone to do it for you is not only cheaper than using a service (e.g., Dun & Bradstreet, Webb, Dunhill) but often results in a better quality list. Try to stay with local companies because a personal visit is often required to land a corporate account. Once you have your list (say, 5,000 companies), you're ready to make your initial contacts.

Traditional Approaches

Cold Calling

Successful cold callers fall into one of two categories: the never-say-die bunch and the cherry pickers. A never-say-die broker will start with an initial list of 5,000 names and will commit to turning each and every one of them into an account. Such a broker will make call upon call and send information after information to a prospect in order to try to land the account. A never-say-die broker will spend large blocks of time with a prospect explaining the intricacies of various investment options, probing endlessly for that opening that will allow him to make a sale.

When a prospect tells a never-say-die broker that he's not interested, the broker will simply put the prospect's name on a list and call again three to six months later. Because most sales are made after the fifth or sixth call, these brokers feel that if they just stay with a prospect long enough they will eventually get the account. These brokers know that sooner or later most of these 5,000 people are going to need or want a new broker, and they want to be first in line when that time comes. The only way to stop one of these brokers from calling on you is to die.

At the other end of the spectrum are the cherry pickers. Successful brokers who use this method call a 100 or so prospects per day with a specific product. If the prospect happens to be interested in that specific product on that specific day, then that prospect becomes a "lead" and the broker mails him the information on the product of the day. If the prospect is not interested in that particular product on that particular day, then the broker races the client to see who can hang up the phone first. Each call takes, on average, about a minute. Because of the sheer number of people who are exposed to the given product by brokers using this method, the law of averages tells us that the brokers will usually find some people who are interested. Two leads generated per hour is about average.

Many retail brokers make a mistake in that they don't execute either system properly. Rather than doggedly pursuing a client through six or seven phone calls, they get disgusted after the third call. Or because they're spending a lot of time on each call, they don't make anywhere near the plus-100 calls a day required to be a successful cherry picker.

Although either method will work with straight retail prospecting, the method of choice for the small business market is the never-say-die approach. Small business owners generally admire persistence. Also, because they are hard to reach, it is doubtful if you can make enough contacts in a day using the cherry picker approach to generate a sufficient number of leads to justify your time and effort. In addition, the needs of business owners are so diverse that a product-oriented approach will probably not be very effective (more about this later).

If you're going to make the initial calls yourself, then by all means, call between 7:30 A.M. and 9:00 A.M., 12:00 P.M. and 1:00 P.M., and 5:00 P.M. and 6:30 P.M. These are the best times to reach business owners. Saturday morning between 9:00 A.M. and 12:00 P.M. is also an excellent time to prospect business owners. It is during these times that you will have the best chance of catching him when he's available to speak with you. During the rest of the day, he will probably be tied up running his business. Besides, owners often respect people who work as hard as they work. Finally, at these hours you're not likely to run into secretaries, assistants, or other "screeners" who can put you off. Cold calling business owners during normal business hours is such a low-percentage game that your time can almost always be better spent doing something else that may prove to be productive.

Remember to use anything you can to add leverage to your cold calling. You've heard the slogan, "Anything's better when it sits on a Ritz." Well, any offer of financial services appears to be more appealing when it comes from a third party.

For example, find out who the presidents of your local builders association, medical association, dental association, manufacturers trade group, contractors trade group, and so on are and arrange a meeting, preferably for breakfast or lunch. At the meeting, explain that your firm is offering a special service such as a pension review, insurance review, tax consultation, or the like. Use whatever area you consider to be your strongest. Explain that you usually charge $500 for this service but that if the association is willing to assist you in your efforts by providing you with a membership roster and by cosponsoring your marketing effort, you will not only reduce your usual fee by 50% for association members but will also split your fee 50—50 with the association.

The membership of the association benefits by having the option to obtain a valuable service form you at half the usual cost. You benefit by obtaining leverage and a current membership roster. The association benefits by collecting half your fee and by arranging for its members to receive a price break on your services.

Be prepared to supply the association management with a list of references (preferably including some members of the organization itself) and a sample report or analysis of the service you plan to provide. Always stress that you will not be doing any type of hard sell on the membership but will simply and professionally offer your services.

Although it may take quite a bit of time to convince an organization's management to act as a co-sponsor, the "leverage" that this will provide to your marketing effort more than makes the time investment worthwhile.

Another kind of cold call that is very effective is the cold call you make in person. Drive up to an industrial park or business zone at 7:30 A.M. and simply go door to door. If you do get to see the owner of a business, then simply introduce yourself and your firm. Let him know that you will be in the area and are ready to assist him with all his investment and financial planning needs. Ask him if he would like to be put on your mailing list. As you're leaving, simply ask if there is any current problem about which he would like to receive some additional information. With a little probing you should be able to find something on which to follow up. If the owner can't see you (or won't see you), then leave some literature and a brief handwritten note that says, "Sorry I missed you! Please review the enclosed, and I'll call you shortly."

Done properly, this approach should allow you to speak briefly with 10 owners a day and to collect valuable information such as the best time to call, the secretary's name, whether or not the company has a pension plan, and so forth on about another 20 business owners. Always try to obtain a cross-referenced directory or an industrial directory for an area before you visit it so that you can ask to see the owners by name and can note any new businesses or other changes as you go.

If you don't want to donate a whole day to this approach, then simply drop in on one business every day, either on your way to work or on your way home.

Mailing

Direct mail is a *very expensive* way to prospect. Although it might pay *you* to do mailings, it often costs your firm more than it's worth. Busy people generally don't respond to junk mail. People with time to waste often respond to every piece of mail they receive. They request the information and then string you along for four or five calls before they simply stop taking your calls.

If a mailing is going to be successful, it should be directed to a very specific audience and reference a timely event. For example, TEFRA (The Tax Equity and Fiscal Responsibility Act) reduced the maximum pension benefits of many highly compensated business owners. A letter such as the one shown in Figure 2-1 sent to the presidents of service companies immediately after TEFRA was passed would probably have a much higher response rate than another run-of-the-mill mailing on a new mutual fund. (Service companies are often in high tax brackets because they cannot use many of the deductions available to industrial companies. This means that deductions for qualified pension contributions are very important to owners of service companies).

Figure 2-1. A Sample Prospecting Letter.

Mr. Jim Jones
ABC Inc.
Anystreet
Anytown, USA 00000

Any date

Dear Mr. Jones:

    You may already be aware that Congress has recently passed its latest revision of the tax code. This new act, called TEFRA (The Tax Equity and Fiscal Responsibility Act) has several important provisions that may directly affect you. If you currently have, or are considering establishing, a qualified retirement plan, then you may be adversely affected by the bill's provisions to limit maximum benefits and to accelerate vesting for employees.
    My firm has just finished preparing a report on how TEFRA will impact qualified retirement plans. If you would like to receive a free copy of it, simply complete and return the enclosed form and return this letter in the envelope provided.
    Let me assure you that both my firm and I stand ready to assist you with all your investment and financial planning needs.

Sincerely,

Stuart R. Veale
Registered Investment Advisor

Prospecting letters should be sent either in envelopes *without* return addresses or with the return address of a third party. Mail bearing a brokerage firm's return address is often trashed before it is even opened. Always personalize each letter. You can quickly and easily put your prospect list on a floppy disk and then merge that list with any letter you wish to send, thereby producing several hundred personalized letters. Athough a ''Dear Reader'' or ''Dear Investor'' letter may work with the general public, business owners expect and deserve a little better treatment.

Always enclose a business card with your mailing. You never can tell who might keep it and call you in the future. Any piece of mail that's not worth following up with a phone call is not worth mailing in the first place. The only reason to mail is to find out who on your list is the most interested in the product or service offered (they will be the ones who return the enclosed form). Always follow up on a mailing promptly, and call everyone to whom you sent a letter. Therefore, mailing more than 200 to 250 pieces at a time is a waste of time and money.

Whenever possible, enclose a glossy brochure that detail the scope of your services or your firm's services. It adds a professional touch and yet costs very little.

Seminars

Seminars can either be very successful or a complete waste of time. The difference is planning, planning, and more planning. The planning starts with the choice of topics and the selection of people to invite. Just as with a mailing, you should have a timely topic and an audience that has a very real bottom-line interest in that topic. Use quality invitations and require RSVPs. Never call it a seminar (sounds too dull); instead call it a "Business Briefing." Mail the invitations three weeks before the scheduled seminar date, and always include a postage-paid response card. As you receive the responses, have your office call each respondent immediately to let them know that you have reserved a seat for them.

This is also an excellent time to ask the respondents if they know of anyone else (partner, friend, accountant) who would also be interested in attending. Then have your office call again two days before the seminar to make sure the respondents know how to get to the meeting's location. In all probability, they already know how to get there. The call is just a way to provide a gentle reminder.

Hold the seminar at the most exclusive and convenient location you can find. The best time to hold a seminar for business owners is in the morning. Once they get to their companies, there is a very real chance that something will come up that will prevent them from attending. When deciding on the menu, always go top drawer; remember, you want this event to be something special. A choice of steak and eggs or eggs Benedict will be appreciated, remembered, and talked about long after two runny scrambled eggs and cold toast are forgotten. The additional cost is usually only about $5 to $6 per person. For 20 attendees, that's only another $100 to $120, or the commission on a one-thousand share trade.

The meeting should start promptly at 7:30 A.M. and end no later than 9:00 A.M. Serving a multicourse breakfast helps keep the attendees from getting antsy. Cover only one topic per meeting, and always give each attendee a folder of reference material to take with him at the end of the seminar. Whenever possible, host the seminar in conjunction with a law firm and/or accounting firm (the more prestigious, the better). If the topic is such that the law firm or accounting firm can expect to pick up some clients as a result of participating, don't hesitate to insist on their picking up half of the cost.

It is also a good idea to charge the attendees a modest fee for attending. A modest charge of say $25 (tax deductible) will not stop anyone who's truly interested from attending, it will, however; deter the dead wood. As with a mailing, immediate follow-up is important. Calling the attendees that *same afternoon* is often the best time to get positive feedback and set appointments.

Creative Approaches

So far we have examined the traditional approaches to prospecting. Now let's examine some of the more creative ways to market financial services to small business owners.

Writing

If you have any talent for the written word, then instead of watching M*A*S*H reruns or catching Carson's monologue, use this time to write some articles about current investment and other financial topics that are of interest to business owners. Local business papers, trade papers, association newsletters, and so on all have a large appetite for quality copy. Consider how much more impact your cold call to a member of a trade group or association would be if you had just published an article on the same topic in the prospect's trade paper or trade newsletter.

Once your articles are published, you can make reprints for future use, which will give you instant credibility. For some reason, people still have a lot more stock in what they read then in what they hear. Even a letter to the editor that takes a pro-business stance on a local topic (zoning or taxation, for instance) can generate you a lot of free publicity and improve your image and reputation.

Chamber of Commerce

Joining your local chamber of commerce may be worthwhile, but it's a good idea to go to a few meetings before you join to see just how active your local chamber is. Some chambers offer excellent ways to meet small business owners through special small business councils, business round-tables, after-hours social gatherings, and financial seminars for the membership. Others consist of three brokers, three bankers, and three insurance agents standing around staring at each other. Given the latter situation, unless you have an insatiable sense of civic responsibility, you would probably be better off spending your time in more productive pursuits.

Joining Local Trade Associations

Another prospecting avenue to consider is joining as many local trade associations as your time and financial resources will allow. Say, for example, you join your local plumbers' association. In exchange for your dues (which are usually just a few hundred dollars), you get the opportunity to prospect by attending the meetings, perhaps making short presentations, and attending the social functions.

After the members get to know you, you can expect to be cornered by one member after another trying to pick your brain for ideas and advice. When this happens, answer the simple questions and *set appointments* for the more difficult ones. After attending four or five monthly meetings, you should know most of the people in the organization. Joining various trade associations is also an excellent way to develop rapport with the officers of the association—which, in turn, should make it easier to get the associations to co-sponsor your marketing efforts.

Teaching

One of the best ways to market yourself and your services is to teach courses and seminars directed to the small business owner market. There are many possible forums for this marketing approach. Almost every area of the country has a college or university that offers night school courses that are strictly informational (i.e., not leading to a degree). Either find a school that offers such a course or if you can't find one, then propose it to the curriculum directors of the schools in your area. Also approach high schools with established adult education programs. Trade associations often run continuing education programs for their members; contact them, too. Nonprofit organizations such as local business councils or local chambers of commerce may also sponsor such programs.

It's hard to imagine a better prospect list than a group of business owners who are sufficiently interested in learning more about a given financial topic than those who are willing to take the time to attend a seminar or course *and* are also willing to pay a tuition fee for the privilege. If you are the instructor for the seminar or course, then you are clearly the expert in their eyes and will have their undivided attention for the duration of the program. Assuming you are a reasonably competent instructor and follow up promptly and properly, your conversion ratio of prospects to accounts should be very high.

Once you become proficient, you can even start charging either the attendees and/or the sponsoring organizations for your services. Having people *pay you* to prospect them beats cold calling anytime.

Newsletters

Offering your clients and prospects a periodic newsletter composed of topics of interest to business owners is a very professional way not only to prospect for new clients but also to reinforce your relationship with your existing clients. Preparing this letter is not as difficult as it sounds. Many of the larger firms already generate newsletters geared toward the small business market. If you are a member of one of these firms, all you need do is mail the newsletters.

If your firm doesn't publish a business letter, then you will have to publish your own. There are three ways to do this. First, you can simply buy a newsletter through one of the many newsletter services. These services will personalize them by placing your name and your firm's name on the masthead. The drawback of this approach is that these letters are geared toward the retail marketplace and will do little to enhance *your* image as a corporate specialist.

The second option is simply to copy articles from other sources into your newletter (after first receiving permission from the original publication). Using this approach, you can match the copy to the audience. Although this approach does have its attractions (low cost, minimal time commitment, and so on), it still will not be a showcase for *your* ideas and expertise.

To obtain the maximum benefit from a newsletter, you must write your own, or at a minimum, write a monthly column in the compendium newsletter described earlier. Each newsletter should cover a basic investment topic, provide some timely information, and gives news of a new investment vehicle or strategy (complete with mail-back coupon for additional information). If your newsletter or column is done properly, the resulting sales should be enough to cover the time and expense involving in preparing, printing, and mailing the newsletter.

The newsletter should be mailed to everyone on your prospect and client list. To avoid the expense of mailing the newsletter to people who don't appreciate receiving it, enclose a response card with every sixth issue that the recipient must fillout and return in order to continue receiving the publication. Also, you may periodically send out a questionnaire like the one shown in Figure 2-2 to better gauge your client's interests and objectives. The information is, of course, also very valuable in deciding what product or service with which to approach a particular prospect.

Depending on how professional your newsletter is, you may be able to charge for subscriptions or trade if for soft dollars (see Chapter 2).

Trade Shows

Marketing your services at trade shows has several advantages. First, it is easy to target the right audience. Almost every group, industry, and special interest has its own trade shows and conventions. If you determine that you particularly like working with partners of architectural firms, then you can attend a convention made up entirely of officers of architectural firms. If your best prospects are corporate cash management officers, they too have their own trade shows. At any one time, there are literally hundreds of trade shows going on all over the country. The large convention centers—New York, Atlanta, Chicago, San Francisco—all have dozens of different shows each week. Space is often booked years in advance, so finding the right show to attend should not be too difficult.

The second reason this approach is successful is that you will probably be the only person there marketing financial services. All the other exhibitors will probably be showing industry-related products and services (with the exception of maybe a few banks). Any approach that can

---

Figure 2-2. A Typical Questionnaire

Dear Newsletter Reader:

A newsletter is valuable only if it provides you, its reader, with the type of information that you want and you need. In order to make sure that my newsletter covers the topics that you are most interested in, I'm asking you to complete and return the enclosed questionnaire. Your answers will be a major factor in deciding what topics will appear in future issues. Thank you for your input!

I would like to see more news items on:

_____ Ways to improve the design of my pension plan

_____ Investment strategies for pension assets

_____ Increasing the rate of return on my surplus corporate cash

_____ Strategies to minimize my personal tax burden

_____ Improving my employee benefit program

_____ Using insurance to solve business problems

_____ Alternative ways to raise working capital

_____ Tips on buying or selling a business

_____ Attractive personal investments

Name: _____

Address: _____

_____

Return to:

Stuart R. Veale
P.O. Box 706
Hoboken, N J 07030

---

put you in the middle of a huge room filled with prospects *without* any competition being present has to be considered attractive.

The third reason trade show marketing works is that it can be very cost effective, assuming you properly design and execute a sensible marketing plan. Any trade show prospecting or marketing effort should be divided into three phases: preshow, during show, and after show.

The preshow phase consists of sending a brief note to each of the people expected to attend, timing the mailing of the note to reach them about three days before the show begins. Lists of the attendees are generally supplied by the sponsoring organization to the companies and individuals who rent exhibit space. The note should simply pique the recipient's curiosity by appealing to either one of man's basic motivators: fear or greed. For example, if you were going to rent exhibit space at a plumber's convention and wanted to attract attention, you might send a note that said simply: "Considering purchasing some new equipment? Let me show you how you can have Uncle Sam pick up *all the cost*. See me at booth 86. Free gift." When the attendees show up at your booth, you of course explain how a tax shelter will generate enough in tax savings to cover the cost of the equipment they desire to purchase. As a free gift, prepare a chart that shows how much of the shelter they must purchase in order to save X number of dollars off this year's tax bill and next year's tax bill.

Planning is also important on the convention floor. Always look your best. Even if it's an open-air affair (a boat show, for example), wear your best suit. Try to rent space close to the center of the convention hall or arena. The closer you are to center, the more times the same people will have to pass by your booth. Even if they don't stop by on their first pass, they may on their second, fifth, or tenth.

If you don't have a portable exhibit, you can easily rent one. Check with the convention organizers for the names of exhibit vendors. Remember, you want a lot of impact. A trade show floor is no place for a reserved approach.

Another technique that works on the trade show floor is having a drawing for a free gift. U.S. government zero coupon bonds work especially well. Who wouldn't stop and drop his or her business card into a fishbowl for the chance of winning a bond with a $1,000 face value. Of course, the bond costs you only a few hundred dollars because you select one that matures well after the second millenium.

When attendees pass by your exhibit, shake hands and ask them how they like the show. Follow that by asking a few blunt probing questions to give you an idea whether they might be a good prospect for your services. Direct their attention to the free drawing, and note the answers to your questions on the back of their business cards as you drop them into the bowl. Then, as quickly as you can without being rude, start talking to someone else. With a little practice, you should be able to approach 15 to 20 people per hour.

Remember that you're not trying to sell on the convention floor. Instead, you should be trying to eliminate people who are not interested in your product (so that you don't waste time later during the follow-up phase) and finding people who are interested so that you can place their names at the top of your follow-up sheets. If you do find someone who's very interested, set an appointment for later that night or for an early breakfast the next day. Do not let hundreds of prospects walk by your booth while you go through an entire sales presentation with one individual.

Because the larger trade shows attract people from all over the country (and sometimes the world), it's important to remember that you're going to be able to offer these people products and services that can be sold only over the phone. Gear your prospecting and follow-up accordingly.

The last step—follow-up—is the most important. Be prepared before the convention even begins. Have your follow-up letters already set up on a word processor so that you need only to enter the names off the cards you've collected, sign 'em and mail 'em. Make sure your calendar following the trade show is clear. If at first you can't get through to your prospect, put the lead away for a week or so, and try again. Remember: Your prospects will also be very busy immediately after the show following up on the contacts *they've* made.

It's a good idea to follow up with a trade show special of one kind or another. If, for example, you're trying to sell a newsletter, you might opt to hand out one free copy at the seminar and then send a letter offering a convention discount for new subscribers.

Assuming you properly handle all three phases of the marketing campaign, using trade shows to market financial services should be very cost effective.

Trade show marketing can be a lot of fun. Conventions are very up-tempo events. It's a pleasant change to participate in a marketing program where interacting with the prospects will raise, rather than drain, your spirits.

The one final point that should be made is that people within a given industry talk to each other far more often and far more openly than they talk to people in other industries. If you find the right group for your product or service and concentrate on providing a high level of service to that industry or group, it won't take long before you're well known and talked about within that industry or group. This is an excellent way to accelerate the flow of referrals.

Advertising

Although most advertising will be handled by your firm, there is nothing to prevent you from doing some separate advertising on your own (as long as all ads are compliance approved)! The best place to run display ads is in business journals and/or trade papers. Ads should be creative and offer a specific product such as a newsletter or a research report. You can often barter advertising space for articles you have written.

Sponsoring Vacation/Meeting Junkets

Once you're established and have a large client and prospect list, you may want to put together a weekend investment meeting at a local resort. A weekend program with seminars in the morning and golf, tennis, and swimming in the afternoon is an easy sale.

An event like this is actually quite easy to arrange. The catering manager at the resort will do almost all the work. By booking a number of rooms in advance, you can obtain substantial discounts for the attendees. All you (or more likely your assistant) will have to do is mail the invitations, collect the money, arrange for guest speakers, and have a good time.

Don't forget to invite (gratis) other speakers with whom you have worked before as a way of thanking them for speaking at your regular seminars or for sending you referrals. For your clients, the weekend provides an opportunity to get away with the spouse and the kids and yet satisfy that inner need to be productive. Part of the fees your clients pay may also be tax deductible.

Hosting meetings like this one will certainly distinguish you from the next phone jockey who tries to ram a mutual fund down your client's throat.

Brochure about Yourself

One often overlooked but very inexpensive and effective prospecting tool is to prepare a brochure about yourself. Your prospects may or may not be familiar with your firm, but it's *you* they're going to do business with. Having a brochure prepared that tells them why they should do business with you is another very professional way to distinguish yourself from your competitors. A brochure should contain a good picture, a brief biography, a general overview of your services, and a copy of your fee schedule (see Figure 2-3).

Hand these brochures out at seminars, mail them along with information to hot prospects, mail one to each new client's accountant and attorney with a letter of introduction. At about $0.40 each, you can afford to be generous with them.

Newspaper Clippings

One of the many benefits of having your clients' names in a relational data base is that you can quickly send out newspaper clippings that you think might be of interest to them. Let's assume you run across an article on a new tax proposal that affects businesses that use the accrual method of accounting. If you set up your data base properly, you should be able with just a few key strokes to generate mailing labels for all your clients (and key prospects) who use this accounting method. Sending them each a copy of the article will often pay for itself many times over in goodwill. To expedite this process, have your printer put "Thought you might find this interesting" on one of the new self-stick note pads along with your name and phone number, as illustrated in Figure 2-4. Selecting articles that favorably present new investment vehicles or strategies will often result in a number of incoming phone calls (and business). Even those that don't result in business will often pay off in future goodwill.

Prospecting the Unreachable

When you are trying to contact someone you really would like to have as an account but simply cannot get through to in order to discuss your ideas, you may have to resort to drastic measures.

Drastic measure No. 1 is to send a humorous card that may pique their curiosity. Harrison Publishing, as well as other companies,

Figure 2-3

CORPORATE CASH MANAGEMENT

The changes that have occured in the field of Corporate Cash Investing have been nothing short of revolutionary. As recently as a few short years ago, investing surplus corporate cash was a fairly simple proceedure. Many companies simply transferred their free cash balances into money market funds or into their banks short term income funds (STIFs). Even for those companies which managed their short term cash investments in house, the procedure was still relatively straight-forward.

First the investment officer would determine the net cash balance available to be invested. Second, based on the company's cash flow and cash requirements, the officer would determine the optimum average maturity and maximum maturity for the investment portfolio. Finally, the officer would evaluate the various short term investment options available in the marketplace (Certificates of Deposit Commercial Paper, T-Bills, Bankers Acceptances, etc.) and select those vehicles which offered the company the highest net yield within the company's parameters for risk tolerance. Once selected, the investment vehicles were generally held until maturity.

As long as interest rates continued to rise, as they did during much of the 1970's and early 80's, this approach was generally sufficient. As investments matured they could be reinvested, generally at higher rates. In fact, when short term interest rates peaked, many companies found themselves earning a higher rate of return on their corporate cash then they did from their ongoing business operations.

That all changed two years ago, however, as interest rates began their sharp decent. Now, in order to obtain an attractive net rate of return, investment officers need to consider vehicles and strategies which, in many cases, were not available just a few short years ago. Artificial Cash Programs, Hedging Programs, Yield Enhancement Strategies, Tax Arbitrage Rollovers, Vehicle Swaps, Adjustable Rate Preferreds, Convertible Adjustable Rate Preferreds, Money Market Preferreds, and Municipal Commercial Paper, are just a few of the investment alternatives that Cash Managers now need to consider in order to maximize the return on their company's cash.

At Independent Investment Advisory we advise investment officers on the relative advantages and disadvantages of the various new investment vehicles and strategies available in today's market. After thoroughly examining your company's cash flow, tolerance for risk, liquidity requirements, and yield objectives, we will help you to design and implement a practical cash investment program to meet your specific needs and objectives.

FINANCIAL PLANNING

Independent Investment Advisory (I.I.A.) offers financial planning services on an individual basis, and as part of company sponsored employee benefit programs. At I.I.A. we take the "problem solving approach", by offering realistic and constructive programs and strategies in the areas of:

(1) Tax Minimization and Management
(2) Retirement Planning
(3) Wealth Accumulation and Investment Management
(4) Protection from the Financial Hardships of Unexpected Illness
(5) Protection from the Financial Hardships of Disability
(6) Protection for Family Members from Premature Death
(7) Estate Planning and Trust Design
(8) Budgeting

Very often it seems, the same people who rise to the top of their chosen fields have neither the time nor the expertise to properly manage their personal affairs. By helping our clients to: set clear and obtainable goals; design a workable plan to achieve those goals; and then implement and manage that plan; we free up our clients time and energy so that they can focus on their chosen careers.

Many employers have come to realize that an employees satisfaction with a given compensation package is directly proportional to that package's ability to meet the employee's needs and objectives. By providing key employees with financial planning as part of their employee benefit package, employers can assist their employees to derive the maximum benefit from their compensation packages. This, in turn, results in greater employee satisfaction, lower turnover of key employees, and higher productivity for your company.

At I.I.A. we will sit down with each client at length and get to know them personally. We determine their needs and objectives in great detail. Starting with their current financial status, we custom design coordinated budget, insurance, investment tax, and estate programs, to meet their individual needs. Since the only constant in this world is "change", we also review the plan when necessary (at least once a year) to assess the level of progress and to make any changes or refinements that may be needed. At I.I.A. we like our clients to know they only need to have one phone number for all their investment and financial planning needs.

PENSION INVESTMENT SERVICES

Few investment areas are as important or require as much expertise, as the successful design and management of a retirement program. As a business owner or professional you have the awesome responsibility of protecting not only your own financial security, but also the financial security of your employees.

Maximizing the effectiveness of your pension program is a two step process. The first step is to select, adopt, and implement the proper type of plan structure for you and your company or practice. At I.I.A. we can recommend, after thoroughly examining your particular needs and objectives, the best plan for you, including:

(1) Non-Qualified Deferred Compensation Programs
(2) Sep-IRA Programs
(3) VEBA's
(4) Profit Sharing Plans
(5) Money Purchase Plans
(6) Target Benefit Plans
(7) Defined Benefit Plans

Very often we find that no one plan can meet all of our clients objectives. In that case we combine two or more separate plans into an overal retirement program.

The second step in managing a successful retirement program is to design, implement, and manage, a sound investment program for your retirement plan assets. Finding the proper balance between pursuing an attractive rate of return on your pension assets, while at the same time protecting those assets, is never easy.

Complicating this responsibility even further is the avalanche of lawsuits being filed and being won against plan fiduciaries by attorneys who claim that the pension assets were invested either too conservatively or too aggressively. In many of these cases the plan fiduciaries themselves are being held personally liable for damages and legal fees.

At I.I.A. we help plan fiduciaries design, implement and manage, prudent investment programs for their pension assets. We work both with companies that manage their assets in house, as well as with those companies that elect to use outside managers.

When designing an investment strategy we take into account the type of plan you have, the anticipated schedule for future cash deposits and withdrawls, the fiduciaries tolerance for risk, and any other special needs or requirements you or your company may have. We can either work with your current actuary and/or attorney, or can recommend competent and experienced professionals for your consideration.

Figure 2 3

THOUGHT YOU MIGHT BE INTERESTED IN SEEING THIS—

STU VEALE
Independent Investment Advisors
201–249–1735

Figure 2-4

specializes in producing, printing, and personalizing this type of card for brokers (see the examples given in Figure 2-5).

If you don't think your prospect will be amused by a card such as that shown in Figure 5, then consider sending a telegram. Telegrams still have tremendous impact when worded like the one shown in Figure 6. This may be all that is required to get you through to the prospect.

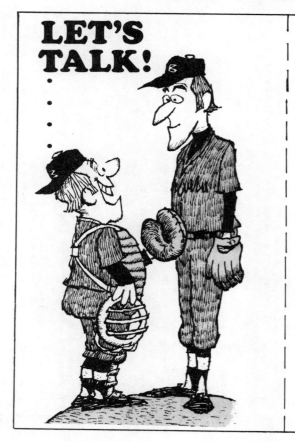

Figure 2-5

Figure 6. A Sample Telegram.

DEAR MR. JONES:

    HAVE TRIED TO REACH YOU FOR LAST MONTH WITHOUT SUCCESS.
I WANT ONLY THE OPPORTUNITY TO BE OF SERVICE TO YOU! PLEASE
CALL ME AT XXX-XXXX. MANY THANKS.

YOUR NAME

NAME OF YOUR FIRM

    Getting through to the business owner often requires getting on the good side of the owner's secretary and/or assistant. Remember that these people screen dozens of calls every day, so be as pleasant as possible. Always try to learn the secretary's first name and use it when you call.

    If the prospect is someone you especially want as a client, consider sending the secretary a small bouquet of flowers or other inexpensive gift.

    About two years ago I unsuccessfully tried to reach a busy executive in New York for more than three months with twice weekly phone calls. His secretary was very pleasant but just kept telling me that her boss simply didn't have time to speak with me. (I knew this individual was one of the busiest men in America, and so I was sure I wasn't just getting the runaround.) Finally, I sent her some flowers to thank her for being so pleasant along with a short note reminding her that I really wanted to talk to her boss. The next morning, I called and was immediately scheduled for an appointment. Twenty bucks worth of flowers accomplished what three months of my best cold calling could not. Since then I have used this approach a number of times, and it hasn't failed me yet!

Chapter 3

Selling
The Small-Business Owner

To become truly successful in the small business market requires that you become a consultant in the truest sense of the word. You will have to earn your clients' trust by always placing their interests above both your own interests and your firm's interests. In addition, you will have to learn to be market-driven rather than product-driven. This is often a very difficult transition to make. Being *market-driven* means that instead of selecting a product and then trying to find someone to sell it to, you first find out what a prospect wants and then find the best product available to meet that client's needs. You must be a professional financial problem solver instead of a securities salesman, which requires an entirely different mindset and attitude on your part.

As a professional, you must always listen (notice that I said "listen," not just wait for your turn to talk) to a prospect and ask question after question until you are sure you have the prospect's problem clearly defined in your own mind. This is difficult because often the prospect cannot clearly articulate just exactly what his problem is, so you will need to pull it out of him. If, after you clearly understand a prospect's problem, you determine that you can't be of any assistance, then say so and move on. Never lead a prospect to believe you can do something for him unless you are sure you have both the training or resources to follow through.

Never be afraid to say, "I don't know, I'll have to check on that and get back to you tomorrow." Nobody expects you to know everything. If you say something that later turns out to be incorrect, you may have a hard time reestablishing your credibility.

Never try to intimidate a sophisticated client into making a decision. You may get the sale, but it will probably be your last one to that prospect. Small business owners are by nature a very proud group of people. It is much better to lead them into drawing their own conclusions than to try to make their minds up for them. Nobody's as "sold" as the prospect who sells himself.

Small business owners also tend to be very opinionated. They often have their own ideas about what they want to accomplish and how it should be done. In this case, rather than disagreeing with the prospect, simply provide him the service of implementing his ideas (assuming, of course, that they're sensible).

The same holds true for economic and market predictions. You may be bearish on the markets, but if your prospect is bullish then recommend and implement a strategy that will be successful in a bullish market and just hedge it whenever it is possible to do so. Your prospect has just as good a chance of being right as either you or your firm's reasearch department do. Remember, you are there to serve your prospect's needs as *he* perceives them—not as *you* perceive them.

Although you may be able to gently temper a prospect's opinion if it is extreme, you cannot disagree with a prospect who holds a sensible position and win. If you argue or debate with your prospect and he wins, you look foolish; if you win, he takes his business elsewhere—a lose-lose situation.

The Importance of Accuracy

Be careful of any claims you make regarding an investment vehicle or strategy so that you do not exaggerate its benefits or minimize its risks (a natural tendency). If, for example, you're calculating how much money a prospect will have in a retirement plan that you are proposing he adopt, make sure you assume a conservative interest rate. If you assume a rate that the client feels is unattainable over a long period, you may severely jeopardize your credibility. Instead, calculate the cash accumulation using an 8% to 9% assumption, and point out that the plan may indeed yield more if the investments prove to be especially successful. Although you might be able to get away with exaggerating to an unsophisticated retail client, small business owners are too knowledgable for that to work. And if your ethics are sound, you will not try to get away with exaggerating, anyway.

Encourage Owners to Talk Business

As mentioned earlier, business owners are a proud group of people and rightfully so. They work very hard and often spend more time with their businesses then they do with their families. Therefore, it's always a good idea when meeting a prospect to ask to take a quick tour of his plant, or ask how the business got started, or ask what new product the company's working on, or any other question that will allow the owner to start talking about his business. Business owners like to talk about their businesses the way grandparents like to talk about their grandchildren.

Aside from being a good ice breaker, talking about the business is an excellent way to learn about the specific types of problem that various businesses face, which can be very useful information. (This is true in any business, of course, but brokers seem to overlook the tactic.) For example, let's assume two of your clients, who happen to be in the printing business, tell you that their biggest problem is recruiting dependable help. The next time you meet a printer you can use this information to get his attention immediately. You might say something like, "I understand that in your business it's very difficult to recruit and retain quality help." A comment like this should immediately strike a responsive chord with the prospect and give you the opportunity to land an appointment quickly.

If the owner agrees that finding good people has been difficult, then you can briefly discuss how a deferred compensation plan can help him recruit and retain good people without increasing his current expenses. Knowing a little about a lot of different types of business can reduce the amount of time it takes to build rapport with a new prospect and probe for a need.

Changing the Way You Do Business

Working in the small business market often requires that you spend time out of the office. It also requires, when you are in the office, that you have blocks of uninterrupted time in which to develop solutions to your prospects' problems and to prepare proposals and presentations. Therefore, you will find it difficult to actively trade stocks, bonds, options, or futures for some clients while you are developing corporate business. Each activity requires an entirely different approach to doing business. A typical day of a small business consultant might look like Table 3-1.

Table 3-1. A Day in the Life of a Small Business Consultant.

Time	Activity
8:00 A.M. to 9:00 A.M.	Meeting with Mr. Jones (a prospect) at his location.
9:15 A.M. to 10:30 A.M.	In-person cold calls in prospect's industrial park.
11:00 A.M. to 1:30 P.M.	Meeting with Mr. Smith (a client) to present pension investment proposal, following by lunch with the client and his accountant.
2.00 P.M. to 3:00 P.M.	Back in the office. Prepare order tickets for Mr. Smith's pension plan, and return phone calls from morning.

3.00 P.M. to 5:30 P.M.   Start work on a deferred compensation agreement proposal for Mr. Jones.

Night   Take 60 to 90 minutes' worth of reading material home (research reports, newsletters, magazines, etc.) to stay current.

There is not a lot of room in a day such as that outlined in Table 3-1 for you to be trading. If you want to become a small business consultant, then you will have to use prepackaged products such as mutual funds, unit trusts, limited partnerships, and investment managers whenever possible. You become an asset collector. Rather than trying to both be a trader and a salesman, you turn the responsibility of selecting individual stocks and bonds over to someone else so that your time is free to help another business owner solve his problem. In effect, you use prepackaged products and managers to leverage your time and efforts.

Many brokers resist this idea but haven't been able to provide a logical reason. Some brokers have indicated that they fear giving up control over their clients' funds. This approach does not require that you give up control over the clients' funds. Instead, you simply make the adjustment from managing individual stocks and bonds to managing the managers. Instead of telling a client, "This stock is not performing as well as I expected, let's sell it and look for a better opportunity," you will say, "This fund/manager is not performing as well as I expected, let's sell it and look for a better opportunity." Rather than selling a stock and buying a bond, you will sell a stock fund and buy a bond fund. With the proliferation of specialty funds, you can build just about any kind of portfolio by using funds made up of the same stocks and bonds that you would use to build an individual portfolio.

There are several other advantages in using this approach. First, your clients' funds are managed by people who have good performance records (assuming you choose your funds wisely). Second, the managers of these funds can literally stare at their quote screen and read research reports all day. Thus, they should be better informed and better able to respond more quickly (except for the largest funds) to any changes in the market than you are.

Third, funds allow even your smallest clients to have diversified portfolios. Although this may not seem to be very important during a raging bull market, it is extremely important during the bear market that inevitably follows. Fourth, by placing a little distance between yourself and the actual individual stock and bond selections, you stand less chance of being blamed by your client should the investments prove to be disappointing. In effect, you place yourself on the same side of the table as your client. No client will tolerate poor performance forever, but you have a better chance of getting a second chance if you did not directly select the investments.

Every time a potential client asks me what I like in the market I say "mutual funds." When asked why, I say, "Because I'm sitting here in your office talking to you. At this moment, I don't know where the market is or in which direction it's moving. To manage a portfolio properly today requires that every investment be monitored all the time the markets are open, and I can't be two places at once. Besides I happen to be a lousy stock picker.'' That usually gets a laugh.

Teamwork Can Pay Off

Because you may be spending a lot of time outside the office, you may want to consider taking on a partner. This inside man/outside man approach is effective and efficient. Some brokers are outgoing, are excellent salespeople, and enjoy working outside an office environment. Other brokers are knowledgable, write well, and are oriented to detail. If you fall into one of these two categories, than teaming up with your alter ego may allow both of you to minimize your weaknesses and leverage your strengths.

Before jumping into a partnership, remember that a partnership is like a marriage: It's best to make sure you're compatible before you make any commitments. If you find someone you think you can work with, then try working together for a few months before entering into any formal arrangement.

If you do decide to form a partnership, have a competent lawyer draw up a partnership agreement. Make sure to include provisions covering what happens to the accounts should either party decide to dissolve the partnership.

Send Business Their Way

One of the nicest and most appreciated things you can do for a small business owner is to send him some business or give him a lead. (Just think how you feel when someone gives you a lead.) As a broker, you come into contact with a large number of people who not only produce a wide variety of goods and services but also require a wide variety of them. Steering one of your clients toward another one of your clients is a great way to build goodwill and is something no discount firm can ever do.

Referring business is simple. You do not need to become a part-time sales representative for your clients. However, if during the course of a conversation a client complains about his current trucking company and you happen to have a second client who owns a trucking company, then providing that lead to your second client can only generate goodwill regardless of whether or not he gets the business. Both clients will know you were thinking of them and will appreciate the thought.

Compensation

Putting out the extra effort to study the latest tax changes, learning about the latest investment vehicles, and providing your clients with the highest level of professional service is worthwhile *only* if you are fairly compensated for your additional efforts. To ensure that you will be fairly compensated for your efforts, you may have to adopt a compensation program other than straight commission. The reason is that there are many problems associated with being compensated on a straight commission basis, especially when you are concentrating on the small busines market.

The first problem is that preparing a proposal for a small business owner can consume many hours of your time. Unfortunately, there are some procrastinators out there who will have you go to the trouble of preparing a proposal, only to let your recommendations collect dust. Either they get distracted by another project that they view as having higher priority, or they really weren't that interested to begin with.

Any broker who has ever heard a prospect say, "Well, it sounded like a good idea when we first talked about it and I do appreciate your preparing the proposal and taking the time to explain it to me, but for right now I'm going to hold off. I'll give you a call when I'm ready," knows just how frustrating this type of prospect can be.

The second problem is that there are thieves who will gladly have you do some work for them while never even seriously considering using you to implement your ideas. These people are the ones who are very friendly when you call, seem receptive to your ideas, promptly schedule an appointment to see you, give you all the information you need to prepare a proposal, listen attentively when you present your recommendation, ask a lot of questions, and then turn around and execute your proposal at their local discount firm or exclusively with no-load products. It's easy to spot this type after you have been victimized. They go from being Dr. Jekyll to Mr. Hyde as soon as they've finished picking your brain. Before you present your ideas, your calls to these people always get placed right through. After your presentation, however, you might as well try to reach the man in the moon.

I believe this type of exploitation happens to brokers more often than they realize. With the proliferation of discount firms and no-load products, the problem is only going to get worse. The difference (in dollars) between executing a large number of securities transactions at discount commission rates versus full service commission rates can be enough to tempt even the most honest of people into forgetting your efforts on their behalf.

The third problem with working on straight commission is that often the amount of securities transactions generated by your recommendations is completely disproportional to your efforts. You can do a lot of work for a client and yet not generate a lot of trades, whereas at other times, a simple piece of advice can result in a tremendous number of transactions. In the past, these two situations tended to balance each other out, but now clients are becoming very aware of their commission costs and are less likely to allow us to be overcompensated for simple work. Of course, they're not nearly as adamant about our being undercompensated. I haven't had a client yet who said, "Hey, you worked hard on this; charge me double your regular commission rates."

The fourth problem, and one that's getting worse all the time, is the perception by the investing public that because brokers are compensated by commission they will offer bad advice if it generates a trade in lieu of good advice that doesn't. The publicity surrounding the onslaught of suits against brokers for "churning" has made the public very leary of brokers' professionalism and objectivity. Charging straight commissions unquestionably creates conflicts of interest between brokers and clients.

A quick look at the phenomenal growth of the "fee only" financial planning business as well as the growth of *Money Magazine, Personal Investor,* and other financial periodicals confirms that an ever-increasing number of investors and seeking impartial financial advice.

A fifth problem with being paid by straight commission is that people simply don't like to pay commissions. They almost always feel that the commissions are too high regardless of how much work you do to earn them. The huge number of financial neophytes who could truly benefit from the services of a good broker but who instead choose to use a discount firm, often to their own detriment, is a testament to the animosity that many people harbor toward paying commissions, even when the commissions are justified.

For all these reasons, I recommend that every broker, especially those concentrating on the small business market, adopt a fee-versus-commission compensation schedule instead of working on a straight commission schedule. With a fee-versus-commission compensation schedule, you charge a set fee for your time (e.g., $100 an hour), and credit your prospects with one hour of time for every $300 in full service commissionable trades they execute through you. If, for example, you spent six hours preparing a deferred compensation proposal for a prospect, then the prospect would have the option of paying you either a fee of $600 or executing $1,800 in full commission rate business with you. If the implementation of the aforementioned plan generated only $900 in commissions, (half of the required commission level), then the client would owe you an additional fee of $300 (half of the minimum fee). If, instead, the plan implementation generated $5,100 in commissions (at full service rates), you could either execute the "surplus" trades at discounted rates or credit the client with 17 hours of your time for future research or projects.

This type of arrangement is mutually beneficial for both broker and client. For the broker, the arrangement eliminates the deadwood. Clients who have only a lukewarm interest in having you do some work for them will not commit themselves to this type of arrangement. A minimum fee also stops the thieves of this world from exploiting you. Finally, charging a minimum fee for your advice makes you appear to be more professional in the eyes of your prospects. People assume, rightly or wrongly, that advice from someone who charges is better than advice from someone who doesn't. A lawyer who charges $300 an hour is perceived as being a better lawyer than one who charges $50 an hour. Thus, your advice is to a large extent worth what you say it is worth.

For the prospect, this kind of arrangement serves to discourage recommending trades solely to generate commissions, a point you should bring up during your initial conversation with a prospect. If, for example, you evaluate a client's employee benefit program and determine that his benefits program is as good as it can be, you can report that to the client without feeling that you have wasted your time and effort.

This approach also benefits both parties in that by tying your compensation to the time and effort you actually spend working on a prospect's behalf, neither you nor your client will feel exploited by the relationship.

Another benefit of this approach to both you and your prospect is that your proposals stand a better chance of being implemented if you adopt this compensation system. The rationale for this on the part of prospects seems to be that as long as they have to pay for it, they might as well get their money's worth. Assuming your advice is sound, implementing the plan should be to your prospect's benefit as well as to your benefit. By quantifying the value of your advice, you also make paying full service commissions more palatable for your prospects.

Remember, in order to charge fees (or to even mention them), you must first become a Registered Investment Advisor (RIA) with both the Federal Securities and Exchange Commission and the state commissions in any state in which you do business. If you have passed your Series 7 Exam, then becoming an RIA is simply a matter of completing Form ADV and returning it to Washington with a check for $150. (A move is under way to require a separate RIA exam and to raise the RIA application fee substantially.) Brokers should check with their own State Securities Commissions for a copy of the state registrations.

Preparing a Business Profile

One of the best ways to convert prospects into clients and to cement new client relationships is to use business profile forms. A business profile is nothing more than a rather lengthy and detailed questionnaire about a company's financial needs and the needs of its owner(s).

Figure 3-1. A Business Profile Form.

STRICTLY CONFIDENTIAL

DATE: _____   Prepared By: _____

BUSINESS PROFILE

Name of Business _____

Phone Number: (Switchboard) _____ (Night Number) _____

Street Address: Mailing Address:

_____   _____

_____   _____

Predecessor Company(s) if any: _____

_____

Related Company(s) if any: _____

_____

Type of Company:

_____ Corporation   If incorporated: State of
_____ Subchapter (S) Corporation incorporation: _____
_____ Professional Corporation
_____ Nonprofit Corporation   If not incorporated: State
_____ Partnership   and county in which reg-
_____ Sole Proprietorship   istered: _____

Company Officers and Managers

Name	Title	Percentage of Ownership
_____	Chairman	_____
_____	CEO	_____
_____	President	_____
_____	Treasurer	_____
_____	Cash Manager	_____
_____	Other _____	_____

Members of Committees
Pension Committee: _____

_____

Employee Benefits Committee: _____

_____

Fiscal Year End: _____

Accounting Method: (Cash or Accrual) _____

(LIFO or FIFO) _____

Assets:

    Cash & Equivalents   _____

    Receivables   _____

    Inventory   _____

    Plant & Equipment   _____

    Real Estate   _____

    Goodwill   _____

Liabilities:

    Current
    Long-Term Debt   _____

Type   *Payable to*   *Interest Rate & Terms*

_____   _____   _____

_____   _____   _____

_____   _____   _____

_____   _____   _____

Available Lines of Credit:

From   *Size*   *Terms*

_____   _____   _____

_____   _____   _____

_____   _____   _____

Approximate Annual Profit (Loss) (Actual Dollars) _____

                                  (As Percentage of Sales) _____

                                  (Return on Equity) _____

Does company have a retained earnings problem?

_____

_____

Does company need financing? _____ For what purpose?

_____ Working Capital   _____ Acquisition

_____ Equipment Purchases   _____ Real Estate

_____ Receivable Financing   _____ Other _____

Would company be interested in:

_____ Secured Bank Loan   _____ Public Debt Offering

_____ Unsecured Bank Loan   _____ Venture Capital

_____ Equipment Sale/Leaseback   _____ Private Equity Placement

_____ Private Debt Placement   _____ Public Equity Offering

_____ Receivables Financing   _____ Real Estate Financing

_____ Federal Programs (SBA, FFCA, OED, etc.)

_____ Other _____

Is company for sale now or in the near future?

_____

_____

Is company seeking any acquisitions?

_____

_____

Income Tax Brackets (Federal) _____ (State) _____

Any tax loss carryforward? _____

Any special tax considerations? _____

_____

Current Number of Employees: _____

Annual Employee Turnover (%) _____

Number and Nature of Employees Covered by Collective Bargaining Agreement:

_____

Existing Benefit Program:

Group Life? _____

         Carrier? _____ Coverage _____

Group Health? _____

         Carrier? _____ Coverage _____

Group Disability? _____

         Carrier? _____ Coverage _____

Group Medical/Dental? _____

         Carrier? _____ Coverage _____

Non-Qualified Deferred Compensation? _____

Qualified Pension Plans:

Type of Plan	*Covering Whom?*	*Annual Contribution*
_____	_____	_____
_____	_____	_____
_____	_____	_____
_____	_____	_____

Who manages plan assets and what has the return been over the past year, three years, five years?

_____

_____

_____

_____

Who administers plan?   _____

Who is plan actuary?   _____

Who is plan attorney?   _____

Where are plan assets held?   _____

Name of company accountant?   _____

Does the company have buy/sell buy/back agreements   _____

Are the agreements funded?   _____ How?   _____

Does the company do any international business and if so is the currency risk

hedged?   _____

_____

Does the company use any commodities (lumber, grain, precious metals), and if

so are they hedged?   _____

_____

Other notes on company: _____

_____

_____

_____

_____

_____

_____

company's financial needs and the needs of its owner's).

Taking the time to visit a business owner and completing a profile form such as the one shown in Figure 3-1 has numerous benefits, including the following:

- It demonstrates to a business owner that you are market driven rather than product driven and that you really care about identifying and solving his problems.

- You obtain, in a minimal amount of time, relatively complete information about a company and its owner so that you can find additional ways to be of service.

- You discover what the owner's most pressing needs are so that you know what services to offer first.
- You learn which bank, accountant, and attorney the client uses so that you can start to establish a rapport with your new client's other advisors.

Done properly, completing a profile form should take less than an hour. After the usual prebusiness pleasantries simply ask;

"Mr. Jones would you mind if I asked you a few questions about your business and its finances so that I can provide you with better recommendations and service?"

Complete the form, and take it back to the office. Have it typed, and have the information put into your computer data base. Mail the owner a copy of the completed questionnaire with a brief cover letter similar to the one shown in Figure 3-2. With service like this why should a business owner even listen to the next phone jockey who's lucky enough to get through to him?

- Insurance specialists.
- Tax specialists.
- Retirement planning specialists and actuaries.
- Trust specialists.
- Corporate finance specialists.
- Venture capital specialists.
- Real estate and mortgage specialists.

It is often preferable to work with specialists within your own firm. You already indirectly pay their salaries because part of your commissions end up in their paychecks. Additionally, these in-house product specialists often have production quotas to meet. Many of them are aggressive and competent sales people.

Working with Product Specialists

No one can be an expert on every financial topic and every investment vehicle. To serve your clients properly will require that you interact with various product specialists. In effect, you act as a "point man" for a wide range of people with a wide range of expertise, calling on the right ones when needed to solve a prospect's problems.

Product specialists can often be found both within your firm and in other companies. Some of the specialists you should line up so that you can call on them when you need them include the following:

Figure 3-2. Sample Letter to Accompany Business Profile.

[YOUR LETTERHEAD]

February 24, 19XX

Mr. Small Business Owner
Name of Company
Street Address

Dear _____:

    Please take a few minutes to review the enclosed
business profile form for accuracy and completeness. I will
be relying on this information when I develop ideas for your
consideration. Please make any necessary changes and/or
corrections and return this form in the envelope provided.
    Let me assure you that both my firm and I stand ready to
assist you with all your investment and financial planning
needs. I will be calling you shortly to schedule our next
meeting. Thank you for your time and attention.

Sincerely,

Your Name

YN:fd

Your income will be dependent, at least in part, on the efforts of
these product specialists, so develop good working relationships with
them. The golden rule for working with product specialists is not to waste
their time. Bring them into the planning only when you have a truly
interested prospect with a solvable problem. Product specialists often
have many brokers competing for their time. If you develop a reputation
for setting quality appointments for your firm's product specialists, you
will always have "first dibs" on their time.

Computerize!

The personal computer (PC) is the most useful business tool since the pencil and the telephone. By using it properly you can dramatically improve your productivity and the productivity of your assistant(s). If you are one of the many brokers who have not yet started using a PC in your business, I strongly recommend that you start. After all this is the 1980s.

Any PC that is fully IBM-compatible and has a hard disk drive (10 million bites minimum) is suitable. However, you may want to invest in one that allows you to connect additional terminals to the processing unit so that you and your assistant can both use the computer at the same time. Add a letter quality printer, and you have all the hardware you will need (at about $2,000).

The only software you need is a word processing program, a spread sheet, and a relational database. With a word processing program that can store any number of standard letters, all you need to do in order to generate a letter is to add the recipient's name and address. Additionally, having a word processor allows you to store copies of the proposals you prepare for your prospects. As you build your library of proposals, you will find that you can use some of the "boilerplate" again, shortening the amount of time it takes you to generate subsequent proposals.

Also, if you plan to write any articles, a word processing program is almost essential.

The spread sheet is used to develop financial projections for pension plans, deferred compensation plans, budgets, portfolios, and the like.

The relational data base issued to store client and prospect files. The advantage of using a data base is that if you want to select those prospects and clients who are both over 50 and have defined benefit plans (let's assume you want to send them each a copy of an interesting newspaper clipping) you can do it by simply hitting a few keys. Once you have selected the names, you can have the computer print mailing labels for all the prospects who meet your criteria by using only a few more keystrokes.

It is important to select software that's "integrated"—that is, software programs that can trade data and files. With integrated software, you can insert the results of a spread sheet into a proposal you're writing on your word processing program. Or if you want to send a personalized letter to all your prospects with dental plans, you can select a list of their names from your data base and automatically merge this list with a letter. All the software to accomplish these varied functions can be purchased for less than $500.

If you are going to publish a newsletter, you may also want to add a publishing program to your shopping list. With this software, you can create mastheads and use different type styles. Many small printers can set the type for your newsletter directly from a floppy disk and print it—thus saving you typesetting charges.

Working with Accountants and Attorneys

Establishing a good relationship with your prospects' accountants and attorneys can be very beneficial. The last thing you want to do is end up in a power struggle for your prospects' respect and attention—a struggle that you will almost always lose. Most power struggles usually start when one professional feels that another professional has encroached on his territory. For example, if you provide your client with a pension document, the prospect's lawyer may resent it. Likewise, if you attempt to implement a complicated tax strategy, the prospect's accountant may feel that you have infringed on his territory.

The easiest way to avoid this type of fight is to involve the prospect's other advisors in your work at your earliest opportunity. Every time you complete a prospect's business profile, send a copy of it to the client's accountant and attorney along with a letter introducing yourself. Follow up with some phone calls to ask for their input about any recommendations you are thinking of making to your prospect. If they don't like an idea, try if possible to change it to their satisfaction. If you make the effort at this point to obtain their approval, you should have it "made" when your prospect calls his accountant and attorney to find out what they think of your recommendations.

Use the accountant's name and the attorney's name in any proposals you prepare. For example, in a pension proposal you might recommend the prospect's accountant by name to administer the plan and the prospect's attorney by name to review it and file it. Some brokers find this process demeaning, but it's always good to remember that before the business owner became your prospect, he was their client. Accountants and attorneys can be your best sources of referral business, assuming you handle them properly. Often this means showing a little humility and deference. Besides, you can make more money in a single day than they make in a month. A good thought to remember when they try your patience.

Chapter 4

Corporate Cash Management

Why Market These Services?

As discussed in Chapter 2, the first step toward doing business with any company is to find a way to "get in the door." Once you have provided the company with that first product or service, it becomes easier to sell the second and even easier to sell the third. The hardest step is often the first one. For this reason, you always want to take the path of least resistance when trying to start a new business relationship. Corporate cash management products and services are ideally suited to "opening doors" because they:

1. are simple and straightforward,
2. have wide applicability,
3. lend themselves to a telemarketing campaign, and
4. offer an immediate benefit to the prospect.

Prospecting with corporate cash management products and services is as simple as calling the appropriate company official and asking, "Would you be interested in improving the performance of your company's (or organization's) short-term investment portfolio?" Follow up this opening question with a few probes about the company's current cash position, current investment portfolio, and tolerance for risk. Once this information is obtained, it is generally fairly easy to find some way for you and your firm to be of service. You may be able to:

1. increase the after-tax return on the prospect's portfolio,

2. reduce the prospect's risk exposure without sacrificing yield, and/or

3. improve or simplify the prospect's record-keeping system.

Because almost every company or organization—large or small, taxable or tax-exempt, profitable or not—can benefit from improving its short-term investment program, these products and services have wide applicability. Also, since short-term cash investment decisions are generally controlled by one person (except in the largest of companies and organizations), lengthly presentations to company "committees" are generally not required. These facts, coupled with the simplicity of many corporate cash management services and products, make these services and products ideally suited to a telemarketing campaign.

Since a better cash management program offers some immediate benefits to the company or organization you are prospecting, closing sales should be relatively easy and should occur relatively quickly. Thus prospecting with corporate cash management services is an excellent way to quickly add new clients to your book.

Aside from the relative ease of opening new accounts, another reason to market cash management products and services is that they are an excellent way to gather information about a company or organization. If, for example, you call on a company and the treasurer tells you that the company is a net borrower and thus has no surplus cash to invest, your prospecting call was still worthwhile. Now that you know the company is a net borrower, you can reasonably assume that the company is interested in alternative ways to raise capital. Maybe all you need to get a corporate finance relationship started is to immediately mail the individual a brief letter that describes your company's corporate finance services and then follow up with another phone call a week later.

Similarly, if a prospect tells you that the company currently has a large cash position, but that its current cash management program is adequate, this is also useful information. If the company has a large cash surplus, you might well assume that the company is profitable. Because profitable companies need to shelter income, you might elect to send the company a letter detailing your firm's pension and tax shelter services.

Any prospecting call that results in your knowing more about a prospective client than you did before is a worthwhile call. Because a company's cash position is often indicative of its operating results, prospecting with corporate cash products and services can direct you to those areas where you and your firm may be of service to a prospect.

The third reason to market these services is that the commissions can be lucrative. Depending on the mix of products you sell, commission levels can run from .10% to 1.00% per year. A diligent marketing effort targeted at the right market can net $100 million in cash under management per year. Assuming an average commission of .25% means you can expect to generate $250,000 of gross commissions from a product you're using as a "door opener." Add to this some higher margin business and you can see that this market can be very lucrative indeed.

Formulating an Investment Policy

After you have opened up a new account with whatever product or service proves to be applicable, try to get the client to adopt a written investment policy regarding the company's surplus cash. From the client's point of view there are two benefits of taking the time and trouble to formulate and adopt a written cash management investment policy. First, it will clear up any confusion the treasurer or cash manager may have about the company's internal policy regarding the various investment vehicles and strategies. Any broker who has worked in this market for any period of time has no doubt run into a number of corporate treasurers and/or cash managers who, although responsible for investing the surplus corporate funds, do not have clear investment guidelines and policies for doing so. Often this confusion on their part expresses itself in an overly conservative investment program, which *reduces both the client's investment return and your annual income*.

Once an investment policy has been established and approved by the board of directors, owners, or whoever has the authority within the organization to approve such things, then your prospect can begin to invest (with you) with confidence.

The second benefit to point out to your new client is that once the company adopts a written investment policy, you will be better able to serve its needs without wasting a lot of time offering the company inappropriate investment vehicles and strategies.

As the client's broker, you enjoy many benefits from guiding your new client through the process of formulating and adopting a written investment policy:

- It will cement the new relationship.
- It will demonstrate to your new client that you are more than just a salesperson "hyping" products.
- It will enable you to learn everything about the client's investment objectives and limitations.
- It will allow you to discover just who in the organization really makes the investment decisions.
- It will provide you with the opportunity to provide your input to the company on just what is and what is not a sound investment policy, helping to ensure that the policy is written so that you can be of ongoing service to your client.
- It will provide you with the opportunity to present and sell additional products and services.

The policy statement does not have to be long or complicated. A few paragraphs that cover the following ten points is often sufficient:

- What types of investment vehicles does the company consider suitable?

- What is the maximum percentage of the company's cash that can be invested in any one vehicle at any time?

- What is the minimum credit rating that the company requires of its short-term investment vehicles? Does every vehicle in the portfolio have to meet this minimum, or does the average rating of the portfolio have to meet this rating? For example, if a company requires an "A" rating for its portfolio, can it have $500,000 invested in "BBB" instruments *as long as* it also has $500,000 invested in "AA" instruments?

- Can the company invest overseas in the Eurodollar market?

- What maximum maturity can any one investment vehicle within the portfolio have? What is the maximum average maturity for the portfolio?

- Can the company enter into "repurchase agreements" (or repos) and "reverse repurchase agreements" (or reverse repos)? If so, with whom and under what circumstances?

- In which of the new corporate cash preferred stock vehicles can the company invest?

- Can the company use the options and futures market to hedge its portfolio?

- Can the company use the options market to facilitate a dividend capture program?

- How aggressively is the company willing to pursue swap opportunities?

Make sure to mention to the client that this policy does not have to be etched in stone. In fact, it should be periodically reviewed to reflect changes in the marketplace and changes in the client's investment objectives and limitations.

Once an investment policy is formulated, copies (including any revisions) should be held by the company, by you, and by your firm's money market trading desk. Working hand-in-hand with your traders (or your trading liaisons) is going to be essential if you are going to be successful in this market.

Providing your traders with your client's written investment policies not only demonstrates to them that you are committed to working in this market, but also allows your firm's traders to seek out attractive investment opportunities for your clients, thus freeing up your time to prospect for new clients. Utilizing your trading desk properly can provide tremendous leverage for your sales efforts.

Investment Vehicles

A wide variety of vehicles are suitable short-term investments for surplus corporate cash. In this section we are going to touch on the basics of the traditional money market instruments. Remember: Any bond that matures, or that can be "put" (or returned to the issuing company in exchange for full face value), within one year is technically a money market instrument, regardless of its date of issue or maturity. For example, if XYZ Corp. issued a 20-year bond 19.5 years ago, then the bond has six months to maturity and is a money market instrument. Often issuers of short-term notes also have outstanding long-term issues that mature at approximately the same time and usually offer a higher return. (This is one of the many quirks that the "efficient market theorists" have trouble explaining.)

To intelligently discuss the yields of money market instruments, you not only need to know their absolute yields but also their relative yields, particularly their historic yield spreads over T-Bills. Because T-Bills are U.S. government securities, they are assumed to have zero credit risk. Every other vehicle, when compared to the T-Bill, therefore has at least some additional credit risk. Much of the analysis of money market instruments centers around analyzing whether, for a given vehicle, on a given day, in a given set of market conditions, the additional yield the vehicle offers, relative to the T-Bill, justifies assuming the additional risk. As we shall see, the relative yields between the T-Bill and the other instruments are critically important to understanding and successfully participating in this market.

Certificates of Deposit

The certificate of deposit (CD) is one of the most popular investment vehicles for surplus corporate cash. There are several reasons for this. First, for a corporation *in a low tax bracket, a properly managed CD portfolio* offers:

- Competitive returns,
- minimal credit risk, and
- good liquidity.

Investors more interested in liquidity than in yield will generally invest only in CDs issued by the top-tier money center banks. The reason: The trading market for the CDs issued by these institutions is very well developed and thus these CDs are liquid. It is possible to buy and sell these instruments at almost any time at a fair price and with minimal transaction costs. The price investors pay for this liquidity is a lower yield.

Investors who are more yield-conscious well generally hire a CD broker to place their CDs with banks and savings and loans (S&Ls) that offer the highest yield, regardless of where the banks and S&Ls are located. Because there is no secondary market for CDs issued by the "Pokomoke Savings & Loan," investors needing their funds prior to the CD's maturity date either have to redeem their CD with the issuing institution (and incur a six-month interest penalty) or sell the CD in the open market at a heavy discount.

Aside from breaking up a large CD investment so that no more than

$100,000 is invested with any one institution at any one time (the maximum insured by the FDIC and FSLIC per account, per institution), a CD broker may provide other services as well. Some CD brokers perform due dilligence research on an institution prior to placing any CDs with it. However, because assessing the quality of a bank's loan portfolio is at best difficult, both brokers and investors should take these "approved for investment lists" with a grain of salt. Remember also that the FDIC and FSLIC only guarantee that insured deposits and interest will be paid in full, not that they will be paid on time. If your client has a CD from a bank or S&L that has a particularly complicated failure (inadequate records or fraud problems), getting paid can take months!

Most brokerage firms either act as CD brokers or work very closely with CD brokerage firms. For their efforts most CD brokers generally charge the clients a fee of 25 basis points, annualized.

Credit risk with the money center banks is negligible since the Fed has stated publicly that these banks are too big to fail. In the event that one of these banks got into trouble, the fed would rescue it and protect all depositors, regardless of size, from any loss. (A case in point is Continental Illinois.)

CDs are available in maturities as short as 7 days or as long as 20 years. They come in discount (zero coupon) form, variable rate coupon form, and fixed rate coupon form. Dollar-denominated CDs are issued by:

- Domestic offices of domestic banks and S&Ls (negotiable and fixed rate CDs)
- Foreign offices of U.S. Banks, that is, Citicorp in London (Euro CDs). Note that the term "Euro CD" encompasses all dollar-denominated CDs issued outside the U.S., not just those issued in Europe.
- U.S. offices of foreign banks (Yankee CDs)
- Foreign offices of foreign banks (Euro CDs or foreign CDs)

Since CDs have such wide acceptance, they are a very attractive vehicle with which to prospect. Few corporate investors will refuse to listen to a presentation about obtaining a higher insured yield via a convenient CD brokerage program. The only major exceptions are companies that are very dependent on their banks for credit and that do not want to jeopardize their banking relationship.

The 1986 Tax Reform Act will have a dramatic effect on the attractiveness of CDs as corporate investments. Under this law, the maximum corporate tax bracket will be reduced from 46% to 33%, and a 10% alternative minimum corporate tax will be imposed. Additionally, many of the tax deductions commonly used by corporations such as investment tax credits, energy tax credits, and certain types of accelerated depreciation will be repealed. Many companies that previously were able to effectively shelter themselves from taxes by using these credits are now going to have to pay taxes, albeit at lower maximum rates. While the net effect of this dramatic tax change on the relative attractiveness of CDs (and other taxable vehicles) is impossible to accurately predict, it appears that, on balance, they will become less attractive to a large number of investing corporations.

Commercial Paper

Commercial paper (CP), sold on a discounted basis, is an unsecured promise by the issuing company to pay to the investor a certain number of dollars on a stated maturity date. If the proceeds are used to finance current transactions and mature in less than 270 days, the issuers are exempted from registering the issue as a security offering.

CP can be divided into two main classifications based on the type of issuer: direct issue paper and dealer paper. *Direct issues* are sold directly by the issuing companies. These companies are so large and so active in the commercial paper market that it is cost-effective for them to build and maintain a dedicated in-house CP sales force. Examples of direct issuers would be the large finance companies and the largest public corporations. Smaller companies, on the other hand, use *dealers* to sell their CP when they are in the market. For this service they generally pay a fee to the dealer of approximately .125% of the offering proceeds.

CP, regardless of the issuer, is usually unsecured debt. This means it is backed only by the full faith and credit of the issuing corporation but not by a specific lien against any specific assets or collateral. For this reason, investors need to pay close attention to the credit ratings of CP issues they own or are thinking of acquiring. CP is rated 1, 2, 3, or 4 by the major rating services. "1" paper is the safest and "4" paper is either already in default, or well on its way. These ratings are expressed as "A1-P2" (meaning Standard & Poor's rates it a "1" and Moody's rates it a "2").

Often a company with a low credit rating will get a letter of credit from its bank guaranteeing the issue or a financial guarantee bond from its insurance company to cover the issue. This way, paper that would have been rated "3" can come to market with a "1." Even after paying the bank or insurance company a fee for providing the guarantee, the company's net cost of borrowing is often reduced by obtaining these third-party guarantees.

CP trades in pieces as small as $50,000 or as large as several $100 million.

Recently, municipalities have begun to enter the CP markt by selling short-term paper to investors who can benefit from the exemption from federal income taxes that this paper offers. Foreign companies have also begun tapping this relatively low-cost source of funds.

Most of the CP that is purchased by investors is held to maturity, partially because, on average, CP has a very short duration (less than 30 days). Another reason is that, while dealers and issuers will usually buy back paper from investors who need to sell it to raise cash, the secondary market for CP is not nearly as well developed as it is for other money market instruments. Thus CP is not suitable for trading.

The relative attractiveness of CP as a short-term investment corporate investment vehicle will be adversely affected by the proposed tax act because it is fully taxable.

Banker's Acceptances

A *banker's acceptance* (BA) is an obligation of a bank to pay to the holder a certain number of dollars on a certain day. A bank creates BAs in a variety of ways, but usually they are created to finance trade.

For example, a wine merchant in New York City wants to import $950,000 worth of wine from a winery in Italy. The merchant would like to buy the wine, sell it, and, from the sale proceeds, pay the winery in Italy. He feels that this cycle will take approximately six months from the date the wine is delivered to New York. First, he presents his proposal to the winery, but for some reason the winery is either unwilling or unable to finance him for six months. The winery informs the merchant that they cannot extend him a trade credit and will require prompt payment if they are going to do business.

Because the merchant has an excellent credit rating, he is able to go to his bank in New York and get a $1 million line of credit (LC) for a term of 9 months. This done, the merchant sends a purchase order to the winery in Italy and instructs his bank to send an LC to the winery's bank in Italy. That bank, upon receipt of the LC, notifies the winery that the LC has been received and that the wine can be shipped. The wine merchant then ships the wine and provides proof of shipment to his bank (bills of lading and the appropriate shipping documents). The Italian bank then forwards these same documents to the merchant's bank in New York.

Assuming the paperwork is completed properly, the merchant's bank then forwards the funds ($950,000) to the bank in Italy, which credits the funds to the winery's account. Thus *the winery has been paid before the merchant has sold (or probably has even received) the wine. At the same time the merchant has received proof that the wine has been shipped prior to releasing any funds to the winery*. This somewhat complicated process, with the two banks acting as intermediaries, has served to protect both parties to the transaction.

The merchant's bank then delivers the shipping documents to the merchant so he can take delivery of the wine upon its arrival in America. If four weeks have elapsed, the merchant has eight months left on his LC. The bank can then expect to receive $1 million in eight months. In the meantime, it has paid out $950,000. In this example the difference between the $950,000 that the bank sent to Italy and the $1 million it will collect from the merchant represents the bank's fees, expenses, and profit.

Should the bank have a better use for those funds, it may elect *to sell the right to receive the $1 million on a discounted basis to an investor*. For the sake of this example, let's assume that, with four months left to maturity, the bank sells the note to an investor for $982,000. The bank, determining that it could make better use of its funds elsewhere, has sold the right to the million in four months for $982,000. In four months, the investor will receive $1 million. The difference between the $982,000 purchase price and the $1 million maturity value represents his return on the investment.

However, in order to make the note salable to the investor, the bank will have to agree to guarantee to the investor that it will make good on its obligation to pay him $1 million in four months, regardless of whether the wine merchant honors his obligation to the bank. It does this by stamping the word "ACCEPTED" on the note. Hence the name, "banker's acceptance."

Banker's acceptances have maturities of up to 270 days and are always sold on a discount basis. Generally BAs are held in bearer form and are fully negotiable.

Because investors must rely on the bank for payment, they generally prefer to deal with either local banks that they are familiar with or with the strongest money center banks. No American has lost a penny of principal in a banker's acceptance since they became popular over sixty years ago.

Banker's acceptances trade in million-dollar pieces, but most dealers will break BAs into smaller pieces for smaller investors. They are an attractive investment for companies that are very safety conscious.

Because BAs are fully taxable, they are likely to be adversely affected by the 1986 tax legislation.

Repurchase Agreements

A *repurchase transaction (repo)* is generally defined as the sale of a security from a seller to a buyer with the simultaneous agreement from the seller to repurchase the same security at a fixed price (or pricing rate) on a specified future date. Thus, while a repo is technically a "sale," functionally it represents a loan from the buyer to the seller with the security being used as collateral.

The most common repurchase transaction consists of a sale by a U.S. government bond dealer of a U.S. government bond to an investor and simultaneous agreement to repurchase the same bonds the next day at a slightly higher price. The difference in price represents the return to the investor. In this type of transaction the dealer is able to use the investor's money to finance his bond inventory at a lower cost than what a bank would charge to finance it. The investor, on the other hand, is able to lock in a fixed return on an overnight investment, generally at a higher rate than he could get from a money market fund.

Although most repos are overnight transactions, corporate investment officers frequently enter into longer-term repo transactions (up to a month or more) if the rate offered them by a dealer is particularly attractive, or if they expect interest rates to decline and wish to lock in a fixed rate.

The repo market is not limited to government securities. Repo transactions can also be done against certificates of deposit, banker's acceptances, high-quality corporate bonds, U.S. government agencies, mortgage securities, or other high-quality, liquid securities. Repos need to be done against high-quality liquid securities because, in the event the seller is either unable or unwilling to repurchase the securities on the agreed-upon date and at the agreed-upon price, the buyer must then sell the securities in the open market in order to recoup his investment. Only high-quality liquid securities offer repo investors real protection in this situation.

If the transaction is done properly, the investor should not have any market risk. If, over the course of the transaction, the market value of the collateral should either rise or fall, the market gain or market loss *accrues to the seller and not to the investor*. The investor, by agreeing *in advance* to a specific repurchase price (or a specific pricing rate), effectively locks in a return regardless of how changing market conditions affect the market value of the collateral.

The principal risks to the investor therefore are twofold. One, in the event the seller fails to repurchase the securities, the buyer must have clear and unencumbered access to the securities so as to be able to sell them. Two, the securities, when sold, must bring a high enough price in the open market to allow the investor to recoup not only his initial investment, but also any costs that may be incurred and a fair return on his investment.

As for the first risk, access to the securities, repo investors must make sure that they take delivery of the securities themselves. When this is either impractical or uneconomic (as in the case of a small dollar volume or an overnight transaction), they must make sure that the securities are properly escrowed for their benefit at an appropriate financial intermediary (such as a commercial bank or clearing house). Thus, if they need to sell the securities, they are free to do so.

The financial press has been full of stories recently about repo investors who either lost money or had to sue a seller in order to try to recoup an investment because they neglected to stringently follow this rule (Lombard Wall, Drysdale, ESM securities, and so on). In some of the more bizarre cases, investors have entered into repos with dealers *who did not even own any securities*, much less have them properly escrowed for the investor's benefit.

To protect themselves against the second risk—recouping their investment plus costs and a profit in the event of a forced sale—buyers need to be sure that they have sufficient "margin" in the transaction. *Margin*, in repo transactions, is defined as the transfer by the seller to the buyer of enough securities so as to slightly *over*collateralize the repo. The benefit to the investor of insisting on having margin is that, if the dealer defaults on his obligation to repurchase the securities at the same time the market value of the securities drops, the investor will have a "cushion" against any loss of principal during the forced liquidation.

The amount of the margin in a given transaction is negotiable. When negotiating margin requirements, investors should take into account the reputation and financial strength of the dealer, as well as the quality, volatility, and liquidity of the securities involved. Top dealers often offer no margin at all, believing that their good name offers investors sufficient security. However, with smaller dealers, obtaining sufficient margin is a must.

Naturally, margin should be a two-way street. If, during a longer-term repo transaction, the market value of the securities being used as collateral should rise appreciably, then the seller should be allowed to recall some of the "excess" collateral.

Recently, at the urging of the Fed and the securities industry, the bankruptcy code was modified and "clarified" to help protect repo investors in certain types of repo transactions involving Treasury securities, government agencies, certificates of deposit, and banker's acceptances. In the event that an investor is ever involved in a repurchase transaction with a dealer who files for bankruptcy, and the investor is thus forced to sell the securities to recoup his investment, the recent changes in the code will help protect the investor from the bankruptcy trustee, should he or she ever decide to try to attach the sale proceeds.

To simplify repo transactions, the Public Securities Association (PSA), a nationwide trade association of securities dealers and brokers, has prepared a prototype repurchase agreement which is rapidly becoming the standard in the industry. This contract spells out in very simple terms the basic structure of a repo transaction and the obligations of both parties. The only real variables left for the parties to negotiate are the type of securities to be used as collateral, the maturity date, the yield, and the margin requirement. Prior to entering into any repurchase agreement with any dealer, investors should demand that the dealer sign a PSA (or similar) repo prototype agreement. Brokers working in this market should familiarize themselves with the PSA prototype contract.

Assuming your firm has a good government security trading desk, and a good reputation, repurchase agreements can be a successful prospecting tool. When you encounter a prospect who is currently doing repos with his local bank, you should be able to offer the prospect a higher yield as well as better security. Should you encounter a prospect who uses a money market fund because of a liquidity need, you can offer the prospect the same liquidity and a higher return by setting him up with an ongoing overnight repo program.

Repos are fully taxable and thus may also be adversely affected by the proposed tax legislation.

Reverse repos (r-repos) are the opposite of repos. An r-repo might be suitable for the client who owns the securities (usually U.S. governments) and who wants to raise cash by borrowing against them. The client will retain a dealer who will "take in" the securities and in turn find an investor to purchase them in a regular repo transaction. The dealer thus acts as a conduit between the client with securities who needs cash and the investor with investable funds who is seeking an investment.

For example, if your client owned $10 million of U.S. government long bonds priced at par and yielding 8%, he might reverse repo them to a dealer who would, in turn, repo them to an investor at a rate of 7%. Thus the "spread" is 1% for the term of the transaction. This 1% is generally split between the client and the dealer.

These transactions are very popular with companies that have seasonal cash needs. These companies generally have a large cash surplus for most of the year and are net borrowers for only a short period each year (from a few weeks up to a couple of months). Rather than restricting themselves to short-term vehicles, which mature prior to their need for cash, these companies invest in *higher-yielding*, longer-term bonds and then reverse repo the bonds when they need cash.

Municipal Investments

Corporations in high tax brackets invest in municipal (muni) securities for the same reason that individuals in high tax brackets invest in them. Interest paid by municipal securities is exempt from federal income tax and, if the issuer and investor are from the same state and/or state and city, the notes can be double or triple tax-exempt, respectively.

Although every municipal security with less than a year either to its maturity date or to its "put" date can be considered to be a money market instrument; however, when investors refer to the municipal money market, they generally are referring to tax anticipation notes (TANs), revenue anticipation notes (RANs), bond anticipation notes (BANs), or muni low-floaters (MLFs). TANs, RANs, and BANs, are distinguished by the source of funds that will be used to pay off the notes when they mature. If a city needs money immediately but does not collect its taxes for six months, it might issue a 6-month tax anticipation note, using the tax revenues, when they are collected six months hence, to pay off the TANs.

Similarly, if a state is going to float a 20-year municipal bond offering but feels that interest rates will be lower in 9 months, it might elect to instead issue 9-month BANs. Thus the state can raise the money it needs now, but doesn't have to issue its long-term fixed rate debt for 9 months. In this situation, the state is betting that interest rates will be lower in 9 months, and thus the cost of the state's long-term financing, when issued, will also be lower. If, instead of moving lower, interest rates should move higher over the next nine months, the state might elect to issue a second series of BANs, using the sale proceeds of the second BAN offering to pay off the first BAN offering. The expectation is that, when the second series of BANs come due, interest rates will then be low enough so that the state can float its long-term bonds without the need for a third series of BANs!

Revenue notes rely on a future revenue source, such as tolls, federal revenue sharing funds, and the like, to pay off the note holders. The specific revenue projections, as well as detailed information on the expected revenue source, can be found in the offering memorandum.

Muni notes are rated by the major credit agencies in a manner very similar to the ones the agencies use to rate CP. After evaluating all the relevant information about an issuer's financial strength and ability to meet its financial obligations on a timely basis, the agencies assign it a rating from P1 to P3 (Standard and Poors) or MIG1 to MIG4 (Moodys). Also like CP, it is very common for municipal issuers with low credit ratings to have a bank issue a letter of credit or to have an insurance company issue a financial guarantee bond so that the issue can come to market with a top credit rating.

Unlike the negotiable CD, where only about a dozen banks are considered prime (see Chapter 12), in the muni note market there are thousands of issues and issurers. Most trade only locally, although the better known ones (such as New York City or the state of California) trade nationwide.

Muni notes are offered in both coupon and discount form. The coupon notes are available in both fixed rate and variable rate form.

One additional vehicle that brokers should be familiar with is the *municipal lease*. Many county and municipal governments have restrictions against borrowing money for a term of more than one year without first holding a public referendum. This is to prevent an outgoing administration from saddling an incoming administration with a high debt load. Because of these restrictions many municipal purchases are technically made as a series of renewable one year leases. For example, if a municipality wanted to purchase a fire truck it might structure the deal as a series of five one-year renewable floating rate leases with the option to purchase the truck for $1.00 at the start of the sixth year.

These leases are written with such onerous cancellation clauses that they are almost never terminated, so the investor is well protected. (Additionally, a municipality will go to almost any length before it will default on its fire truck payments.) These leases offer substantially higher rates of return (although less liquidity) than other short-term municipal investments. Brokers offering municipals to their clients and prospects should become familiar with municipal leases.

Equity Investments

U.S. corporations that invest in the equity securities of other U.S. corporations can exclude 80% of the dividends they receive from federal taxation, assuming that they hold the securities for at least 45 days and that they did not borrow money specifically to purchase the securities. This tax break results in a maximum corporate tax on dividends of 8.00% (20% of the dividends received taxed at the current maximum corporate tax rate of 40%). Note that the maximum corporate tax rate is expected to decline to 34% by 1988 making preferred stocks even more attractive. This exceptionally favorable tax treatment has resulted in equities being a favorite investment vehicle for corporations that find themselves in the higher tax brackets. Because preferred stocks generally pay a higher dividend yield than common stocks, most of the attention from corporate investors has been focused on the preferred market.

In many ways equities are some of the most exciting, and potentially lucrative, vehicles for brokers to present to their clients and prospects. During an economic upturn, more companies have more cash to invest than they normally would have. Further, more companies find themselves in the higher tax brackets, increasing the relative attractiveness of these vehicles. These factors, taken together, mean that brokers should have no trouble finding suitable prospects for these vehicles during good times.

The following sections describe the various types of preferred stocks available in the marketplace today.

Straight preferred stocks are fixed-rate, long-term (sometimes even perpetual) securities. Like any other fixed-rate, long-term fixed rate security, they are susceptible to both credit risk and interest rate risk. When interest rates were relatively constant (at least by current standards) in the 1950s and 1960s, fixed-rate preferreds were a very popular corporate cash investment vehicle.

OPEC and the 1970s put an end to the "buy and hold" strategy used by many of the corporations that invested in fixed-rate preferreds. When the prime rate reached 21%, many corporate investors saw the market value of their fixed-rate (4–5%) preferreds holdings drop by 60% or more. While the dividend exclusion remained attractive, the extreme market volatility resulting from the violent interest rate swings made these issues too speculative for most companies to hold in their short-term investment portfolios.

The two exceptions to this rule are:

1. Companies wishing to speculate with a portion of their surplus cash by trying to "time" the market. Using this approach they would buy straight preferreds when they expected interest rates to fall, and retreat to cash when they expected interest rates to rise.

2. Companies that are comfortable using the futures markets to hedge a straight preferred portfolio against adverse interest rate moves.

Adjustable-rate preferred stocks (ARPs) were issued by the investment banking clients by Wall Street firms, in response to the changing market conditions, including wildly fluctuating interest rates, as early as 1981. Like fixed-rate or "straight" preferred stocks, the dividends from these securities are 80% excludable from federal income tax calculations when received by another U.S. corporation.

Unlike straight preferreds, however, these preferreds' yields are not fixed, but rather are free to *float* in relation to a "basis rate." In most cases, the *basis rate* is defined as the *highest yield* offered by *either* the 90-day T-Bill, the 10-year U.S. government bond, or the 20-year U.S. government bond. Thus, when the yield curve is positive, the yield offered by the 20-year U.S. government bond defines the basis rate. However, when the yield curve is either inverted or humped, the basis rate is determined by either the T-Bill or the 10-year note, respectively.

The yield on an individual ARP issue is based on the issuing company's credit rating. Most issues yield a fixed basis point spread under or over the basis rate. A company with an excellent credit rating may be able to fix its yield at 300 basis points *below* the basis rate, while a company with poor credit ratings might have to offer investors yields that are fixed at 100 basis points above the basis rate in order to attract buyers. So if the basis rate is 8%, the ARP with the high credit rating would yield 5% and the ARP with the low credit rating would yield 9%. If the basis rate rises by one percentage point, so would the yield offered by both the higher and lower rated ARPs. Most ARPs' yields are adjusted quarterly.

In theory, a preferred stock that pays a floating rate should always trade at or near par, and thus ARPs should be an excellent vehicle for preserving principal. Unfortunately, the actual market behavior of these securities has deviated markedly from the early theoretical predictions. Unfortunately, many of the early investors in ARPs (and their brokers) found this out the hard way.

Two principal factors can adversely affect the market value of an ARP and disturb its theoretical par, or near par, value. The first factor, which of course can affect any security, is *credit risk*. Unfortunately for the early investors in the ARP market, many of the early issuers of ARPs were banks. In a classic example of Murphy's Law at work, almost immediately after the first ARP issues hit the street, we had what is now commonly referred to as the "Latin American banking crisis." As the crisis unfolded many of the early ARP issuers had their credit ratings downgraded, which in turn lowered the market value of the ARPs they had just issued.

The second risk, which is a risk unique to adjustable securities, is what is referred to as *bracket risk*. Although these securities are adjustable, most issues have a maximum and a minimum yield that the issue can pay, that is, its "bracket." Bracket risk is the risk that, once an ARP reaches the upper limit of its yield range, it will cease to adjust in response to any further rises in the basis rate. Thus the ARP becomes, for all practical purposes, a fixed-rate security with the same corresponding *interest rate risk*. For example, right after the banking crisis, the prime rate hits record highs, and since most ARPs could not pay yields above the 12–14% range, they became effectively, "fixed rate" securities.

The combination of the interest rate risk to which they were now exposed, and the unexpected downgrading of their credit ratings, resulted in many ARPs dropping to 75%–80% of their issue prices in the secondary market. Investors were understandably angry at experiencing losses of this magnitude from a vehicle designed to protect principal. Since those early dark days, interest rates have fallen dramatically and the ARP market has not only recovered but has gone on to grow into a $12 billion + market.

When interest rates are low enough, ARPs offer investors a bracket "gift" instead of bracket risk. Because ARPs generally also have a *minimum yield*, once that yield is reached, even if the basis rate should continue to decline, the ARP's yield remained fixed at a now *above-market level*. Thus any further decline in interest rates should result in the ARP's market value appreciating (exacting the reverse of bracket risk). Should interest rates turn around and start to rise, then the ARP's yield will float up with the now rising basis rate, so as to preserve principal.

Thus, when interest rates have dropped to the level where the ARPs are either at, or are close to, their minimum yields, then ARP investors are in a win-win situation. Further declines in the basis rate will result in the investors' receiving an above-market yield and possibly market appreciation. However, should interest rates start to rise, the investors then own a security that will keep pace with the rising rates and thus preserve principal.

Two further derivatives of the ARP are the *collateralized adjustable rate preferred (CARP)* and the *convertible adjustable rate preferred (CAP)*. CARPs and CAPs are simply ARPs with some additional security features. In the case of the CARP the security comes from the fact that the issuing institution, usually either a bank or an S&L, places into trust a sufficient quantity of Ginnie Maes or other high-quality security to guarantee the timely payment of dividends and the redemption of the ARP in the event of a *dividend* default. To do this, the issuing institution usually creates a separate subsidiary and capitalizes it with the Ginnie Maes; this subsidary then issues the CARPs. Since these ARPs have Ginnie Maes behind them, they are practically immune to credit risk. Standard & Poor's has examined this structure and has rated securities that use this "collateralized" approach as "AAA."

CAPs get their additional security from the fact that they are convertible into a fixed *dollar* amount of the company's common stock (*not* a fixed number of shares as in the case of conventional convertible stocks and bonds). Suppose, for example, that the market value of a CAP declines from $100 to $90. The investor then has the option of converting a CAP share into $100 dollars worth of the issuer's common stock, regardless of the number of shares that may be required to do so (within certain relatively wide limits). Of course, just the fact that a given CAP is convertible goes a long way towards mitigating any significant price fluctuations. Investors seeking this "conversion option" generally have to give up between 100 and 200 basis points in yield relative to nonconvertible ARP's with an identical credit rating.

The *money market preferred* is another evolutionary concept in the preferred stock marketplace. First appearing in 1984, it was designed to provide the ultimate in principal stability. By 1986, this market had grown to a $6 billion market. By 1987, this market had grown to a 15-billion market, and its growth is expected to continue at a very high rate for the several years.

Unlike the previous generations of preferreds, an MMP's yield is determined by the *investors themselves*, via a Dutch auction process. Every seven weeks the preferreds are put out to bid. The various potential buyers submit bids, through their brokers, which state the *minimum yield* they will accept on the shares for the next seven weeks. The agent handling the auction, usually Manufacturers Hanover, ranks the bids from the lowest required yield to the highest required yield. The *lowest required yield, at which all of the available shares can be purchased, becomes the new yield for all the shares for the next seven weeks.*

Bidders who required a minimum yield above the yield determined by the auction are closed out of the auction. Bidders who bid at or below the yield auction-determined will receive the rate determined by the auction for the next seven weeks, when the entire process is repeated. Thus bidders know in advance that they will either get shares with at least the yield they bid at or not have to purchase any shares.

The auctions occur at 7-week (49-day) intervals because a corporate investor has to own the preferred for at least 45 days in order to claim the 80% dividend exclusion. These MMPs are not for the small investor since the shareprices run in either $100,000, $250,000, or $500,000 denominations. Corporations that already own shares of the preferreds being auctioned and wish to continue to hold their shares for another seven weeks, regardless of what the new yield turns out to be, can enter a *hold order*. These investors will continue to own the securities and will receive whatever yield is determined by the auction.

To protect both issuer and investor, most MMPs have minimum and maximum yields. To protect the issuer, most MMPs cannot pay a yield higher than the AA-rated commercial paper rate as published by the Federal Reserve Bank of New York. (Otherwise it would be cheaper for the issuer to borrow funds in the commercial paper market.) To protect the investor, MMPs cannot yield less than 59% of the same commercial paper rate. At a yield equal to 59% of the AA CP rate, MMPs offer corporate investors in the 46% tax bracket the same after-tax return they would earn if they had invested in AA-rated CP. Auctions typically go off somewhere between these two limits.

In the unlikely event that there are not enough bidders to buy all the shares offered for sale on a given auction date, the auction is then considered to be a *Failed Auction* and the preferreds would then *pay a higher* dividend rate (often 150% of the AA CP rate), until the next auction date. As of early 1987, every auction, for every issue, has been successful. Both the Wall Street firms and the issuing corporations have a vested interest in seeing that no auction ever "fails," and so both have worked very hard to support this new preferred vehicle. However, potential investors should be made aware that the possibility exists of not being able to sell these shares on a given auction day.

Like other preferreds these shares are redeemable, generally at 103 the first year, 102 the second, 101 the third, and at par from thereon. In the event that the yield determined by the action ever exceeds the AA commercial paper rate, as in the case of a failed auction, many MMP issues are then immediately callable at par.

To participate in an auction for a given issue, a corporate investor must first sign and file with the agent handling the auction the *Purchaser's Letter* found at the back of the prospectus for the issue. In this letter, the buyer acknowledges, among other things, that the shares are issued only in book entry form. Once this letter is on file with the agent, the investor has his broker submit the proper bid form to the proper place, by the proper time, in order to participate in the auction. Settlement is made on the next business day.

These MMPs offer yields that are approximately 50–100 basis points higher on an after-tax basis (assuming a 40% tax bracket) than the more traditional short-term investment vehicles (CDs, BAs, T-Bills, repos, CP, Eurodollars, etc.). MMPs allow the issuing corporations to borrow money at rates below the rate in the CP market, *at the same time* giving the investing corporations the opportunity to obtain a higher net after-tax return than they could in the CP market.

Rollover Programs

One way for corporation to enhance the yield of preferreds stocks even further is to implement a preferred stock rollover program. In a preferred rollover program an investor generally purchases preferred stocks just prior to their going ex-dividend (or X). The investor then collects the dividend, holds the stock for the required 45 days, sells it on the 46th day (usually at a small market loss), and then immediately reinvests the sale proceeds in another stock about to go X. The objective of this strategy is for the investor to collect additional dividends during the year in exchange for negligible trading losses.

In basic form, a preferred stock rollover program is nothing more than a tax arbitrage strategy. While the dividends are tax-advantaged, the short-term capital losses can be written off, resulting in a net higher after-tax return to the investor.

For example, an investor can go into the market today and purchase a stock that we'll call "preferred A" for $100 a share and that offers a 10% yield. The investor who simply buys it and holds it for a year should receive a 9.2% after-tax rate of return, assuming that he is able to sell it for the same $100 at the end of the year. (This oversimplified example is used only to illustrate the concept of a preferred roll program.)

If instead of just purchasing one preferred, let's say that our investor was able to purchase two preferreds: preferred A and preferred B, both selling for exactly $100 a share and both yielding 10%. In addition, both are going X exactly 46 days apart; that is, A goes X on June 1, and B goes X on July 15. If our investor was then to roll back and forth between these stocks for one year, he would collect eight dividends instead of four for a total of $20 in dividends received.

However, we know that when a stock goes X, it generally opens the next day for trading at a price that is lower by the value of the dividend just paid. In our example, since the stock was $100 and paid a $2.50 quarterly dividend, we would expect it to open for trading the next morning at $97.50. Over the next three months the price of the stock would rise as the dividend "builds up" in its market value, and by the next X day we would expect it to be back up to $100.

Thus, if we were to sell the stock half-way through its buildup period, i.e. on the 46th day, we would expect to recoup only about half of this dividend buildup or about $41.25. In effect, over the course of a year, we would buy each of the preferreds four times, at $100 a share, and sell each of the preferreds, four times, at $98.75 a share. Over the course of a year the investor would experience eight trading losses of $1.25 each for a total loss of $10. At year-end, the investor would have collected $20 in dividends and had $10 in trading losses.

At first glance the investor's net return appears to be the same regardless of whether the investor just buys and holds preferred A or rolls A and B. This, however, is before the different tax treatment of dividends and trading losses are taken into account. Since the $20 in dividends is taxed at 8%, we are left $18.40 in after-tax gains. Since the losses are tax-deductible we lose only $6.00 from our $10 trading losses. Subtracting net after-tax losses from net after-tax gains yields a final net after-tax return of $12.40 or 12.40%. Thus by rolling dividends we were able to increase the client's *after-tax return* by 3.2% (12.4% net from the roll program minus 9.2% net from simply buying and holding).

Now that we understand the theory, let's examine this approach using real market conditions. The chances of being able to actually collect eight dividends during a year are small (February always seems to upset the cycle!). However, *collecting* six or seven is very possible. In addition, in our theoretical example we used only two stocks. In a real rollover program we would constantly screen through the entire universe of quality, liquid preferred stock issues to find appropriate candidates to "roll" (including *ARPs*!).

Notes on Preferreds in General

Fortunately brokers do not need to trade these securities themselves in order to offer them to their clients. Several firms have started in-house preferred stock management and rollover services. Also, some mutual funds are geared specifically to the corporate market. Aside from offering the diversity and professional management that every mutual fund offers, these funds also allow corporate investors to:

1. Redeem their shares and have the proceeds wired directly to their bank on settlement day.
2. Borrow their money out of the fund to meet a short-term cash need without incurring a second sales charge when they reenter the fund.

For the broker these funds offer:

1. Freedom from having to follow the market on a minute-by-minute basis.
2. Reasonable commission structures including trailing commissions to compensate brokers for ongoing account servicing.
3. Sales assistance, sales literature, and other marketing support.

Brokers generally have neither the time nor the resources to properly invest clients' funds into these vehicles on their own. The preferred stock trading community is very close knit. All the "players" know all the other players. An insider can get better information, better bids, and better offerings than any "outsider." Additionally it is very time-consuming to follow this market, and your time could be better spent looking for new clients.

Regarding additional compensation, most money managers and mutual funds will, in addition to paying you their stated commission rate, also run trades through you if you place a significant amount of money with them. This is called *soft dollar compensation* and another way to leverage your sales effort.

Swaps

Swaps are nothing more than selling one investment and replacing it with another. There are many reasons for preferring one vehicle over another. Some of the *many* possible examples include:

1. Sometimes two securities with the same credit rating and maturity are trading at different prices, thus offering different yields. If you happen to own the higher-priced (and thus lower-yielding) security, you might sell it and buy the lower-priced (and thus higher-yielding) security.

For example, let's suppose that Company A and Company B both have commercial paper outstanding that is rated A1-P1 and matures in 60 days. Company A's paper is priced to yield 6.62% whereas company B's paper is priced to yield 6.74%. There is an almost infinite number of reasons for this discrepancy in prices. Company A may be buying back its own paper; Company B may have done a poor job of distributing its paper, and so on. As long as the reason for the discrepancy is not that company A is about to have its credit rating revised upwards or that company B is going to have its credit rating revised downwards, the reason is relatively unimportant. What is important is that, *with the proceeds from selling A, an investor can buy more of B and obtain a higher yield, without either sacrificing the quality or lengthening the maturity of the investment.*

2. Another popular reason for swapping securities is to lengthen or shorten the average maturity in anticipation of an expected change in interest rates. If an investor expected interest rates to rise, he would shorten the average maturity of his portfolio. This way his investments would mature sooner and he would be able to reinvest his funds at the then higher yields. If an investor expected interest rates to fall, he would lengthen his portfolio so he would have fewer vehicles maturing and therefore would continue to remain invested at the current higher rate.

3. One more reason investors swap securities is that they believe that one segment of the market is temporarily out of line with another. Suppose that A1-P1-rated commercial paper has historically yielded 25 basis points more than a BA from a top-tier bank. One day, for whatever reason, an unusually large amount of BAs come to market and, due to the law of supply and demand, the market value of the BAs drops to the point where their yield is the same as that of the A1-P1 CP. The investor, believing this to be a temporary aberration, sells his CP holdings and buys BAs. Sure enough, a few days later the BA selling spree is over and BAs rise in value again until their historic yield spread is regained. The investor would then have significant capital appreciation on his BAs in addition to achieving the same current yield as he was getting from his CP.

One of the most common mistakes corporate officers make is being overly conservative with their corporate cash portfolios. Far too many treasurers and financial officers simply buy securities and hold them to maturity, never looking to exploit the endless series of price aberrations that occur daily in the money market. Corporate officers far too often remark, "We make our money in our business, we're not really interested in the yield on our corporate cash." If you encounter this attitude (and you will), two strategies are possible:

Strategy 1: "Well Mr. Jones, if your company had four divisions would you operate three of them for profit and one for laughs? Of course not! But that's just what you're doing by not maximizing the rate of return on your corporate cash. Think of your corporate cash as a separate profit center. All I ask is that you let my firm and I attempt to increase your yield without increasing your risk. That's not too much to ask, is it?''

Strategy 2: If that doesn't work, simply compute the amount of additional dollars you *conservatively* estimate that a better investment program might yield Mr. Jones and then ask for a check for that amount.

If the amount was ten thousand dollars, say ''Well Mr. Jones, I'm sorry you're not interested in our services, could I please have a check for ten thousand dollars.''

Mr. Jones will of course say, ''Ten thousand dollars, for what?''

To which you respond: ''Well Mr. Jones, by my calculations by sticking with your current investment program instead of using our rec-ommendations, I estimate the cost to you will be ten thousand dollars. Now since ten thousand apparently doesn't matter to you, and since it matters a great deal to me, I would really appreciate it if you would write me a check. By the way would you like to see how I came up with that figure of $10,000?''

Either Mr. Jones will have had his curiosity piqued and will want to review the figures—or he will throw you out of his office. So be it.

Program Trading

One of the most controversial topics on Wall Street, *program trading* is nothing more than a simple arbitrage using the future value of a stock index versus the cash equivalent of the same index. In a program trade, an investor buys a representative, properly weighted portfolio of the stocks that make up an index on which futures are traded. Note that the investor doesn't have to buy all the stocks that make up an index, rather he purchases a representative sample that closely mirrors the performance of the index. For example, instead of buying the 1,500-plus stocks that make up the NYSE Index or the 500 stocks that make up the Standard & Poor's Index, an investor need purchase only 30–40 stocks to closely mirror the performance of each index.

At the same time the investor is purchasing the equivalent of the index in the cash market, he sells the same index for a higher price in the futures market. For example, let's say that the NYSE Index is at 134.50 on June 15 and the September NYSE Index Future is selling at 144.50 next door at the New York Futures Exchange. An investor who buys the index equivalent portfolio and at the same time sells a futures contract on that index has locked in' a guaranteed profit of 5,000 per contract ($144.50 minus $134.50 times $500 per point).

On the last Friday of September (expiration day for the September future contract), the cash market and the future market must, by defini-tion, be equal. It doesn't matter at what level the market closes because the investor is hedged. If the market drops the investor may lose a small fortune on the stock portfolio where he is long, but will make the same small fortune plus $5,000 on the futures position. In the reverse situation, if the market should rise, then the investor will lose a small fortune on the futures transaction but make the same small fortune plus $5,000 on the stock portfolio. Hence, once both sides of the transaction are in place, the transaction is "riskless" and is suitable for short-term corporate cash, pension assets, or any other conservative funds.

Where this strategy becomes even more attractive is when, because of market conditions, the investor doesn't have to wait until September to realize the $5,000 profit. If, for example, on July 1 the NYSE Index and the September future are trading at the same price, the investor would sell the stocks, cover the short futures position, and make the same $5,000—but in a shorter period, *thus increasing his annualized return*. If the price of the September futures contract should again rise to a high premium relative to the cash market, then the investor would again buy the stocks and sell the futures and lock in another guaranteed profit.

The controversy about program trading stems from the fact that each of the large investment firms is executing these programed trades on a massive scale. Some experts believe that program trading may be responsible for 40% or more of all trading on the floor of the New York Stock Exchange. Since program traders are interested only in the spread between the value of the cash index and the price of the futures contract, the absolute value of the securities is almost irrelevant to them. Thus when they are selling stocks, as long as the spread between the cash market and futures market remains low enough, they will continue to sell stocks even if their selling pushes the market down by 30–40 or more points.

A small investor, who has the unfortunate luck to purchase a stock just prior to the time the program traders start dumping it, often gets (understandably) upset at watching his investment get crushed. Because it takes sophisticated computers as well as numerous floor brokers acting in concert to execute a program trading program successfully, the small investors are starting to feel that the deck is stacked against them.

Theoretically, as more players enter the program trading game, the spreads between the futures and the cash markets should become more stable, but this has not occurred as of this writing.

If your firm offers pooled program trading accounts and your clients are sophisticated enough to understand program trading, you have an excellent sales opportunity. Program trading pools are currently yielding a *risk-free* return of about 6% over T-bills. That's easy to sell and tough to beat.

Selecting Investment Managers

As discussed in Chapter 2, working with either in-house or outside investment managers is essential. No one person can be an expert on every type of investment. Further, no sales representative has the time to properly follow even one market, much less all the markets in which their clients will need to participate in order to maximize the performance of their short-term portfolios.

Your role as a salesperson is to listen to your clients, identify their problems, develop solutions to those problems, explain your proposed solutions to your clients' satisfaction, make any necessary changes in your proposal, implement your proposal, monitor its progress, and update the program when necessary. Period.

In many cases your firm will be able to help you find appropriate managers. You may, however, have to go outside your firm to find appropriate managers who specialize in the various instruments covered in this chapter.

Case Study

During a day of cold-calling, you contact Mr. Smith, a food distributor. Mr. Smith mentions in passing that, because he handles some new items that have proven to be very popular (premium ice creams and low-calorie frozen dinners), his business is growing very rapidly. In fact he is about to exhaust the tax-loss carry-forward he built up when he first started the business three years ago.

Recognizing an opportunity, you immediately mention that *now* is when he needs to consider moving the cash he is generating from taxable to tax-advantaged investment vehicles. After asking a few more questions, you find out that his current cash balance is $500,000 and that it is expected to grow to $2.5 million within one year. Currently his funds are evenly divided between 30-day CDs and money market funds.

You promise to send him some information and set an appointment to talk again four day later. You quickly prepare a one-page report showing the relative *after-tax* return between his current investment portfolio and your recommended portfolio. One possible proposal is as follows:

- $100,000 into overnight repos for liquidity.
- $100,000 into brokered CDs.
- $150,000 into muni notes.
- $150,000 into a preferred stock mutual fund.

In your report you include a calculation that details how many *additional* dollars he will have in just one year if he implements your suggestions. You enclose your firm's promotional literature as well as the appropriate prospectuses and account forms.

During the next phone call you answer Mr. Smith's questions and make a $50,000 CD sale. Because Mr. Smith's office is near your office, you arrange to personally deliver a copy of the trade confirmation the next day at 5:00 P.M.

While you are there, you complete the basic corporate survey form (see Chapter 2) and get a commitment for the balance of Mr. Smith's cash account. As you're leaving you mention that you'll be putting some information in the mail to Mr. Smith about establishing a pension program.

Chapter 5

Retirement Planning

Whenever a survey is taken to determine what our population believes its most important financial goals or greatest financial concerns are, "planning for a comfortable retirement" is always at or near the top of the list. There are several reasons why planning for a comfortable retirement is consistently cited as one of the most important financial concerns by such a large percentage of our population.

First, there is the widespread publicity about the financial struggles of many of our current elderly people. (Only three out of every 100 people who reach retirement age are financially secure.) This publicity has made many people take a hard look at their own retirement programs.

Then there is the fact that people are living longer because of advances in medical and health care. This means that retirees' accumulated savings, retirement plan benefits, and benefits from government programs must be sufficient to support them for a longer time.

Also to be considered is that many people are rightfully concerned about the stability and solvency of the Social Security system. It is doubtful that in light of the current budget deficits Social Security payments will be regularly increased to keep up with the cost of living. What is worse is that for those people with individual savings and/or company retirement plans, Social Security benefits may in the future be reduced or even eliminated. This trend has already started with the taxation of a portion of the Social Security benefits that people with moderate supplemental incomes receive.

Because of the current federal budget deficits, many people are concerned about the return of inflation. Many people who are either currently retired or who will be retiring in the near future are on fixed incomes. A return to high levels of inflation could therefore be devastating.

Another factor is that many companies, as part of their efficiency and productivity drives to meet both domestic and foreign competition, are encouraging their employees to retire early (under threat of termination) or are laying them off in large numbers. Many of these people are unable to find comparable employment elsewhere and yet are not financially prepared for retirement.

When a person chooses to retire or is forced to retire, the question always is not, "How much money do I have," but "How long will my money last?" With the governmental programs caught in the budget squeeze and with the cost of living so high that few people can build up substantial personal savings, more and more of the burden of providing for the financial needs of the retirement community is falling to private employers and the pension benefits they provide.

A good pension plan is one of the most sought-after employee benefits. Therefore, in order to attract and retain good people, many companies have had to offer this benefit to their employees. Additionally, Uncle Sam, through the tax code, provides a number of incentives for both employers and employees to establish and participate in pension programs. In fact, because of the new tax legislation's devastating effect on many other tax shelters, retirement plans may be the small business owner's best remaining vehicle with which to shelter income.

Employer-provided retirement programs can take many forms, depending on the needs and objectives of the company, its owners, and its employees. Because each business has its own objectives and limitations, designing the best type of retirement program for a given business requires a great deal of creativity as well as knowledge of the options. Some of the many factors that must be considered when designing a retirement program include the following:

- How stable are the company's cash flow and earnings? Can the company afford to obligate itself to make set contributions for a number of years, or does it need the flexibility of having a plan that can be easily modified or cancelled?

- What is the employer's major motivation for installing the plan? Is it to shelter taxes, to provide for his own retirement, or to attract, retain, and reward key employees?

- Does the owner want the plan's benefits to accrue mainly to those employees he feels are his key people, or does he want all his employees to share proportionately in the plan's benefits?

- What percentage of the employees' salaries (and his salary!) does he want the plan's eventual benefits to replace?

- Does the employer want to tie his employees's retirement benefits to productivity increases?

- Does the employer want to encourage or discourage early retirement?

In high tech firms, for example, it's often advantageous to entice employees to retire early so that they can be replaced with new people who may be more up to date. Also, employers with persons in occupations that require tremendous physical or mental exertion may wish to encourage early retirements. In occupations for which experience is critical (e.g., law firms), however, you may want to structure the plan so as to economically discourage employees from taking early retirement.

- What type of retirement benefit does the employer want to provide the employee and/or the employee's family in the event the employee becomes disabled or dies prematurely?
- What administrative duties is the owner willing to perform?
- What is the age differential between the owner and the employees?
- What is the ratio of key employees to other employees?
- Does the owner believe that employees should pay part of the cost of the program?

Most retirement plans fall into one of three categories: qualified plans, nonqualified deferred compensation plans, and plans that invest primarily in the employer's stock. Each of these plans has its own advantages and disadvantages. In the next few chapters, we are going to cover in very basic terms each of these three types of plan and illustrate situations in which each type of plan would be appropriate.

Qualified Plans

When most people think of retirement plans, they are thinking about qualified plans. Included in this category are the following:

- Defined benefit plans.
- Target benefit plans.
- Money purchase plans.
- Profit sharing plans.
- SEP–IRA plans.
- Some employer stock plans.

For a plan to be qualified, it must meet the requirements of Section 401 of the Internal Revenue Code as well as any other applicable rules and regulations. The principal advantages of "qualified" plans are the wide variety of tax breaks provided to both the employers who establish them and the employees who participate in them. These tax breaks include the following:

- The opportunity to deduct contributions and administrative costs in the year they are incurred.

- The tax deferral of interest and capital gains on plan investments, which allows the plan assets to grow and compound much faster than they could outside a qualified environment.

- The opportunity to roll over pension distributions into an IRA for continued tax deferral.

- The eligibility of distributions from qualified plans for favorable 5-year averaging for income tax purposes.

- The fact that employer contributions on behalf of an employee are not taxable to the employee until they are actually received by the employee.

- Various tax breaks in the event an employee dies or becomes disabled before reaching retirement age.

However, Uncle Sam does not just indiscriminately hand out tax breaks unless they also help Uncle Sam achieve his objectives. In order to take advantage of the tax breaks afforded by qualified plans, employers must agree to abide by a wide-ranging set of rules created in part by the following federal tax acts:

- Employee Retirement Income Security Act of 1974 (ERISA)
- Economic Recovery Tax Act of 1981 (ERTA)
- Deficit Reduction Act (DRA)
- Tax Equity and Fiscal Responsibility Act (TEFRA)
- Retirement Equity Act (REA) of 1984
- The 1986 Tax Reform Act

Additionally, there have been numerous Internal Revenue Service private letter rulings and revenue rulings, Department of Labor guidelines, various court rulings, and so on, that have had an impact on qualified pension plans.

The overriding themes and objectives of this collective legislation have been to accomplish the following:

- Ensure that the plan assets are managed solely for the benefit of the plan participants and their beneficiaries.

- Accelerate the vesting of benefits so that employees earn nonforfeitable benefits in a shorter time.

- Increase the percentage of employees in a given company who are included in the company's plan.

- Decrease the difference in retirement benefits earned by highly compensated employees/owners relative to the rank and file.

- Increase the rights of both women in the work force and women who are homemakers.

● Reduce the maximum benefit that qualifies for favorable tax treatment.

In summary, these acts have collectively increased the obligations of, and reduced the attractiveness of, qualified plans to business owners. They have also helped achieve Uncle Sam's goal of shifting a greater portion of the burden of providing for the population's retirement needs on to the business community and away from both government programs and personal savings. These trends are expected to continue in any new legislation. Despite the onslaught of this collective legislation, however, qualified plans are still *very* attractive to many small business owners, *assuming the plans are designed properly*!

A well-designed qualified plan will often allow a small business owner to cover his employees with a retirement plan *and* increase his own retirement benefit for a smaller dollar commitment than it would cost to cover himself alone with a nonqualified plan.

For example, if a 45-year-old business owner contributes $50,000 a year to a qualified pension plan and 55% of the contribution is earmarked for his personal benefit and another 9% is credited to the benefit of his wife (who works as a part-time bookkeeper), then their combined interest in the plan is 64%, or $32,000. Initially, it might appear that the cost to the business owner of covering his employees is $18,000 ($50,000 contribution minus the $32,000 earmarked for the owner and his wife), but this is not the case. The cost is actually much less when the tax savings are considered. The calculation is as follows:

	Owner's Cash Flow
Pension Contribution	− $50,000
Tax Savings (33% bracket)	+ $16,500
Owner's Portion	+ $27,500
Owner's Wife's Portion	+ $ 4,500
Plan Administration Costs (after tax)	− $ 1,000
Net gain (loss) for owner	− ($ 2,500)

Thus, it *now* appears that the cost to the business owner of providing $18,000 of pension contributions for his employees is $2,500, but even this is not the whole story. Because both the interest earned and the capital gains received on investments held in a qualified plan are allowed to grow and compound with the tax deferred, the plan's assets can grow much faster in a qualified plan than they could out of a qualified plan.

Let's compare how much $32,000 (the owner's portion plus the owner's wife's portion) will grow to if it's invested in a qualified as opposed to an unsheltered account. For the purposes of this example, we'll assume a 10% return compounded annually for a period of 20 years (i.e., until the owner reaches age 65).

In a tax-sheltered account, $32,000 would grow to $215,280. Assuming a 30% tax bracket, the owner could look forward to a $150,696 after-tax pension benefit from this one year's contribution. (The tax becomes payable when the money is withdrawn from the plan.) If the owner maintained the plan for a number of years, the after-tax retirement amount would be much higher. Thus, as a result of his one year's cash contribution of $51,000 (plan contribution plus expenses), the owner was able to cover his employees with a retirement plan and provide himself with a benefit of $150,696.

In contrast, if the owner had elected to forgo establishing a qualified plan and had instead taken the same $51,000 and invested it out of the plan at the same rate of interest, he would have: $51,000 times 0.7 (to account for 30% taxes up front) leaves $35,700 available to invest. Assuming the same 10% pretax interest rate (7% after tax), this $35,700 would grow to only $138,148 at the end of the same 20-year period.

Thus, by establishing a qualified plan, the owner was able to (1) cover his employees, and (2) provide himself with an additional $12,548 from the same initial sum.

For all these reasons, selling business owners on the advanages of establishing a qualified retirement plan is not difficult. What is difficult and/or time-consuming is to do the following:

- Design the best type of plan (or plans) to meet the owner's needs.
- Convince the business owner that your proposal is the best one to achieve his objectives.
- Implement and administer the plan.
- Successfully invest the plan assets.

Major Requirements

Before we can start to design plans, we must first become familiar with the definitions, laws, rulings, and structures of qualified plans. The best place to start is always at the beginning. So let's examine some of the major requirements a plan needs to meet in order to become qualified *and remain* qualified. Some of the major requirements are as follows:

1. The plan must be a written plan.

2. The plan must be adopted by the employer (although it may be funded by the employees).

3. The plan must be communicated to the employees. This means the employees must be provided with: a. Access to the plan document in its entirety, b. A summary of the plan's benefits and features within 90 days of becoming a participant in the plan (120 days for a new plan) c. An annual statement of account balances and/or accrued benefits d. "Native language" plan summaries if the company has a high portion of workers for whom English is not the primary language.

4. The plan must be nondiscriminatory. That is, it must not provide benefits that are disproportionately higher to the highly compensated employees of a company than to the rank and file (within certain limits).

5. The plan must have its assets held by a trust company, an insurance company, or in certain cases a fiduciary. The trustees must be named in the plan document or appointed by a fiduciary named in the plan document.

6. The plan must not provide benefits or contributions that exceed

the maximum benefits and contributions allowed by law. To do so for even one employee may disqualify the plan for the year in which the legal limits were exceeded. Additionally, plan years need not correspond to calendar years (just as accounting years may be different from calendar years).

Plan years are referred to as *limitation years*. If your client has a limitation year that's different from the calendar year and should he inadvertently overfund the plan for an employee or for himself, then the deductions are disallowed for any calendar year that contains any part of the plan's limitation year. Thus, overfunding will result in the loss of two years' worth of tax deductions. Repeated offenses will result in complete disqualification of the plan. This is one good reason for making the limitation year the same as the calendar year.

Furthermore, for the purposes of calculating maximum benefits and contribution levels, the value of *all* qualified plans maintained by the employer (and any affiliated employers) must be combined.

7. The plan must base contributions, benefits, and other calculations on each employee's entire compensation, including wages, salaries, commissions, tips, bonuses, earned income, and any other income that is "reportable for income tax purposes."

These records can be kept on either a "cash" or on an accrual basis. The advantage of using the accrual basis is that it allows an owner to include, in the previous year's calculations, a bonus paid in January but earned over the previous year. Adopting a cash method does not allow this flexibility.

8. The plan must meet *either* one of two coverage tests for at least one day each quarter.

a. Coverage Test One: Does the plan cover at least 70% of all employees, *or* does the plan cover at least 80% of all *eligible* employees, assuming that at least 70% of all employees are eligible. Thus, a plan that covers 70% of all the company's employees meets the coverage test. Also, a plan that covers 80% of the eligible employees also meets the coverage test, assuming that the eligibility requirements do not exclude more than 30% of all the company's employees (i.e., 80% of 70%, or a minimum of 56% of the employees).

b. Coverage Test Two: The second test is not nearly so precise. It requires that any plan proposal not discriminate in favor of the highly compensated employees, the stockholders, or the officers of the company can be qualified. For example, a high tech design and manufacturing firm might find that, in order to attract and retain engineers, it has to offer them a pension plan. However, the same firm may not have any trouble attracting assemblers to build the components, and so, it may not want to incur the expense of extending the plan to cover them. If the engineers are not the highest paid employees of the firm and if they are not major shareholders or officers, it will likely be acceptable to set up a plan that covers only the engineering staff.

If, however, the engineers are also the shareholders, or the officers, or the highest paid, the plan probably will not qualify. Plans that attempt to qualify under Test Two are examined on a case-by-case basis. A plan that covers a good cross section of employees has a better chance of being approved by the IRS.

For purposes of these two tests, employees who (a) haven't met the minimum age or service requirements, (b) are covered by a collective bargaining agreement (assuming that a pension plan was the subject of good faith bargaining), and (c) are nonresident aliens, can all be excluded from consideration.

Because of the nature of small businesses (and because many are top-heavy, which is discussed later) they usually end up having to cover most, if not all, of their employees.

9. The plan must set aside contributions or accrue benefits for *all* participants. Any common law employee who is not specifically excluded from the plan (see the foregoing discussion of the coverage tests), has more than one year of service (1,000 hours or more per plan year), and is at least 21 years old must be allowed to participate.

Independent contractors are excludable as are "leased employees" if the leasing firm covers them with a plan comparable to that of the client. For defined benefit plans, employees who are hired when they are within five years of the plan's normal retirement age are excludable, although they must be included in any defined contribution plan.

Employees must continue to participate until they reach age 70 under the Age Discrimination Employment Act (ADEC), although contributions and/or benefits for an employee over age 65 can be actuarily reduced by an amount sufficient to bring them down to what it would cost to cover a 65-year-old employee. Companies with fewer than 20 employees are not bound by the ADEC, so many small businesses can avoid making contributions for employees over 65 (or whatever the plan adopts as its normal retirement age). Also, senior executives with accrued pension benefits in excess of $27,000 per year are not covered by the ADEC regardless of their company's size.

10. The plan must provide credit for past service when the plan is continued by a successor employer (i.e., when a new owner buys the business). If, however, the new owner discontinues the plan for more than five years, then past service can be ignored.

11. The plan must provide an acceptable vesting schedule. An employer may make a contribution to a qualified plan for an employee's benefit, but this does not mean that the contribution belongs to the employee. Most plans require that an employee remain with the company a number of years before he or she can take title to his or her proportional interest in the plan. The schedule by which assets are transferred from the plan to the employee is called the *vesting schedule*. If a benefit is 60% vested, then an employee who quits or is fired will forfeit 40% of the contributions or benefits accrued on the employee's behalf. (Depending on the type of plan the employer adopts, these forfeitures are either used to reduce future employee contributions or are distributed to the remaining participants.)

The ERISA defined four minimum vesting schedules that an employer can adopt for a qualified plan, although more liberal (read "faster'') vesting schedules can always be adopted. These four schedules are as follows:

(a) Cliff Vesting: Cliff vesting is 0% vesting until the tenth year, at which time the employee becomes fully vested in all contributions and accruals. (Note—the 1986 Tax Reform Act reduces the maximum number of years to 5 years after 1988.)

b. Graded Vesting: Graded vesting is 25% vesting in all contributions and accruals after five years, followed by 5% additional vesting for five years (i.e., 50% vested after 10 years), followed by 10% additional vesting for the next five years (i.e., 100% vested after 15 years).

c. Rule of 45: This rule requires the faster of the following:

(1) 50% vesting in all contributions and accruals after 10 years, followed by 10% additional vesting for the next five years (i.e., 100% vested in 15 years).

(2) 50% vesting in all contributions and accruals when the sum of the employee's years of service plus the employee's age equals 45, followed by 10% additional vesting for next five years.

d. Class Vesting. In class vesting, each individual contribution must be 100% vested within five years. For example, at the end of year three of vesting, an employee might be 60% vested in year one's contribution and investment return, 40% vested in year two's contribution and investment return, and 20% vested in year three's contribution and investment return, and so on. (The Tax Reform Act also places serious restrictions on class vesting—check with a tax attorney or actuary regarding the applicability of "class vesting" to a proposed plan.) Note, however, that the IRS can impose a more stringent vesting schedule if it feels the plan will likely be discriminatory. In this case, the IRS usually imposes what is called a "4–40" (four/forty) vesting schedule (40% vesting after four years, followed by 5% additional vesting for the next two years, followed by 10% vesting for the next five years (100% vested in 11 years).

Vesting must start at age 18. Say a company hires an employee when he is 17. When that employee reaches age 21, he will already have had three years of service for vesting purposes. Thus, it is often the case that employees start vesting in future contributions even before the employer is required to start making contributions for the employee.

Any employee contribution (whether mandatory or voluntary) is always immediately fully vested. If the employer elects not to make a contribution to a plan that requires employee contributions, then the employee will not receive any credit for the year for vesting purposes.

Although it should go without saying, an employer cannot fire someone just to avoid having the person vest in the company pension plan. This is a sure way for the owner to get the plan disqualified and find himself embroiled in a very nasty lawsuit. (Don't laugh; I've had several business owners ask if they could do this.)

Should an owner ever decide to change vesting schedules, any employee with five or more years of service must be given the option of choosing to remain under the old vesting schedule.

12. The plan must provide credit for past service to employees who

leave the company's employ and then return at a future date. Basically, an employee cannot lose credit for past service for either participation or vesting purposes provided his break in service was not longer than the longer of five years or the number of years he actually worked for the employer. So if an employee worked for three years, he would have to return within five years or lose his accumulated service credit. However, if an employee worked for eight years, he could return as late as eight years later and still get full credit for his past service. An employee who works more than 501 hours in a year (i.e., a partial year) will not have a break in service until the following year. Thus, the following rules apply:

a. An employee who works more than 1,000 hours must be credited with one year's service for participation and vesting purposes.

b. An employee who works between 501 and 1,000 hours will not be credited with a year of service for participation and vesting purposes but cannot be considered as having a break in service either.

c. An employee who works fewer than 500 hours is considered to have a break in service.

Employees, both male and female, must receive up to 501 hours of credit in the first year they need it to avoid a break in service when either they have or they adopt a child. Thus, a woman who worked for two months (320 hours) and left to have a baby would get credit for that year. A woman who left after eight months of service would not need the 501 hours to avoid a break in service for the year she left and so would be credited with those hours the following year.

13. The plan must be funded (i.e., money must be contributed on an ongoing basis to meet projected expenses). An unsecured promise to pay benefits will not entitle the plan to qualification. Furthermore, contributions must be made to the plan within 2½ months after a plan's limitation year unless an extension (for up to six months) is obtained from the IRS.

14. Loans can be made from a qualified plan to a vested employee providing that:

a. The plan specifically allows loans.

b. The loan is for an amount between $10,000 and the *lesser* of 50% of the employee's vested interest, up to $50,000.

c. The loan is repaid with a reasonable rate of interest and within five years unless the loan was to buy or add to the employee's (or his family's) principal residence.

d. Loans are available to all participants on the same terms.

e. Any pledge of an employee's interest in the plan is considered a loan.

f. The loan is not to a self-employed owner in a Keogh plan (which is prohibited).

Any loan judged to be improper will be considered a distribution and thus will be taxable.

15. The plan must not allow voluntary employee contributions that are higher than 10% of the participant's compensation. Employee con-

tributions are not tax-deductible but are allowed to grow and compound tax-deferred.

16. The plan may be, but is not required to be, integrated with Social Security. By integrating a plan with Social Security, an employer can reduce the benefits paid to lower paid employees relative to higher paid employees without disqualifying the plan. The justification for allowing business owners to integrate their plans is as follows. Social Security is partially supported by employer contributions (50% of the contributions to an employee's account are paid by the participant's employer's social security taxes). Social Security retirement benefits replace a greater percentage of a lower paid employee's salary than they do for higher paid employees. The fact that employers provide *proportionally* higher benefits to lower paid employees with their FICA taxes (and thus discriminate against their higher paid employees) is not lost on our policymakers. Because Social Security is discriminatory *against* higher paid employees, employers are allowed to adjust their pension programs to correct for the inequity of the Social Security system.

The dividing line between lower paid and higher paid employees used to be left the employer's discretion but the 1986 TRA limited integration to the Social Security taxable wage base (i.e., the amount of income that is subject to Social Security taxes, currently $42,000). Thus, an employer *can* provide higher benefits to any employees who earn more than $42,000. We will examine this very flexible tool in some detail when we review the specific types of plans later.

17. The plan must file on an annual basis a Form 5500 with the IRS. The filing is usually done by the administrator of the plan. Form 5500 provides the IRS with the relevant data concerning a plan.

18. The plan must provide joint and survivor annuity benefits unless both the employee *and the employee's spouse* agree in writing to select another payout formula (either a lump sum or an annuity on the employee only). The agreement to select another payout formula must be witnessed by a plan official, or it must be notarized. The justification for this requirement is that, in Uncle Sam's opinion, too many women have not been covered by their husbands' pensions after the husbands have died. Although a joint and survivor annuity will be smaller because of its longer expected life, the government feels that spouses, particularly wives, deserve this protection.

In addition, employers must provide employees and their spouses with written summaries of their retirement benefits prior to the employee's retirement.

Determination Letter

When the company and its attorney feel that they have drawn up a plan that is qualified, they can *and should* submit it to the IRS for review. If the IRS agrees that the plan meets the necessary requirements to be qualified, it will issue to the plan sponsor a favorable determination letter. Although applying for a determination letter is not required, it is prudent for every company to do so. An ounce of prevention. . . .

Types of Plans

Qualified plans generally fall into two categories: the defined benefit plan and the defined contribution plan. Some types of plans have characteristics of each, however. As we shall see, each type of plan has its own advantages and disadvantages and is appropriate in different situations.

Defined Benefit Plan

In a defined benefit plan, each employee's pension benefit is determined in advance by the benefit formula adopted by the plan. This formula is usually expressed as a percentage of the employee's average pay multiplied by a factor to account for the employee's length of service. Some plans use the average of the employee's pay over his entire career. For example, if an employee worked for a company for 25 years, then the pay component of the formula would be the average of the employee's earnings over that 25-year period. Because inflation tends to diminish the value of the employee's eventual retirement benefits under a career formula, plan many companies have instead adopted formulas based on shorter periods. The average of the five highest paid consecutive years or the three highest paid years are the most common formulas used today.

For example, 1% of the employee's average pay for the highest paying five consecutive years for each year of participation is very common. If an employee averaged $30,000 a year over his highest consecutive five years of employment and worked for 25 years, his benefit would be derived as follows:

1% of $30,000 (or $300) times the number of years an employee participated in the plan (25) equals a $7,500 annual pension benefit.

For the reasons we have discussed earlier, many defined benefit plans integrate Social Security Benefits into their Benefit Formula. This is done primarily in one of two ways. The first way is to credit a different percentage of pay for compensation that is in excess of the social security taxable wage base than for compensation that is below the social security taxable wage base. This is referred to as a *step-up* plan.

The step-up, or differential, can be as large as 1.4% of pay for a plan that uses career average pay, or as large as 1% for a plan that uses the highest consecutive five-year average pay. For example, a plan that uses career average pay might credit 1% of pay for earnings below the breakpoint and 2.4% for earnings above it *or* a plan that uses a highest five consecutive years formula might credit 1.5% for earnings per year for earnings below the taxable base and 2.5% for earnings above the taxable wage base.

The second way that defined benefit plans are commonly integrated is by means of the offset method. When this approach is used, the employee's retirement benefit is reduced by an amount that is a percentage of the employee's Social Security retirement benefit.

For example, an employer might provide a benefit of 60% of the average compensation earned during the employee's best consecutive five years *minus* 50% of the employee's Social Security benefit. Because, on a percentage basis, this reduction will reduce the benefits of lower paid employees more than those of higher paid employees, it helps to compensate for the discrimination of Social Security against higher paid employees. The maximum percentage of Social Security that can be offset is 83.3%. Any defined benefit plan that is integrated with Social Security must use an average pay period of at least five years.

Regardless of whether or not the plan is integrated, the maximum annual benefit that anyone can receive from a defined benefit plan is $90,000 or 100% of the average of the highest three consecutive years' (limitation years or calendar years) compensation, whichever is lower. Plans that allow early retirement before age 62 must actuarily reduce the maximum benefit ($75,000 maximum benefit for a retirement age of 55). Plans that allow later retirement can, *but are not obligated to*, actuarily increase the maximum benefit ($135,000 at age 70).

Should an employee's average highest three-year compensation be below $10,000, then the employer is not bound by the 100% maximum and can receive a benefit of up to $10,000 instead.

Because the employee is guaranteed a predetermined benefit, the burden of investment performance falls on the company if it adopts a defined benefit plan. If the company earns a high rate of return on its pension assets, then it will have to contribute less money to the plan in order to fund the predetermined benefits. If, however, the company earns a low rate of return on its pension assets, then it must contribute more money in order to fund the benefits. With a high enough rate of return, some companies can entirely eliminate some of their annual pension contributions.

In addition to the employer's promise to pay benefits, an employee covered by a defined benefit program is also protected by the Pension Benefit Guarantee Corporation (PBGC). The PBGC was created by Title IV of ERISA and insures pension benefits for participants of defined benefit plans only, not defined contribution plans.

Insurance by the PBGC is not insurance in the typical sense of the word. First, it is not voluntary. Any plan that applies for a determination letter is required to buy the insurance. The cost was recently raised from $2.60 per participant to $8.50 per participant per year. (Many small professional groups that never had more than 25 participants are exempt from obtaining PBGC coverage.)

Second, PBGC insurance does not cover all losses. The insurance insures benefits up to only $1789 a month. Participants entitled to receive benefits larger than this maximum are insured only up to this maximum. Furthermore, the PBGC does not use its own funds unless it absolutely has to. Instead, the PBGC first looks to the employer and can require an employer to forfeit up to 30% of the company's net worth to meet its underfunded pension obligations. Only if this 30% is not sufficient does the PBGC commit its own funds to pay the benefits.

Determining How Much to Contribute. Each year an actuary evaluates the plan to determine how large a contribution the company must make in order to have enough money in the plan to pay the future benefits that the plan promises. When an actuary determines the required contribution, the law requires that he use a set of assumptions that are both consistently applied and, when considered together, reasonable. Some of the factors that the actuary considers are the age of the plan participants, whether or not the plan will cover more participants in the near future, the sex of the participants, the historical and expected employee turnover, any past service liability, the expected and actual return on plan investments, early retirement liabilities, as well as any other significant factor that may affect the plan's ability to provide the promised benefits in full and on time.

All defined benefit plans have an actuarily calculated Funding Standard Account, which starts at zero and is credited and debited each year based on the plan's performance and parameters. If the value of this account is negative, then the plan is underfunded. If the value of this account is positive, the plan is overfunded. Each year the account is debited with the following items:

- The present value of the future benefits earned over the plan year.

- The amount necessary to amortize any unfunded past service liability. For example, if a company starts a plan in 1986, it may want to give credit to its employees who are about to retire although it has not been setting money aside for them. Any benefits paid would be an unfunded pension liability and would have to be amortized over 30 years. Older and multiemployer plans may be able to amortize these liabilities over 40 years.

- The amount necessary to fund any additional costs caused by changes in plan amendments or changes in actuarial assumptions, amortized over 30 years.

- Any "net experience" losses, investment or otherwise, amortized over 15 years.

- Interest charges on liabilities at a reasonable interest rate, prorated for the period the liability actually existed.

Credits are added to the account in a similar manner except for cash contributions, which are not amortized but are credited in full.

An actuary must evaluate the plan at least once every three years and more often if the IRS determines that closer scrutiny of the plan is advisable (for example, if the plan is seriously underfunded or borderline discriminatory). Also, a valuation is generally required whenever the plan has a significant amendment, the number of participants increases by more than 20% in a single year, or the plan is affected by a spin-off, merger, or acquisition.

There is also a variety of ways in which actuaries can value a plan's assets, including the assets' fair market value and the average market value of the assets over a multiyear period (the lookback method). For valuation purposes, bonds and/or instruments of indebtedness can be carried at face rather than at market value. The justification for this is that because defined benefit programs are long-term plans and because a bond's market value must equal its face value when it matures, ignoring intermediary price fluctuations will not be harmful to the plan's ability to meet its future obligations. Because stock prices do not have a "face value," they do not receive this favorable valuation treatment.

If the account value is negative, the plan is technically underfunded; if the account value is positive, the plan is technically overfunded. A plan that is overfunded or underfunded is not necessarily a problem so long as the gap between the plan's assets and liabilities does not get too large. If the plan is overfunded by too much, the IRS may contend that the plan is not being used to fund only the future benefits but is in fact being used to shelter profits in a tax-deferred fund for eventual reversion. In this case, the IRS may move to disqualify the plan.

If the account is too underfunded, the IRS will impose a 5% penalty excise tax and send the company a notice of funding deficiency. The company then has 90 days to correct the deficit or it will be liable for a 100% penalty (neither penalty is tax deductible). If after this 90-day period, the company still fails to make the required contribution to the plan, the Pension Benefit Guarantee Corporation will declare the plan to be "insufficient" and may move to seize control of the plan and its assets.

Because the implications of underfunding a defined benefit plan are so severe, any business owner who considers establishing a qualified retirement plan should be totally aware of the implications of underfunding before he adopts a defined benefit plan. Currently, more than 80% of the new plans being started are *not* defined benefit plans, and the onerous penalties for underfunding is one of the main reasons why business owners are not selecting them.

However, the rules for defined benefit plans are not completely inflexible. In the event a business is experiencing true hardship, it can take a number of steps to reduce or postpone its required current pension contribution, as discussed in the following several paragraphs.

1. The company can apply to the IRS for a one-year waiver of its required contribution. To have its contribution waived, the company must convince the IRS that it cannot make the payment without incurring undue hardship. Under no circumstances can the company apply for waiver more than five times in 15 consecutive years. Any waived contribution must be amortized over the following 15 years, and none of these amortized payments can be reamortized even if the company receives another waiver in a later year.

2. The company's actuary can adopt an Alternative Minimum Standard in lieu of the funding standard. By adopting this standard, the company is allowed to fund its plan on a slower schedule. However, switching to this schedule does have some drawbacks. Most notable is the

requirement that if this schedule is adopted and the company cannot make even the reduced payment required, it will have to revert to the regular funding schedule and amortize any waived contributions over five years instead of 15 years.

3. The company can apply for an extension (of up to 10 years) of its amortization period. Notice that neither any previously waived contributions nor any plan using the alternative funding schedule is eligible. The burden is on the plan sponsor to convince the IRS and PBGC that if the company obtains the extension it will then be able to meet its future obligations.

4. Finally, the company can elect to adopt retroactive plan amendments that are designed to reduce future benefits and thus current costs. No amendment can be made, however, that will reduce already accrued benefits or that is retroactive for more than one year.

Voluntary Termination. If, despite the hardship rules, the company either can no longer afford the plan or simply decides to discontinue the plan, the company can move to voluntarily terminate it. Before this decision is made, however, the company needs to make sure that it has had the plan in place for more than a few years (at least enough years to convince the IRS that, when the plan was established, it was meant to be permanent). If the plan is relatively new, the plan may not meet the qualification requirement of "permanency." In this case, if the company applies to have the plan terminated, the IRS may retroactively disqualify the plan and disallow all the previous tax deductions the company took for contributions.

Assuming the company has met the permanency requirement and wants to terminate its plan, the first step is to file Form 5310 with the PBGC at least 10 days before scheduled termination and to notify all interested parties (participants, retirees, and so on) using a form created for this purpose by the PBGC. After notifying the PBGC and the interested parties, no benefits can be paid to retirees for 90 days unless prior approval is obtained from the PBGC.

After notifying the PBGC and the interested parties, the next step in the termination process is to determine the value of the plan's assets and obligations to see if the plan has sufficient assets to meet its existing obligations. For termination purposes, pension benefits are ranked into six priority categories as follows:

1. Benefits accrued from voluntary employee contributions.
2. Benefits accrued from mandatory employer contributions.
3. Benefits in "pay status" for three years before termination.
4. All other vested benefits guaranteed by the PBGC (includes most benefits except those recently added).
5. All other vested benefits.
6. All other nonvested benefits.

If the assets are sufficient to meet all the obligations of categories 1 through 4, then the plan has sufficient assets so far as the PBGC is concerned.

If the plan has sufficient assets, then the company must distribute the assets or buy annuities within 90 days and then report back to the PBGC within 60 days of the distribution date. Only after the plan has met all the obligations of all six benefit priorities can it recapture any excess plan assets, and then only if reversions are specifically allowed by the plan document. If reversions are not specifically allowed, then the assets must be distributed to the participants in a nondiscriminatory manner. Notice also that if the participants were required to make any mandatory contributions, they must share in the reversion pool on a prorated basis. The theory behind this requirement is that their contributions helped to over-fund the plan and so a portion of any excess assets belongs to them.

If the plan has insufficient assets but the company itself is solvent and does not want the PBGC taking over the plan, then the company can agree in advance to make up any shortfall in assets needed to meet the first four benefit priorities. All amounts contributed are tax deductible. The company, however, needs to be very sure of just what its obligations will be because once it agrees to make up any shortfall it becomes *fully* liable for the shortfall.

If the plan has insufficient assets and the company does not or cannot guarantee to make up any shortfall, then the PBGC will usually become a trustee of the plan. The PBGC has the authority to seize up to 30% of the company's net worth to meet any shortfall. Also, any transfer of company asssets or large distributions from the company's plan to an owner within the 120 days previous to the termination may have to be repaid to the company or the plan.

The company must prepare a comprehensive net worth statement and furnish the PBGC with financial statements for the previous five years. Companies that refuse to provide complete information to the PBGC in a timely manner may lose the 30% liability limit and may find themselves liable for 100% of the plan's shortfall. Spinning off divisions, changing the company's name or location, changing the state of incorporation, selling the company, or converting to a defined contribution plan will not limit liability.

Any liability must be payed promptly although the PBGCmay allow installment payments if it feels that its chances of collecting funds are improved by allowing installment payments.

Involuntary Termination. The PBGC can *force* a company to terminate a plan if any of the following conditions obtain:

- The plan is too underfunded.
- The plan can't pay benefits owed in full and/or on time.
- An owner takes a large distribution that leaves the plan underfunded for its vested benefits.
- Any other reason that leads the PBGC to believe it will have to cover a loss in the future.

Tracking and Notification. To keep track of established defined benefit plans and to identify potential problems early, the PBGC requires plan administrators to notify it within 30 days of certain events pertaining to defined benefit plans. The notification should include the following:

- A copy of the plan document.
- A copy of the latest actuarial report.
- Identification and explanation of the event.
- A copy of the lastest IRS determination letter.
- Any other paperwork appropriate to the event.

The events that must be reported include the following:

- Any amendment that reduces already accrued benefits, or benefits that would have been accrued if not for the change.
- Dramatic decrease in the number of participants.
- Minimum funding levels not met.
- Inability to pay benefits in full and on time.
- Distributions to owners that leave plan underfunded.
- Bankruptcy, liquidation, or any indication that the company will go out of business.
- Changes in sponsorship or in the control group.

Advantages of Defined Benefit Plans. In spite of the restrictions and administrative requirements of defined benefit plans, they are still the plan of choice for many situations.

First, because a defined plan allows a participant to fund a large retirement benefit in a minimal amount of time, it is often the plan of choice for owners who do not start their plan until they are over age 45. For this same reason, these plans are very popular with people who earn a large amount of money in a short time (e.g., professional athletes and entertainers).

Second, because the benefits are determinable in advance, because the benefits are predictable, and because the investment burden falls on the company, this type of plan is often the favorite of unions.

Forfeitures in defined benefit plans must be used to reduce future contributions and cannot be used to increase benefits.

Defined Contribution Plan

As their name implies, defined contribution plans are plans in which the contribution and not the eventual retirement benefit is defined in the plan document. In these plans, the company makes a dollar contribution to a separate account in each participant's name and invests the funds in what it believes to be a prudent manner (more on investments in a later chapter). This separate account is separate for bookkeeping purposes only. Plan assets are generally held in one pooled account, although some companies do give employees a choice over how funds in their individual account are to be invested.

An employee's benefit is determined solely by the amount of the employer's contribution to the employee's account and by the rate of return earned on the account's investments. The pension benefit is thus as large or as small as the value of the employee's account on retirement day. Thus, with defined contribution plans the selection of investment managers, strategies, and vehicles usually rests with the employers, and the investment risk and investment reward fall to the employees.

The principal advantage of defined contribution plans is their flexibility. Unlike a defined benefit plan, to which the owner is obligated to make actuarily determined contributions, in a defined contribution plan the owner determines the size of the contributions irrespective of investment performance or eventual benefit.

The maximum annual addition to a defined contribution plan is generally $30,000 or 25% of compensation, whichever is lower. The annual addition is defined as *the sum of* the following:

1. New contributions.
2. Forfeitures (in a defined contribution plan forfeitures can be used either to reduce future contributions or can be reallocated in a nondiscriminatory manner).
3. The lessor of 6% of employee pay or half of any voluntary or mandatory employee contributions. Contributions, whether mandatory or voluntary, are ignored for annual addition calculations unless they equal 6% or more of employee compensation.

The only liability that an owner has in the event a defined contribution plan is terminated, assuming all required contributions have been made, is that all employees immediately become 100% vested in their separate accounts.

Defined contribution plans are of several kinds, as follows:

Target Benefit Plans. A target benefit plan resembles a defined benefit plan in that the plan attempts to provide a stated benefit. However, rather than guaranteeing the benefit itself, the plan guarantees to make contributions that *should* be sufficient to provide the employee with the targeted benefit, assuming a reasonable rate of return is achieved on the plan's investments. So long as the employer makes the contributions, however, the employer cannot be held liable if the target benefit is not achieved. The IRS can impose excise taxes on the company if it fails to make the required contributions. Because the benefit is "targeted," any forfeitures are used to reduce future contributions.

The contribution level is determined actuarily by using the benefit desired, the investment return expected, and the participant's age. Many pension experts like to describe these plans as defined benefit plans without the administration and termination restrictions. This is not really true, however, because the maximum contributions allowable are much lower than is the case with defined contribution plans. A target benefit plan can be integrated with Social Security.

Money Purchase Plan

A money purchase plan is considered a pension plan as opposed to a profit sharing plan. An employer who adopts it incurs an ongoing obligation regardless of the company's profitability or financial condition. Under a money purchase plan an employer agrees to make a fixed contribution, usually expressed as a percentage of pay for every participant every year. The percentage can be any amount up to 25% of compensation or $30,000, whichever is lower.

The plan can be integrated with Social Security using a "differential" of 5.4%. This means that, whatever the contribution percentage is for compensation below the Social Security Taxable Wage Base (currently $42,000), the contribution percentage for compensation above the taxable wage base can be 5.4% higher. Thus, if a company contributes 9% of compensation below the wage base to a plan, it can contribute 14.4% of compensation above the taxable wage base. If the company contributes 0% of compensation on salaries below the taxable wage base, it can still contribute up to 5.4% of compensation above the taxable wage base.

Profit Sharing Plans

Profit sharing plans are the most flexible type of qualified plan an employer can adopt. While they are similiar to other qualified plans, they have a number of important differences.

The most important difference between defined benefit plans (and money purchase plans for that matter) and profit sharing plans is that the contribution formula for profit sharing plans can be very flexible. Profit sharing plan contribution formulas generally fall into one of two categories.

1. *Predetermined share of the profits formulas:* This type of compensation formula must (a) define what the company means by profits (that is, before-tax or after-tax, including or excluding capital gains, and so on) and (b) determine whether a certain threshold figure needs to be met before profit sharing begins. For example, many companies only allow employees to share in profits above some predetermined return on equity, such as 30% of profits above those required to maintain a 10% return on equity. This is done to place the interests of shareholders ahead of the interests of employees.

2. *Discretionary formulas*: This type of compensation formula al-

lows the company's management or board of directors to decide on an annual basis what, if any, the year's profit sharing plans contribution will be. This type of formula is, of course, the more flexible of the two. However, any company adopting this contribution definition will need to be very careful to ensure that the plan's contributions are both "substantial and recurring." The reason for this rule is to prevent a company that has a windfall year from sheltering its profits in a profit sharing plan without any inclination of ever making any additional contributions to the plan. If the IRS determines that the plan's contributions are not substantial and recurring the plan may be disqualified.

The second major difference between profit sharing plans and other types of qualified plans is the treatment of forfeitures. With most other types of plans, any forfeitures are used to reduce future employer contributions. With a profit sharing plan, forfeitures may, at the option of the company as detailed in the plan document, be credited to the remaining participant's accounts in a nondiscriminatory manner. Usually "nondiscriminatory" means on a basis proportional to the *participant's compensation*, not the participant's "account balance," which is what is usually used to proportionally credit investment gans and losses.

The third major difference is the *current* contribution limits for a profit sharing plan in any given year. For profit sharing plans, the annual current contribution limit is 15% of the participant's compensation. In those years where the number of dollars that the employee is entitled to receive under the benefit formula exceeds this 15% maximum, the excess can be "carried over" to another year in which the employer's contribution *again* exceeds 15%. Then the company can credit the participant's account with the carry-forward up to the full $30,000 or 25% of compensation defined contribution plan limit.

For example, Joe Jones earns $100,000 a year. In year one of his participation in his company's profit sharing plan, his share of the company's profits is computed to be $30,000 based on the contribution and allocation formulas stated in the plan document. However, because of the 15% limit on *current* contributions, Joe Jones can receive only $15,000. The other $15,000 is carried forward to the next year. If in year two Joe is still earning $100,000 and his share of the profits is again $30,000 then Joe may be credited with $25,000, which represents his maximum contribution from the current year (15%) plus $10,000 from the carry-forward on the previous year, bringing his total contribution up to the defined contribution maximum of 25% of compensation. The carry-over going into the third year is then $20,000 ($5,000 from year one and $15,000 from year two). Contribution carry-forwards can be carried indefinitely.

Any forfeitures credited to a participant's account must also fall under the maximum defined contribution limits. In the preceding example, if Joe was credited with $5,000 of forfeitures in the second year, then he would have been able to use only $5,000 of his contribution carry-forward before he reached his $25,000 maximum. Therefore his contribution carry-over into the third year would be $25,000 instead of $20,000.

Profit sharing plans are integrated with Social Security the same way as money purchase plans.

Profit sharing plans are often the favorite plan type of small business owners for a number of reasons.

1. Small business owners, not being sure of their company's future cash flow are reluctant to commit to making the required contributions of either defined benefit or money purchase plans.

2. Owners believe that, when an employee has a direct interest in the profits of the company, the employee becomes more productive. Indeed, many studies have shown that employees who participate in the company's profits are significantly more productive. This is in direct contrast with other types of plans where the employees get their contributions regardless of productivity or profits.

3. Allowing employees to share in the company's profits may help eliminate the "we-versus-they" attitude towards management that is so prevalent in the American work force.

4. Installing a profit sharing plan may reduce employee turnover and encourage employees to suggest ways in which the business can be improved.

5. The IRS often takes a more liberal view of profit sharing plans from a "coverage" point of view. This means that plans that cover only certain groups of employees often have a better chance of obtaining a favorable determination letter when they are profit sharing plans as opposed to defined benefit plans or money purchase plans.

6. Profit sharing plans are allowed to invest more of their assets (up to 100% under certain circumstances) into employer securities and employer real estate and indeed even provides a tax break for doing so.

Hybrid Plans

Hybrid plans are defined benefit plans that maintain separate accounts for each employee. They are designed to allow any favorable investment results above the anticipated rate to accrue to the participants, while guaranteeing that if the investment results are unfavorable, the company will step in and provide some minimum predetermined benefit. These plans are considered to be the most favorable of all to the employees because they both guarantee a benefit and credit employees with any unusually successful investment returns.

SEP–IRS Program

A SEP–IRA plan does not fit either of the foregoing two categories. It is really a combination of individual IRA accounts that are funded by an employer. Every employee who has provided any service to the employee in three out of the past five years must be a participant. All participants must receive the same percentage of payroll contribution (up to 15% or $30,000—($7,500 after 1986 per Tax Reform Act). If the plan is integrated with Social Security, the employer is allowed to subtract the number of dollars actually paid in Social Security taxes from each employee's contribution. If compensation is excess of $100,000 is taken into account, then the owner must contribute at least 7.5% of payroll to prevent discrimination. The principal advantage to the employer is that a SEP–IRA plan requires a minimum amount of paperwork and administration. For the employee, the principal benefit is 100% vesting.

Combination Plans

A business owner can often improve his pension program by combining different types of pension plans into an overall "pension program." The benefits that can be obtained by combining plans include the following:

- Increasing flexibility.
- Increasing the percentage of pension contributions that accrue to the owner.
- Increasing the total number of dollars that the owner is allowed to contribute (and deduct) for his own benefit.

You will often encounter small business owners who will have one or more of these benefits as objectives for their pension programs.

Although combination plans can be integrated with Social Security, they cannot discriminate against lower paid employees in regard to *either* contributions or benefits. Although exploring all the ways that plans can be combined and all the rules that apply is beyond the scope of this book, the following will illustrate some acceptable plan combinations that achieve the three benefits listed.

The *combination of profit sharing and money purchase* is one example of a combination plan. For example, if an owner has earnings (for pension purposes) of $150,000 a year and were to put in a straight profit sharing plan, he would be able to set aside only $22,500 (15%). If the owner were to establish a money purchase plan, he would be able to set aside the full $37,500 (25%) but would then be required to make 25% contributions each and every year—a restriction he may not want.

If the owner were to establish a money purchase plan calling for a 10% contribution ($15,000), however, and then also established a profit sharing plan and contributed 15% ($22,500), he would be able to make the maximum $30,000 contribution while obligating himself to only 10% contributions on an ongoing basis. Thus, he has both flexibility and the ability to make the maximum contribution allowable under the defined contribution rules.

Another kind of combination is that of *defined benefit and defined contribution plans*. Employers who do not want to be bound by the $30,000 limit of defined contribution plans may opt to be covered by defined benefit plans. When these plans are used in conjunction with a defined benefit plan and are integrated with Social Security, they can increase not only the percentage of the contribution that accrues to the owner and his key personnel but also exceed the maximum contribution limits of single plans. When a defined contribution and a defined benefit plan are adopted in combination, the contribution limits are increased. The dollar contribution limit is increased by 1.25, and the percentage of compensation is increased to 1.40. For example, to use the 1.25 multiple the formula is as follows:

dollars contributed to defined contribution plan − defined contribution + dollars contributed to defined benefit plan − contribution limit

Let's assume an owner is contributing $65,000 to a defined benefit plan and wants to know how much he can contribute to a profit sharing plan. From our formula we know:

$$\frac{?????}{\$30,000} + \frac{\$65,000}{\$90,000} = 1.25$$

After doing the math, we find that the owner can contribute $15,834 to the defined contribution plan, which brings the owner's allowable pension contribution up to $80,834 (assuming that is not more than 140% of the owner's compensation).

Broker Compensation

As usual, there are several ways in which you can be compensated for your services.

First, you can charge fees for your design services and for the preparation of proposals and projections. Most firms have departments that can help you with this, or you can establish relationships with outside administrators and actuaries. Your fee schedule can be fixed (e.g., $250.00), or it can be based on the type of plan and number of participants (e.g., $150 plus $10 per employee).

The second service for which you can charge is providing your client with prototype plan documents for his attorney to review. Having pension plan documents prepared from scratch can cost $2,500 or more, so charging a client a few hundred dollars for a copy of a document that needs only to be reviewed and customized is reasonable. Copies can usually be obtained from your own firm's pension department, any major insurance company, or a book of current legal forms.

Remember always to get the client's attorney involved in the plan adoption process to protect your interests and your client's interests, to handle the plan filing, to obtain the determination letter, and to build another potential source of referrals for you and your services.

You can also be appointed as the company's retirement planning counselor. Your duties would be to meet with each employee as he or she retires and provide counseling on how to budget and handle their financial affairs during their retirement years. You may be retained by the company, charge the company a fee for each retiree, charge the retiree a fee, and/or earn commissions from securities transactions resulting from your advice.

Top-Heavy Plans

One of the principal goals of TEFRA was to make sure that the relative difference between the benefits paid to key people and those paid to the lower paid employees was never too large. To do this, TEFRA includes what are known as the *top-heavy provisions*. These provisions primarily affect small businesses, and a large percentage of small businesses are affected by them. For this reason, it is essential that any broker concentrating on the small business market become familiar with the top-heavy rules.

A plan is deemed to be top-heavy in any year in which more than 60% of the contributions are earmarked for the key employees, or 60% of the benefits accrue to the key employees. This percentage calculation must include both voluntary and mandatory employee contributions in addition to employer contributions. (For the purposes of determining whether a plan is top-heavy, all the employer's qualified plans must be considered in the aggregate.) A key employee is defined as any one of the following:

- An officer of the company or one who has the duties of an officer. (Thus, not giving someone a title will not exempt him from this definition.)
- or one of the 10 largest shareholders.
- or a person who is at least a 1% owner and earns more than $150,000 a year.

Restrictions

If a plan is top-heavy in a given year, certain restrictions will be placed on it.

Vesting. The company must adopt a *faster vesting* schedule. The IRS has approved two schedules (although an employer can always adopt a faster schedule).

- *Cliff vesting:* Employees are 0% vested until the end of the third year of participation. At the end of the fourth year, 100% vested.
- *Graded vesting:* Employees are 20% vested at the end of the second year, 40% at the end of the third, 60% at the end of the fourth, 80% at the end of the fifth, and 100% at the end of their sixth year of participation.

In the event a company plan is top-heavy and in a later year ceases to be top-heavy, all vested benefits accrued in the top-heavy year remain vested to the employees.

Minimum Benefit. The plan must provide a *minimum benefit*.

For a defined benefit plan, 2% of an employee's five highest-paid consecutive years of service for up to 10 years is the minimum benefit. Thus, an employee who averaged $40,000 over his best five years and worked for 10 years would be entitled to a benefit as follows:

$$2\% \times \$40,000 \times 10 = \$8,000$$

For a defined contribution plan, a minimum contribution is equal to the *lower* of 3% of compensation or the highest percentage credited to a key employee. Thus, if a key employee received 6%, the non-key employees would have to receive at least 3%. If the top rate paid to a key employee was 2%, then the plan would have to contribute at least 2% to the lower paid employees.

Although top-heavy plans can be integrated with Social Security, the integration cannot be used to reduce the minimum benefits.

Maximum Compensation. The *maximum compensation* that can be used to calculate the compensation percentages for key employees is $200,000. Thus, if the owner earned $300,000 and his secretary earned $10,000 and he set aside $30,000 for himself, then his percentage is not 10% (30/300) but is 15% (30/200) because only the first $200,000 can count. Thus he would have to make a contribution of 15% of his secretary's salary for her benefit (adjusted for Social Security if the plan is integrated). For purposes of percentage of compensation calculations, only the first $200,000 of compensation is counted in top-heavy plans.

Combined Plans. A top-heavy employer can *combine plans* and provide the minimum required contribution for his employees in only *one of the plans*. Under most circumstances, the plan where the minimum contribution is made is the defined contribution plan because it is usually the plan under which providing the minimum benefit will cost the employer less. If the sum of his (dollar allocation to his defined benefit plan/defined benefit maximum + dollar allocation to defined contribution plan/defined contribution maximum) is equal to one or less (instead of 1.25 in non-top-heavy plans). Then the combination is usually acceptable. For example, if the owner were to contribute $5,000 to his profit sharing plan and $68,000 to his defined benefit plan:

$$\$5000/\$30,000 + \$68,000/90,000 = 0.2 + 0.76 = 0.96$$

the combination of the plans is allowed. If the sum of the two ratios can be raised even to 1.25 if the employees get an extra 1% in whichever plan their minimum requirement is (4% in a defined contribution and 3% per year in a defined benefit) *and* the key employees don't receive more than 90% of the total.

Distributions to Key Employees. If a key employee receives a distribution from a top-heavy plan before age 59½, the distribution is subject to a 10% excise tax. The reason for this is to discourage key employees from removing funds from a top-heavy plan in order to convert it into a plan that is not top-heavy.

Despite being top-heavy, pension plans (especially if they are combination plans) can be very attractive for a small business owner as the following examples illustrate.

Illustration: Effect of Different Types of Pension Plans on a Typical Small Business

To reinforce the advantages of the different types of plans discussed, let's consider a typical small business and develop a pension plan for it. Consider the following hypothetical census data for ABC Manufacturing Inc.:

Name	Age	Start date	Salary	
Joe Owner	50	1/1/65	$200,000	
Jill Owner	49	1/1/65	$ 70,000	
Sam (Outside Sales)	40	1/1/76	$100,000	Comm.
Jack (Plant Mgr.)	58	1/1/78	$ 30,000	
Fred (Assembler)	35	1/1/78	$ 25,000	
Bob (Assembler)	26	1/1/80	$ 23,000	
Sally (Office Help)	32	1/1/81	$ 22,000	
Bonny (Secretary)	22	1/1/81	$ 12,000	
Bill (Ship. Clerk)	19	1/1/86	$ 11,000	

The company is fifteen years old, fully incorporated, and all the employees work full time.

From this data we can design a number of different plans. Assume our goals are to:

● *Maximize the number of dollars we can contribute to the plan to increase the size of the company's tax deduction.*

● *Increase the percentage of those dollars that accrue to the benefit of the owners.*

There is a variety of plans we can try to use to achieve these goals.

Plan Alternatives

Plan 1

The simplest plan is a SEP–IRA plan under which the same percentage of assets is set aside for all employees. Since some trust companies require that these plans include outside commissioned sales representatives, we have included Sam in the plan. Under this plan a maximum of 15% of payroll, up to $7,000 in 1987, can be set aside.

Currently, under this plan the maximum total contribution is $34,510 of which $19,198 (55.63%) accrues to the owners.

Plan 2

The next plan is a nonintegrated profit sharing plan in which the maximum percentage of payroll (15%) is contributed. Because commissioned sales representatives are excludable, no contribution needs to be made for Sam. Sam is also excluded from all subsequent plans. This reduces the maximum contribution that the company can make to the plan ($57,300) but increases the percentage of the contribution that accrues to the business owners: $40,500 or (70.68%).

Plan 3

Plan three is a profit sharing plan that is "integrated" at the $42,000 level. This means that the employer can contribute a lower percentage of payroll for those employees who earn less than $42,000 than for those who earn more than $42,000 (5.4% less). The net effect of integrating the plan is that the percentage of benefits that accrues to the owners and other highly paid employees increases. Thus in this plan the same number of dollars is set aside ($57,300), but more of them accrue to the business owners ($41,482 or 72.39%).

Plan 4

Plan four is a money purchase plan under which the maximum contribution is made (25% of payroll). The plan is nonintegrated, and thus the benefits accrue evenly to all the employees. Under this plan the maximum contribution is $75,500 of which $45,890 accrues to the owners (62.91%). Thus while the percentage of the contribution that accrues to the business owners decreases, the number of dollars that can be contributed increases.

Plan 5

Plan five is another money purchase plan, but integrated at the $42,000 level. Because the plan is integrated the maximum contribution is reduced to $68,760, but the percentage that accrues to the owner's benefit is increased to 66.74% ($45,890).

Plan 6

Plan six is a combination of a money purchase and profit sharing plan integrated at the $30,000 level. Under this combination plan the contribution is $50,844 of which $39,420 (or 77.53%) accrues to the owners. Thus by combining plans you can dramatically increase the percentage of the plan's contribution that accrues to the owners. (Note: The

Tax Act of 1986 requires companies to integrate their plans at the then current social security wage base.)

Plan 7

Plan seven is a target benefit plan sets aside the maximum number of dollars for the owner's benefit. This plan is not integrated but still dramatically increases the percentage of assets that can accrue to the owner's benefit. By switching to a target benefit plan, the company also increases the number of dollars that can be contributed to the plan. The contribution is $54,018 of which $44,906 accrues to the owners (83.13%).

Plan 8

Plan eight is the same as plan seven except it is integrated at the $42,000 level. This reduces the maximum contribution to $48,538, but increases the owner's percentage of the contribution to 88.13% ($42,777).

Plan 9

Plan nine is a defined benefit plan is not integrated and uses a 10-year cost basis. Under this plan the maximum contribution increases dramatically to $66,040, and the percentage that accrues to the owners remains high at 86.15% ($56,893). Of course, as detailed in the preceding chapter, an owner who establishes a DB plan incurs some long-term liabilities in exchange for being able to make larger contributions.

Plan 10

Integrated Plan 11 at $42,000. This increases the percentage that accrues to the owners but also reduces the contribution. In this plan the contribution is $59,638 and the employee's percentage is 90.76% ($54,127).

Thus we can see that the choice of plan has a very dramatic effect both on the size of the contribution and on the percentage that accrues to the owners. It is also easy to see why employers and employees frequently disagree over what type of plan to install.

Again, different companies with different objectives are best served by different types of plans. For this reason it's essential that you have someone who is an expert in plan design review each case.

Chapter 6   *Funding Qualified Plans*

Investing pension assets involves a special set of rules that must be strictly observed. ERISA and a host of subsequent Department of Labor rulings, IRS rulings, and court-imposed guidelines have created exacting guidelines that plan sponsors, investment managers, consultants, and brokers must follow. Considered collectively, these rules and regulations serve to protect the participants of qualified plans. (Notice that these rules do not apply to nonqualified plans.)

Rules for Fiduciaries

The law defines those individuals who are responsible for the safeguarding and investment of a qualified plan's assets as *fiduciaries*. Falling under this definition is anyone who exercises any discretionary control over, or in certain circumstances, managerial administrative responsibility for, a qualified plan. Such persons include the following:

- The company's officers and the company's directors if they are involved in directly managing the plan's assets or administering the plan or if they are responsible for selecting, hiring, managing and/or terminating investment managers, actuaries, pension consultants, and brokers.
- The members of the company's pension committee.
- Any investment managers hired by the plan.

- The plan's actuaries.

- Pension's consultants, if a plan fiduciary either formally or informally delegates to the consultant any of the aforementioned responsibilities and duties.

- Brokers, if they provide any investment advice to the plan. *Investment advice* is defined as any advice regarding which investments to purchase (or sell), what quantities to purchase (or sell), or when to purchase (or sell). Brokers are not included in the definition of a fiduciary if they only execute transactions and are instructed what to buy or sell, how much to buy or sell, and when to buy or sell. (Notice that brokers may be given five days discretion with regard to timing an execution of a transaction without falling within the definition of a fiduciary.)

No official title is required to be a fiduciary. Anyone who performs the functions covered by the definition of a fiduciary is considered to be a fiduciary regardless of the person's title.

Certain people and organizations that are involved with pension plans are exempt from being included in the definition of a fiduciary. These include the following:

- Accountants and attorneys, provided they restrict their activities to their traditional services and do not provide investment advice or administrative services to the plan.

- Mutual funds, if they do not provide investment advice and accept contributions only for the purpose of purchasing shares. Thus, for example, if a plan sponsor decides to place 100% of the plan assets in a mutual fund that invests only in gold stocks (an improper strategy), the mutual fund cannot be held responsible.

- Insurance companies, if the benefits their policies or annuities offer are guaranteed. If, however, the insurance company offers a variable policy or annuity, which pays a benefit that is dependent on investment performance, then the insurance company is a fiduciary for the variable portion.

A fiduciary is required to meet certain standards and follow certain rules when managing a qualified plan and its assets.

First, the cost of any security or investment purchased on behalf of the plan cannot exceed its *fair market value* at the time of purchase. This is to prevent fiduciaries from overpaying for securities to the detriment of the company or the plan participants. Any security or investment purchased must offer a fair return (or potential for growth if that is the objective of the investment) commensurate with the prevailing rates and market conditions at the time of purchase. Again, this rule is designed to protect the participants.

The plan must maintain *sufficient liquidity* to meet its disbursement requirements. For example, investing 100% of the plan's assets in real estate, which might take months or even years to sell, would violate this rule. If the plan did not maintain sufficient liquidity, it might be forced either to sell assets at distress prices or to delay scheduled disbursements, either of which would be detrimental to plan participants.

The plan's investments must be prudent. *Prudent investments* are defined as those investments that a person familiar with such matters would select if he or she exercised care, skill, and diligence when selecting them. Notice that the definition specifies that the investment decisions must be of the same caliber as would those made by someone familiar with the vehicle. Thus, ignorance of an investment vehicle's characteristics is no excuse for poor investment selection and performance. Also, because the definition states that investment decisions must be of a caliber that someone exercising "care, skill, and diligence" would make, any negligence or unprofessional oversights are also not acceptable as excuses for poor investment selection or performance. Naturally, the circumstances at the time the investments are made are considered, which prevents accusations of breaching fiduciary duty that are based solely on 20–20 hindsight.

Plan fiduciaries must also install reasonable safeguards for the protection of the plan and its assets that may include the following:

- Having the plan's investment results audited on a regular basis.
- Having the plan's investment stratagy reevaluated on a periodic basis.
- Adopting certain minimum guidelines for the quality of plan assets (credit ratings, size of company, etc.).
- Putting other safeguards in place, depending on the circumstances.

The plan's investments also must be diversifed except when it is clearly not prudent to do so. Remember that a qualified plan's investments must not be selected so as to try to "hit a home run" but instead must be designed to reduce the risk of loss. Diversifying a plan's investments reduces the potential reward (because only one investment can be the best, using two or more must reduce the maximum return), but diversifying also reduces risk. A plan's investments must be diversified to the point at which the plan is not exposed to large losses from any one investment.

The question most often asked about the requirement for diversification is: "If the plan has a well diversified portfolio of stocks, is this enough diversification to satisfy the diversification rules, or does the plan need to be diversified with regard to types of investment as well as individual securities?"

The attorneys I've talked to about this question are split on the issue. Some feel that a well-diversified stock portfolio is sufficient to meet the diversification requirements. They argue that the combination of dividends and the expected long-term growth of the American economy provides the plan participants with adequate protection. Other attorneys, however, believe that to be properly diversified, a plan must invest in various investment vehicles as well as various securities.

For my money, I would rather not have to explain to a jury why I had a client 100% invested in equities during a market decline. I strongly doubt that the jury members would have the sophistication to understand the market theory involved. I always, therefore, recommend diversification among different investment vehicles for qualified plans.

Another rule is that no fiduciary can allow a company to withdraw money from a qualified plan for any purpose other than paying benefits or justifiable expenses. One of the reasons for this rule is to prevent a company from retrieving a contribution after it has been made. There are some exceptions to this rule, however. First, a contribution made to a plan in anticipation of the plan's becoming qualified can be removed if in fact the plan does not become qualified (assuming the right to remove assets is allowed in the plan document). Second, a contribution that is the result of an error of fact (such as an arithmetical error) can be removed. In both cases, however, the funds must be removed within one year of the date the contribution was made.

Parties in Interest

A plan cannot transact business with a party in interest except in certain special situations. A *party in interest* is anyone who might have a conflict of interest and be in a position to exert undue influence on a plan, possibly to the detriment of the plan participants. For example, a plan's advisors, its administrators, anyone who qualifies as a fiduciary, anyone who provides services to a plan, anyone who owns 10% or more of the company's stock, any officers of the company, any controlling parties, any union officials (if the plan is a union plan), even relatives of any of the aforementioned parties, may be considered parties in interest, depending on the circumstances.

Anyone who is a *party in interest* cannot represent an adverse party, cannot trade assets with the plan, cannot borrow assets from the plan (except for his or her own vested interest under the rules covered in Chapter 7). For this reason, employers (who are parties in interest) cannot fund a plan with their own debt obligations (except in circumstances that are detailed later). A company cannot use the assets in its pension plan to guarantee or obtain a bond or as a third-party guarantee for its own purposes.

Plans cannot furnish goods or services (such as the use of facilities) to a party in interest except when necessary for plan business. No party in interest can transfer property to a plan if a mortgage has been placed on the property in the past 10 years. This is to prevent a party in interest from effectively circumventing the rule barring sales of property to plans. Thus, a business owner who is prevented from funding a plan with a piece of property worth $100,000 because it would exceed the 10% rule (described later) cannot go out and refinance the property, take out $80,000 in cash, and then fund the pension plan with he property, claiming it to be a $20,000 contribution.

The current rules do allow a party in interest to be paid by the plan for services rendered, providing such services are necessary and the pay is reasonable. Full time employees of the sponsoring company, however, cannot be paid for any service they provide to a plan; they can be reimbursed only for any expenses they actually incur.

The 10% Rule

Generally, a plan cannot invest more than 10% of plan assets into employer securities or employer real estate. The exceptions are plans that by design encourage investment in employer securities as a way of meeting the plan's objectives. Such exceptions include profit sharing plans, stock bonus plans, employee stock purchase plans, and thrift savings plans if and only if these plans' documents specifically allow such investment.

Business owners can apply to the Department of Labor for exemptions to the 10% rule for plans that would usually be prevented from exceeeding the 10% limit, such as defined benefit plans, target benefit plans, and money purchase plans. Exemptions are granted if and only if the Department of Labor feels that granting the exemption is in the best interest of the plan participants and beneficiaries. When determining whether or not granting an exemption is in the best interest of the plan participants and beneficiaries, the department considers the following:

- Whether the proposed transaction offers the participants an attractive return relative to the risk that it entails.
- Whether the proposed transaction offers the participants sufficient security (i.e., whether the transaction is collateralized).
- Whether the proposed transaction is the type that can be properly administered.
- Whether the alternative to allowing the exemption is the termination of the plan.

The current rules allow a plan to pool its assets with the assets of other companies' plans if the fiduciaries exercise due caution and if they believe that using a pooled fund would offer the participants an advantage such as reduced administrative cost or increased diversity.

Penalties for Violations

Fiduciaries who violate any of the rules that govern their role, whether inadvertently or intentionally, are subject to penalties and can be held personally liable. If a fiduciary violates any of the rules, he is personally liable to restore the plan to the condition the plan would be in had the infraction not occurred. In addition, a fiduciary must pay a (nondeductible) penalty tax equal to 5% of the value of the improper transaction(s). If the problem is not corrected within 90 days of when the fiduciary is initially notified of the violation, the Labor Department may impose a second tax that is equal to 100% of the value of the improper transaction(s). Because the penalties are so severe, many fiduciaries elect to purchase liability insurance against breach of duty claims arising out of errors, omissions, or negligence.

A case charging breach of fiduciary responsibility can be initiated either by a plan participant or the Department of Labor, usually in a U.S. District Court. Because of the complexities of these cases and the expense of litigation, almost all of them are brought by the Department of Labor, which has full power to subpoena any relevant documents from the company, its administrator, and its investment advisors.

Investment Strategies

Often, one of the best ways to design an investment program for a small business (15 employees or fewer) is to ascertain the return the owner will require to reach his individual retirement goal and then to implement an investment program that is designed to achieve that return. This assumes, of course, that the return the owner needs to reach his goals is both reasonable and obtainable.

Consider, for example, the case of Mr. Jones, who is the owner of a small machine shop. Eight years ago Mr. Jones started a money purchase plan for himself and his employees. His current account balance in the plan is $350,000, resulting from both generous past contributions and some successful (but very risky) investments.

After talking with Mr. Jones, you find out that he fully expects to be able to contribute the legal maximum (in his case, $30,000) to his plan every year for the next 15 years. Furthermore, he wants his plan to pay him a benefit upon retirement (15 years hence) that will give him the same buying power as a $7,000 a month benefit today.

Recognizing an opportunity, you ask the prospect if he has designed his investment program specifically to achieve the return he needs to reach his goal. The answer in such a case is almost always "no." You then offer your services to create an investment program that will do the following:

- Meet all the current legal requirements.
- Have a high probability of providing the return the client needs to achieve his objective.
- Take a minimum amount of risk in achieving that objective.

I recommend that you charge a small fee for this service as a way of separating those business owners who are truly interested from the merely curious. A fee of $100 to $500, based on the individual circumstances, would be appropriate.

Step 1

First, you compute the number of dollars the prospect will need at retirement to provide him with the same buying power as $7,000 a month would currently provide. Assume an inflation rate, and perform a simple future value calculation (any calculator like the Hewlett-Packard 12–C can do this calculation with just a few keystrokes). I recommend that you let the prospect select the inflation rate you use (so long as it's reasonable) in performing this calculation. The prospect will always place more faith in the results when they are based on *his* assumptions as opposed to your assumptions. Using the prospect's own assumptions also helps the prospect to sell himself.

Step 2

Assume that the benefit the owner will need is $11,000 a month when he retires in order to have the same buying power as $7,000 currently. The next step is to calculate how much money a prospect will need at retirement to purchase a joint and survivor annuity that will provide a benefit of $11,000 a month. After checking with various insurance companies, you find that the approximate purchase price of this annuity is $1.2 million. Of course, the client will need more than $1.2 million because he must pay taxes on his pension distribution. Allowing for taxes, you determine that the prospect will need to accumulate $1.7 million in his retirement plan in order to have the $1.2 million after tax that will be necessary to purchase a joint and survivor annuity that will pay a benefit of $11,000 a month.

Step 3

The next step is to calculate what rate of return the prospect needs on his pension plan assets in order to have $1.7 million on retirement. Doing the present value/future value calculations (again with the help of a calculator), you determine that the plan needs approximately an 8% rate of the return. If the plan's current investments are designed to seek a higher rate of return than 8%, the owner is probably taking a greater investment risk than he needs to. Conversely, if the plan's current investment program is designed to obtain a lower rate of return than 8%, the owner will probably not achieve his retirement goal.

Step 4

Now you must design an investment program that will achieve a 8% return while assuming a minimum amount of risk. One of the many possible portfolios you might consider is shown in Table 8-1.

After you perform the required calculations, you sometimes end up being the bearer of bad news. If an owner wants a benefit that is simply not reasonably obtainable, then you must go back to him and let him know that his plan will probably not provide the type of benefit he wants or is expecting. When this happens, show the owner the benefits his current plan is likely to provide him. Then suggest some alternatives that may help him achieve his goals, including the following:

Table 8-1. An Investment Portfolio for a Pension Plan.

Portfolio Percentage	Investment Vehicle	Expected Income	Expected Growth
10%	Closed-End REIT (15-year maturity)	8%	?
10%	Ginnie Mae	8%	0
10%	High-Quality Utility Mutual Fund	8%	3%
25%	Quality Corporate Bonds (Average 15-year Maturity)	9%	0
25%	Option Writing Mutual Fund	10%	3%
20%	Convertible Bond Mutual Fund	7%	5%

- Working past the normal retirement age. Working for a few extra years will often allow a business owner to meet his objectives.

- Redesigning the pension plan itself. Converting to a different type of plan will often allow an owner to reach his objectives.

- Installing a nonqualified deferred compensation plan. If an owner cannot meet his objectives for a reasonable cost with a qualified program, he may need to add an unqualified deferred compensation program for himself.

- Reducing his expectations of his plan. Sometimes all you can do is lower a prospect's expectations. This is still a valuable service, however, because it gives the owner an opportunity to increase his personal savings rate, a way to reduce his current expenditures, and/or the time to plan for retiring on a lower income.

This "work-back" approach to designing an investment program has some very definite benefits, including the following:

- It is logical, and logical approaches have a natural appeal for many people. Given the choice between a helter-skelter program and a logical one, most business owners will select the logical one.

- It is a customized program developed specifically for the small business owner. It uses *his* assumptions to achieve *his* goals, and thus he should receive it well.

- Once the program you design has been adopted, the owner should be relatively uninterested in being approached by your competitors.

This approach also has some potential drawbacks, most notably the potential for abuse in designing the investment program solely to meet the objectives of the business owner to the detriment of the other participants in the plan. Sometimes the investment objectives of the business owner may be different from the objectives that would benefit the other participants. A plan must, by law, be managed for the benefit of all the participants.

This problem can be largely avoided if, when you design an investment portfolio, you never design one that should yield less than what long-term Treasuries are yielding or more than what is realistically obtainable over the long term in light of current market conditions. Every pension investment program must be periodically reevaluated at least on an annual basis. A reevaluation should take into account whether:

This type of investment program, like every pension investment program, must be periodically reevaluated on an annual basis. A reevaluation should take into account whether any of the following conditions obtain:

- The owner's goals and objectives have changed.

- The actual rate of inflation has been higher or lower than the client's assumed rate.

- The actual performance of the portfolio has been better or worse than your expectations.

- The investment expectations and overall objectives remain reasonable, obtainable, and fair to the other participants in light of changing market conditions.

- The tax rates assessed on plan distributions have changed.

The sooner you start a program like this, the better the chances of achieving the client's goals because you will have more time to adjust your initial assumptions and recommendations.

Besides the owner's objectives, there are other factors that you must take into account when you are designing an investment program.

1. The type of plan must be considered. For example, a company that puts in a defined benefit plan is generally better served by an investment program that offers both predictable and consistent investment returns. In this way, the company can accurately budget its annual required pension contributions. Conversely, with defined contribution plans, the investment return does not affect the contribution. Therefore, an investment strategy can be more aggressive, erratic, and unpredictable without hurting the plan.

2. The length of time the owner will be in the plan is another factor that should be considered. For example, if an owner establishes a plan just a few years before he's planning to retire, you don't want to invest it heavily in vehicles like stocks, real estate, or long-term bonds. The reason is that these vehicles could drop sharply in value over a short term, and the business owner might wind up with a pension benefit that's less than his initial contributions. Although these vehicles are appropriate for plans with longer terms, plans with shorter terms should stick with certificates of deposit, floating rate notes, intermediate term bonds, and annuities.

3. You must consider the total retirement program offered by the employer. For example, if the company offers both a defined benefit plan and a defined contribution plan, it can afford to adopt a higher risk-to-reward ratio with its defined contribution plan because the company's

employees have the defined benefit plan on which to rely. However, if the company offers only a profit sharing plan, it should adopt a more conservative investment program for the protection of its participants.

4. The owner's preference for various investment vehicles and strategies must be taken into acount. Within reasonable limits, you can adapt an investment program to the owner's investment preferences. For example, some owners are partial to real estate, junk bonds, gold stocks, and the like. ERISA does not prevent you from modifying a pension investment program to accommodate the preferences of the owner so long as the modified strategy remains both prudent and reasonable.

5. When you design a pension investment program, remember that not being wrong is more important than being right. Not losing money is more important than making money. Although getting a client a tremendous return may make you a hero, losing a client a lot of money will not only cost you a client but may also cost you a lawsuit and your licenses. For this reason, if you must err, err on the side of being too conservative rather than too aggressive.

Investment Vehicles

Because investments are already your specialty (or should be if you are a broker), there is really no need to discuss them as part of this chapter. There are, however, some investments with characteristics that make them especially well suited for pension plans and so deserve a brief mention.

Mortgage Participation Programs

Mortgage participation programs are usually packaged either as limited partnerships or as real estate investment trusts (REITs). In these programs, the investors lend mortgage money to developers an interest rate close to current market rates. In addition, the investors retain a small interest in any appreciation in the property's value. Because it can take many years for a building to appreciate and because the value of real estate can fluctuate, these programs are appropriate only for plans with long-term investment horizons. The best time to invest in these programs is when interest rates are high because this is when the programs' managers can negotiate the highest participation interests with the developers. Always look for programs with set termination dates as opposed to open-ended programs. The advantages of mortgage participation programs as a pension investment are current income and the potential for appreciation in one investment vehicle.

I personally prefer using REITs as opposed to limited partnerships (either public or private) because REITs are usually more liquid and easier to analyze. Anyone who has ever tried to sell a limited partnership before its scheduled termination knows how important it is to have a liquid market. The only time I prefer purchasing partnerships is when they have fully disclosed real estate portfolios and I can buy them on the secondary market at a sharp discount to their book value.

Mortgage Appreciation Programs

Mortgage appreciation programs use the investor's funds to buy mortgages on buildings that are selling at a discount to their remaining balances. These programs seek to buy mortgages on buildings that have a high probability of being converted to condos or co-ops. When a building "goes condo," the purchaser must usually pay off any remaining balance on the outstanding mortgage on the property. If the program has bought the mortgage at a discount to its remaining balance, then when it's paid off the investors have a gain in addition to the current income. Like mortgage participation programs, the best time to buy these programs is when interest rates are high because that is when the mortgages will sell at the largest discount. They are usually available only as limited partnerships.

Convertible Securities

Convertible securities offer pension plan investors several advantages. First, they usually offer a higher current yield than the corresponding common stock. This higher yield in turn reduces the downside risk of the security by establishing a floor price equal to the value of the security without the conversion feature. The drawback of convertibles is that they usually trade at a premium on their conversion value, which can under certain circumstances reduce the security's appreciation potential. However, because the objective of investing pension assets is to limit risk and not to try for maximum appreciation, convertibles are appropriate investment vehicles. A number of mutual funds and pooled accounts invest in convertibles.

Option Writing

Writing options against a portfolio is always more conservative than simply holding a portfolio. Option writing increases the predictability of cash flow, provides a partial hedge against market declines, and increases current income. The risk of installing an option writing program is that the stocks may be called away shortly into a long bull market. A strategy that can be very successful is to write options against a progressively larger percentage of the portfolio as the market rises. For example, if a client had 50% of his total portfolio invested in stocks, then as the market rose, you would write options against a higher percentage of the stock portfolio. This strategy can also be used with mutual funds. In a mutual fund strategy, you would progressively shift your client's assets from a growth fund to an option-writing fund, as market prices rise.

Hedged Ginnie Maes

Similiar to writing options against stocks is writing options against a portfolio of Ginnie Maes. This approach has the same benefits and drawbacks as writing options against stocks. The strategy in this case, however, is to shift a higher percentage of a client's bond portfolio into the hedged portfolio as interest rates get lower. A hedged portfolio should generate about 1½ points of extra current income per year over an unhedged portfolio, but will also have less appreciation potential.

Equipment Leasing Programs

Equipment leasing programs can be very attractive pension investments if they are structured properly. Because pension plans are tax-exempt structures, they cannot benefit from the depreciation deductions allowable against new equipment. Instead, pension plans are interested in cash flow. Therefore, unleveraged or slightly leveraged programs are the programs of choice. These programs can offer a very high yield because companies that lease equipment are willing to pay a high rate of interest to acquire equipment in an "off balance sheet" transaction.

The type of programs that are preferable for pension plans are those that do the following:

- Use short-term leases.
- Lease low-technology equipment.
- Lease equipment only to creditworthy companies.
- Are 100% amortizing over the life of the lease.
- Have experienced management.

Two points about equipment leasing programs: First, the new tax act will probably eliminate the investment tax credit. This will mean that leasing programs will probably offer slightly higher interest rates in the future to compensate. Second, a leasing program may expose a plan to the unrelated business tax. This is a tax on pension plans that are involved in ongoing businesses, which is what the government considers many equipment leasing programs to be. The tax is usually negligible, but you should obtain an accurate estimate of what it is likely to be from the program's general partner before you recommend the program to a client.

Insurance Programs

When selecting investment vehicles for small businesses you should consider using insurance as a funding and investment vehicle. First, for businesses which cannot afford to offer group life, this may be the only way to provide both the owners and employees with insurance coverage. Second, the underwriting requirements are fairly lax for insurance policies that are issued as funding vehicles for retirement plans. Thus, by funding a retirement plan with insurance, you may be able to get protection for an owner who is otherwise highly rated or even uninsurable.

Also, insurance companies prepare dynamite presentations and proposals for your use with a minimum of effort on your part. Finally, some owners really like the guaranteed cash value offered by insurance products and the safety of having their pensions guaranteed by one of the large insurance companies.

Services You Can Provide. There are a number of ways you can be of service to a small business owner regarding the funding of his retirement program. The first way is to provide the client with a performance study in which you compare the client's investment return against the standard benchmarks (the Standard & Poors 500, the Shearson Lehman Bond Index) as well as against a portfolio with the same risk factor as the client's portfolio.

The second service you can provide is to offer a portfolio evaluation. Many firms have in-house portfolio evaluation software services. In the portfolio evaluation you can suggest ways a client can try to obtain the same return while taking less risk or how to try and obtain a higher return while taking the same risk.

- Vehicles that the client can use to diversify his portfolio.
- Substitute vehicles for the investments the clients currently has that may offer some advantage in light of changing market conditions.
- Ways in which the client can limit his exposure to any one risk (credit, interest rate risk, inflation risk, etc.)

You can also include recommendations on how the client's portfolio can be restructured to more accurately match the client's investment objectives. You may also want to include a section that discusses whether the client's current investments, both individually or collectively, meet his fiduciary requirements.

I recommend that before you do any study you either receive a fee or a commitment for soft dollar compensation. Otherwise, you may spend a lot of time and effort working for no compensation. Of course, you can also broker transactions, but you already know that!

Compensation. The design, implementation, and management of investment programs is an area on which every broker should concentrate, particularly those brokers keying in on the small business market. There are several reasons for this. First, retirement plans are currently the largest pool of assets in the nation and the pool is growing rapidly. Second, for many people (business owners included) the balance in their retirement plan is often their largest liquid asset. Third, many business owners who confidently invest their personal assets without any outside advice still seek professional advice when they are investing the assets in their company's pension plan.

Retirement plans generally incur three kinds of charges: charges for advice, charges for asset management, charges for the implementation, or execution, of purchases and sales. Depending on the services you provide, you may be entitled to one or all of these.

You should charge for advice (such as performance studies or portfolio evaluations) on an hourly basis. Fees of $100 an hour for small plans are reasonable for this kind of work.

Fees for providing investment management services are usually based on the size of the asset pool, the level of activity in the account, and often the performance record of the manager. Obviously, a large account that merely buys and holds a weighted portfolio of the Standard & Poors 500 will demand a lower percentage fee than a small account that employs a complicated investment strategy. Investment management fees generally range from a high of about 2.5% down to 0.25% for very large accounts that employ simple strategies.

For executing transactions most plan sponsors require discounts on commissions. For small accounts, the discounts can be small; larger accounts demand and receive executions at only pennies a share. It is the responsibility of the plan sponsor to negotiate the lowest net transactions costs possible.

Just because there are the traditional methods of compensating those who provide services to retirement plan sponsors does not mean that you need to be compensated in the traditional manner. You can, instead, use either of the following three methods alone or in combination. Each method has its own advantages and disadvantages.

1. Full service commissions.

2. Fees in lieu of commissions.

3. Combination of fees and commissions.

Providing these services in exchange for full service commissions has the advantage of being the simplest method and perhaps the easiest method on which to close a sale. Also, for many brokers who work for firms that do not allow their brokers to charge fees, it is the only option they can use. Unfortunately, this method has a high potential for abuse in that you can spend a lot of time working for clients in exchange for commissions that never materialize. If you are going to use this method, for your own protection have the prospect sign an agreement similar to the one shown in Figure 6-1. A client who really intends to send the business through you will not object, but a client who's not really interested or who is planning to do the business through a discount firm will refuse to sign it. Although it is probably not legally enforceable, it is a useful tool to separate those who are truly interested in your services from the merely curious.

Figure 6-1 Compensation Agreement.

Whereas: _____, hereafter referred to as the "client," desires to have _____, hereafter referred to as the "broker," perform such service(s) as detailed below and to compensate the broker for providing these service(s).

Whereas: the broker desires to perform the service(s) detailed below for the client and desires to be compensated for rendering such service(s).

Therefore both parties hereby agree to the following terms and conditions.

The brokers agrees to perform the following service(s):

_____

_____

_____

_____

_____

_____

The broker agrees that the time required to provide the above services will not exceed _____ hours.

The broker agrees that the services performed will be of a quality that is acceptable to the client.

The client agrees to compensate the broker by either paying the broker at the rate of $_____ per hour for a maximum cash price of $_____.

or

By using the broker to execute securities transactions in such a quantity that the commissions generated (at the broker's firm's regular posted commission rates) by the securities transactions is equal to or greater than three times the maximum cash price as detailed above.

The client agrees to settle this account (either in cash, commissions, or some combination thereof) within _____ months of the completion of the above mentioned service(s).

By signing this contract both parties acknowledge and agree to the terms outlined above:

_____	_____
client	broker
_____	_____
date	date

Compensation from Investment Managers. Before you refer a client to a professional money manager, it is essential that you have a clear understanding about how the manager will compensate you. It is important to reach an agreement about what percentage of the trades in the client's account will be executed through you. Agreeing that between 70–80% of the trades generated in a client's account will be executed through you is very reasonable. (Some managers may promise you 100% of the commissions, but because investment managers usually buy research or their quote service with commissions, that promise is usually broken fairly quickly.)

I also recommend that you find your own managers so that the manager's first loyalty is to you and not to your firm. In the event you ever change firms, having managers that are loyal to you instead of to your firm can be important.

You should also agree in advance on a discounting structure if the manager requires one so that there are no misunderstandings. Of course, any compensation you receive from a manager must be disclosed to the client in advance.

Chapter 7   *Nonqualified Deferred Compensation*

In a previous chapter we covered qualified plans in some detail, including the numerous features and tax benefits that make them attractive. Although qualified plans are fairly flexible and have wide applicability, there are still situations in which a qualified plan is either inappropriate or insufficient. In these cases, a nonqualified deferred compensation plan (a plan that does not meet all the requirements of a qualified plan) often does a better job of meeting a business owner's objectives. The situations discussed in the following sections are examples of such cases.

Not All Employees Covered

A small business whose owner either cannot afford to cover the majority of his employees or can afford to cover them but simply chooses not to is a candidate for a nonqualified plan. This situation often arises in companies that have large unskilled work forces. Because of the coverage requirements for qualified plans, these minimum wage employees are often not excludable from a qualified plan, so the owner will not install a qualified plan despite its advantages. However, the lower paid employees are excludable from a nonqualified plan, and so the owner may be willing to install a nonqualified plan.

Keeping Key Employees

A small business that wants to provide a compensation package to its key employees that is structured so as to discourage the employees from resigning is a good candidate for a nonqualified plan. In this situation, an owner can enter into a "golden handcuff" nonqualified deferred compensation agreement with his key employees. Under the terms of this agreement, the owner usually agrees to provide the employees with additional compensation at some point in the future in exchange for the employees current services. To discourage the key employees from resigning in order to work for a competitor or from simply retiring, these benefits are forfeitable unless the employees remain with the company for a stated period.

For example, ABC Manufacturing has a key salesman who brings in 60% of the company's business. The business's owner is concerned that his star salesman (age 55) will be recruited away by one of the company's competitors. If this happened, ABC Manufacturing would suffer a significant loss. The salesman is well paid, and the owner does not want to increase the salesman's current compensation.

After talking with you, the owner decides to install a nonqualified deferred compensation plan for the salesman. Under the terms of the agreement, the owner agrees to pay the employee an extra $10,000 a year for every year the employee continues to work, the money to be paid to the employee in 10 equal installments beginning at age 65. Thus, if the employee were to work for five more years, he would be entitled to $5,000 a year for the first 10 years after retirement. If he were to work to age 65, he would be entitled to a payment of $10,000 a year for the first 10 years after retirement. As a condition of the contract, the employee would forfeit all accumulated future benefits if he should leave to work for another company. Also, should he retire in less than five years, he would lose his accumulated benefits. Thus, if the employee left six years later to work for a competitor, he would forfeit $50,000 of future benefits. If he retired four years later, he would forfeit $40,000 of future benefits. If he retired six years later, however, he would be entitled to 10 yearly payments of $6,000, beginning at age 65.

From the employer's point of view, structuring the employee's compensation plan in this manner has accomplished several goals, including the following:

- Any competitor that tried to recruit the employee would find it more difficult and expensive to do so.

- The owner has been able to make the employee's compensation plan more attractive without increasing the company's current payroll.

- In the event that the employee were still to decide to leave the employer, the employer would have a future liability eliminated, thus reducing the cost of the loss. If, for example, the employee were to leave five years later to work for a competitor, the employer would save $50,000 in future payments, which would soften the financial blow to the company of the salesman's resignation.

All the terms in a nonqualified deferred compensation "golden handcuff" agreement are subject to negotiation between the employer and the employee. Naturally, because of the serious financial ramifications of these contracts, they should be written only by experienced legal counsel. A contract that is ambiguous in any major detail can turn out to be disastrous for the company, the employee, or both.

Many variables must be taken into account when negotiating a nonqualified "golden handcuff" agreement.

1. The *length of time* an employee must work before he is entitled to receive benefits is important. A relatively young employee may not be interested in waiting until retirement to receive his benefits and may want to be able to draw on the benefits earlier. Also, if the employee feels that the company is not financially stable and therefore may not be around in the future to pay the promised benefits, he may want a shorter maturity on his plan. When a company is financially weak or unstable, the nonqualified deferred compensation agreements are frequently structured as a series of one-year optionally renewable agreements instead of as a multi-year agreement.

2. Any *performance goals* that the employee must meet in order to be eligible for the future benefits must be clearly specified in the contract. For example, in the case of a salesman, will the salesman have to reach a certain quota each year in order to earn the benefit? If so, how is the quota to be determined so that it will be obtainable by the salesman during business downturns and yet remain challenging during business upturns?

3. Any agreement should include *protective covenants* for any employee covered by the plan. Because an employee will generally not receive any benefits unless he stays with the employer for a certain time, the employee will need some guarantees that he will not be indiscriminatingly fired before becoming eligible for the benefits.

4. The means by which the lan is *funded* (if it *is* funded) must be addressed (see discussion later in this chapter).

5. The *benefits the employee's beneficiaries will be entitled to* should he die prematurely is another point that needs to be addressed. Most nonqualified deferred agreements call for the company to pay the employee's beneficiary the accumulated benefit the employee has earned regardless of whether the service requirement has been fulfilled. For example, let's assume the salesman in the preceding example died after two years of service under the deferred compensation agreement. In this case, most plans would allow the salesman's beneficiary two years of deferred earnings ($20,000 in the example).

6. The benefits the employee will be entitled to should he become either partially or permanently disabled during the time he is covered by the agreement must be specified. These benefits are usually similar to the ones outlined in the section of the plan that relates to premature death, with full benefits paid for complete disabilities and partial benefits for partial disabilities.

Supplement to Owner's Retirement Fund

A small business owner who cannot accumulate enough money under his qualified plan savings to fund his desired retirement benefit may implement a nonqualified plan to supplement his retirement. If, for example, an owner figures that his qualified plan will provide him with a retirement benefit of $4,000 a month and if he wants a retirement income of $6,000 a month, he might install a plan for his own benefit that is designed to provide him with a supplemental benefit of $2,000 a month.

Solution to Retained Earnings Problem

A small business with a retained earnings problem is also a candidate for a nonqualified plan. Retained earnings taxes are imposed on businesses that accumulate more capital than they really need to operate. The federal government imposes the taxes to encourage business owners to take additional salary or declare dividends, both of which are taxable. If, in the government's opinion (based on certain formulas) a small business has more capital than it needs to operate, the IRS interprets the excess capital as a "tax avoidance strategy" and imposes a retained earnings tax.

However, retained earnings that are accumulated to pay future deferred compensation benefits are excluded from retained earnings calculations. Thus, a business owner who does not want to declare a dividend or increase his salary might elect to install a nonqualified plan to avoid the retained earnings tax. The reasonable compensation limits still apply, and nonqualified plan benefits must be included in an owners total compensation package for reasonable compensation purposes.

Although we have focused on "money" plans, businesses can also set up nonqualified plans that provide for the employees to receive stock instead of cash as the plan benefit. We cover these stock plans later.

Qualified Vs. Nonqualified Plans

One of the principal differences between a nonqualified plan and a qualified plan is the timing of the company's tax deduction for its contributions. A company that has a qualified plan can take the tax deduction when it makes a contribution to the plan. If the company has a nonqualified plan, it takes the deduction when it pays out the benefit. Allowing for the time value of money almost always makes the qualified plan more attractive than a nonqualified plan from a tax point of view.

A nonqualified plan can also have a number of advantages relative to a qualified plan. The relative attractiveness of these two types of plans is dependent solely on the specifics of the situation to which they are applied.

1. A nonqualified plan can include or exclude any employee without regard to salary, job description, title, percentage of ownership, or any other factor that affects qualified plans. A nonqualified plan can even cover just the owner himself if he so desires. Furthermore, if the owner elects to cover other employees with nonqualified plans, he can negotiate separate deals with different terms, conditions, and benefits for each employee solely on the basis of the owner's opinion of the employee's value to the company. If the employer wants this flexibility, then a nonqualified plan may be superior. If, however, the owner plans to cover most of his employees with the same benefit (proportionally), then a qualified plan is often a better choice.

2. In a nonqualified plan, the owner can negotiate any service requirement directly with the plan participants without taking into account the minimum vesting schedules required of qualified plans. If an owner wants to establish a vesting schedule that would be unacceptable for a qualified plan, a nonqualified plan may be the better alternative.

3. A nonqualified plan can provide any benefit within the realm of reasonable compensation and thus is not limited by the contribution or benefit limits of qualified plans. If the owner plans to make contributions that are under the maximums for qualified plans, he may be better off with a qualified plan. If, instead, the owner wants to exceed those limits, then either a nonqualified plan or a combination of a qualified and a nonqualified plan may be a better choice.

4. The amount of paperwork required to set up and administer a nonqualified plan is minimal, unlike the oftentimes burdensome paperwork requirements of qualified plans. For a nonqualified plan, all the owner needs to do is send a letter to the Secretary of Labor informing the Secretary that a nonqualified plan has been installed, the number of employees it covers, and stating that the company will provide the department with a copy of the plan if requested to do so. For very small plans, the cost of administration may exceed the extra tax benefit of a qualified plan, and so a nonqualified plan may be a better choice.

5. A nonqualified plan does not have to be funded. In fact, as detailed later, there are some serious restrictions pertaining to the funding of nonqualified plan(s). If the employer is short of cash, his only option may be to establish a nonqualified plan because he may not be able to meet the funding requirements of a qualified plan.

Doctrine of Constructive Receipt

Under current law, an employee is taxed on income when he is in *constructive receipt* of it, which means that employees are taxed when they either actually receive the funds or when they acquire nonforfeitable rights to the funds. Thus, to defer taxation of nonqualified benefits to the employee until they are actually received by the employee, the company cannot escrow the funds in any way (i.e., the employee must always have substantial risk of losing the benefits).

Deferring taxation can be accomplished one of two ways. First, the company can provide the employee with a naked promise to pay the future benefits out of future earnings. If the company were to go out of business before the time when the benefits were payable, the employee would lose his benefits. The second way to prevent current taxation of the benefits to the employee is for the company to accumulate assets to pay future benefits but keep them in the name of the company. Again, if the company were to declare bankruptcy the employee's claim would be that of a general creditor.

The constructive receipt rule prohibits the establishment of any kind of separate trust for nonqualified plan assets as is required with most qualified plans. Thus, from an employee's point of view, a nonqualified plan is always riskier than a qualified plan.

Using Insurance to Fund Nonqualified Plans

If a company is going to set aside assets to fund a nonqualified plan, far and away the best vehicle to fund it with is a permanent insurance product (whole life, tax deferred annuity, or universal life). There are three specific benefits of using insurance.

1. The investment income in the policy is free to grow and compound tax deferred, resulting in much faster growth of the asset pool. This, in turn, reduces the required contribution that the company must set aside to fund the future benefits.

2. Should the employee die prematurely, the company will have a ready source of tax-free funds with which to pay the employee's accumulated benefits to the employee's beneficiary plus some additional funds to help compensate the company for the loss of the employee's services. Any payments to the employee's beneficiaries are tax deductible to the company even though the company has received tax free funds from the insurance policy with which to pay them.

3. The company can pay an employee his benefit by borrowing against the cash value of the policy and still take a tax deduction for the payments although it incurs no tax liability by borrowing the cash value. If the company leaves enough cash value in the policy to keep the policy in force, the company can often recoup all of its costs for the deferred compensation plan plus a positive return when the employee dies.

Consider the example of assigning the benefits to another party. Situations commonly arise in which an individual who is entitled to some future benefits under a nonqualified plan wishes to transfer those benefits to a third party. This transfer can result in a number of tax consequences.

Changing the beneficiary will not result in any *gift tax* consequences unless the beneficiary designation is irrevocable. If the designation is irrevocable, then the usual gift tax rules and exclusions apply.

If an employee should "give" his future benefits to a third party, the employee will still have to pay *income tax* on the benefit when the assignee receives the payments. For example, if Joe Jones, who is entitled to receive $5,000 a month for four years as a result of his participation in a nonqualified program, should assign those benefits to his children, he will still be liable for the income tax on the $5,000 when it is paid to his children.

So far as the IRS is concerned, Joe Jones is still the recipient of the plan's benefits; after he receives them, he is then giving those benefits to his children. The justification for this position is that otherwise a beneficiary could shift his benefits to a person in a lower tax bracket to reduce his tax liability (which is known as income shifting).

If a plan participant should sell his future benefits, the sale proceeds are taxable as ordinary income. For example, if Joe Jones was entitled to a benefit of $5,000 a month for a five-year period but instead wanted his benefit in a lump sum, he could sell his future benefits to his employer (or anyone else) for a lump sum, all of which would be taxable as ordinary income.

Compensation

A nonqualified plan is often the plan of choice for a small business owner, either as a standalone program or in combination with a qualified plan. The flexibility of nonqualified plans is such that they can be used to achieve a wide variety of objectives in a wide variety of circumstances.

You can be of service to a small business owner by designing a plan that is customized to his needs and objectives. Naturally, you should charge the client for this service on an hourly basis. Most of the major insurance companies have software that is designed to help you design the best plan proposal to meet a client's objectives.

After you have helped a client to adopt a properly designed plan, then you can sell the client the insurance product required to fund the plan properly. Because the insurance business is still highly regulated, the commission structure is still very high (up to about 80% of the first year's premium).

A nonqualified plan is also an excellent way to throw some business to an attorney with whom you have rapport. Although legal fees can vary widely, a fee of $200 to $600 to draft a nonqualified agreement is standard, depending on the complexity of the document.

The examples that follow illustrate how insurance can be used to fund a nonqualified deferred compensation plan.

In the first example (Table 7-2), a 55-year-old male contributes $50,000 a year for 10 years into a nonqualified plan that earns 10.96%. Beginning at age 65, the individual begins drawing $25,000 a year out of the plan, using the policy loan provision. Despite the policy loans, the policy's cash value and death benefit continue to grow.

Table 7-2 Monarch Life Insurance Company Variable Life Insurance (VLI).

*Illustration of Death Benefits, Investment Base, Cash Surrender Values
and Accumulated Premiums Assuming Current VLI Mortality Charges*

For: Applicant
Age/Sex: 55/Male   *Prime Plan V*

Underwriting: Simplified

	Single Premium	Face Amount	Initial Investment Base
Class: Nonsmoker	50,000	91,927	50,000

Guarantee
Period: For Life

Policy Year	Payments(1)	Total Payments Made Plus Interest at 5%	End-of-Year Death Benefit (2) (3) Assuming Hypothetical Gross Annual Rate of Return of 0.00%	6.00%	12.00%
1	$50,000	$ 52,500	$ 91,927	$ 93,636	$ 99,347
2	$50,000	$ 107,625	$171,665	$ 187,147	$ 203,195
3	$50,000	$ 165,506	$249,847	$ 280,249	$ 312,993
4	$50,000	$ 226,282	$322,846	$ 373,093	$ 429,325
5	$50,000	$ 290,096	$390,976	$ 465,751	$ 552,733
6	$50,000	$ 357,100	$454,576	$ 558,348	$ 683,872
7	$50,000	$ 427,455	$513,756	$ 650,753	$ 823,136
8	$50,000	$ 501,328	$568,742	$ 742,968	$ 971,106
9	$50,000	$ 578,895	$619,706	$ 834,937	$1,128,325
10 Age 65	$50,000	$ 660,339	$666,417	$ 926,051	$1,294,597
15	0	$ 842,779	$561,965	$1,000,915	$1,848,914
20 Age 75	0	$1,075,622	$526,041	$1,082,221	$2,638,513
25	0	$1,372,797	$554,030	$1,189,469	$3,827,522
30	0	$1,752,075	$621,015	$1,314,102	$5,581,650

Policy Year	End-of-Year Investment Base (2) (3) Assuming Hypothetical Gross Annual Rate of Return of 0.00%	6.00%	12.00%	End-of-Year Cash Surrender Value (2) (3) Assuming Hypothetical Gross Annual Rate of Return of 0.00%	6.00%	12.00%
1	$ 48,794	$ 51,771	$ 54,737	$ 45,644	$ 48,621	$ 51,587
2	$ 97,183	$ 105,431	$ 113,981	$ 91,458	$ 99,706	$ 108,256
3	$144,489	$ 161,100	$ 178,992	$136,514	$ 153,125	$ 171,017
4	$190,732	$ 218,876	$ 250,372	$180,832	$ 208,976	$ 240,472
5	$235,904	$ 278,821	$ 328,745	$224,404	$ 267,321	$ 317,245
6	$280,017	$ 341,024	$ 414,819	$267,242	$ 328,249	$ 402,044
7	$322,945	$ 405,400	$ 509,154	$309,220	$ 391,675	$ 495,429
8	$364,621	$ 471,921	$ 612,425	$350,271	$ 457,571	$ 598,075
9	$404,959	$ 540,519	$ 725,303	$390,309	$ 525,869	$ 710,653
10 Age 65	$443,605	$ 610,735	$ 847,972	$428,980	$ 596,110	$ 833,347
15	$403,185	$ 715,574	$1,319,072	$399,935	$ 712,324	$1,315,822
20 Age 75	$407,929	$ 839,230	$2,046,089	$407,929	$ 839,230	$2,046,089
25	$459,604	$ 986,743	$3,175,181	$459,604	$ 986,743	$3,175,181
30	$543,729	$1,150,561	$4,887,010	$543,729	$1,150,561	$4,887,010

Table 7-2 *(cont.)*

Hypothetical rates of return are illustrative only and should not be deemed a representation of past or future rates of return. Actual rates of return may be more or less than those shown and will depend on a number of factors, including the investment allocations made by an owner, prevailing interest rates and rates of inflation. The Death Benefit, Investment Base and Cash Surrender Value for a policy would be different from those shown if the actual gross annual rates of return averaged 0.00%, 6.00% and 12.00% over a period of years, but also fluctuated above or below those averages for individual policy years. No representations can be made by Monarch or the Series Fund or the Trusts that these hypothetical rates of return can be achieved for any one year or sustained over the period of time.

Illustrated values may vary slightly from actual values due to rounding.

This illustration is invalid and incomplete unless accompanied by "Illustration Notes" at the end of this table and dated 01/01/1980 which explains any numbered references on this page.

Policy Year	Payments(1)	Total Payments Made Plus Interest at 5%	End-of-Year Death Benefit (2) (3) Assuming Hypothetical Gross Annual Rate of Return of 0.00%	6.00%	12.00%
1	$50,000	$ 52,500	$ 91,927	$ 93,141	$ 98,831
2	$50,000	$ 107,625	$170,339	$ 185,605	$ 201,519
3	$50,000	$ 165,506	$247,209	$ 276,875	$ 309,189
4	$50,000	$ 226,282	$318,488	$ 366,996	$ 422,189
5	$50,000	$ 290,096	$384,642	$ 456,011	$ 540,892
6	$50,000	$ 357,100	$446,123	$ 543,961	$ 665,696
7	$50,000	$ 427,455	$503,379	$ 630,888	$ 797,030
8	$50,000	$ 501,328	$556,863	$ 716,835	$ 935,355
9	$50,000	$ 578,895	$607,026	$ 801,851	$1,081,175
10 Age 65	$50,000	$ 660,339	$654,328	$ 885,987	$1,235,027
15	0	$ 842,779	$554,294	$ 932,766	$1,718,662
20 Age 75	0	$1,075,622	$521,755	$ 978,783	$2,380,957
25	0	$1,372,797	$552,108	$1,026,644	$3,297,813
30	0	$1,752,075	$620,400	$1,076,875	$4,568,707

Investment Base Policy Year	End-of-Year (2) (3) Assuming Hypothetical Gross Annual Rate of Return of 0.00%	6.00%	12.00%	End-of-Year Cash Surrender Value (2) (3) Assuming Hypothetical Gross Annual Rate of Return of 0.00%	6.00%	12.00%
1	$ 48,549	$ 51,514	$ 54,469	$ 45,399	$ 48,364	$ 51,319
2	$ 96,476	$104,609	$ 113,088	$ 90,751	$ 98,884	$ 107,363
3	$143,048	$159,257	$ 176,913	$135,073	$151,282	$ 168,938
4	$188,291	$215,461	$ 246,375	$178,391	$205,561	$ 310,449
5	$232,268	$273,231	$ 321,949	$220,768	$261,731	$ 310,449
6	$275,047	$332,566	$ 404,133	$262,272	$319,791	$ 391,358
7	$316,699	$393,444	$ 493,442	$302,974	$379,719	$ 479,717
8	$357,305	$455,827	$ 590,407	$342,955	$441,477	$ 576,057
9	$396,973	$519,680	$ 695,606	$382,323	$505,030	$ 680,956
10 Age 65	$435,824	$584,945	$ 809,626	$421,199	$570,320	$ 795,001
15	$397,726	$667,075	$1,226,375	$394,476	$663,825	$1,223,125
20 Age 75	$404,606	$759,017	$1,846,361	$404,606	$759,017	$1,846,361
25	$458,010	$851,669	$2,735,753	$458,010	$851,669	$2,735,753
30	$543,191	$942,857	$4,000,128	$543,191	$942,857	$4,000,128

Table 7-2 (cont.)

Policy Year	Payments (1)	Total Payments Made Plus Interest at 5%	End-of-Year Investment Base (2) (3)	End-of-Year Death Benefit (2) (3)	End-of-Year Cash Surrender Value (2) (3)
1	$50,000	$ 52,500	$ 54,737	$ 99,347	$ 51,587
2	$50,000	$ 107,625	$ 113,981	$ 203,195	$ 108,256
3	$50,000	$ 165,506	$ 178,992	$ 312,993	$ 171,017
4	$50,000	$ 226,282	$ 250,372	$ 429,325	$ 240,472
5	$50,000	$ 290,096	$ 328,745	$ 552,733	$ 317,245
6	$50,000	$ 357,100	$ 414,819	$ 683,872	$ 402,044
7	$50,000	$ 427,455	$ 509,154	$ 823,136	$ 495,429
8	$50,000	$ 501,328	$ 612,425	$ 971,106	$ 598,075
9	$50,000	$ 578,895	$ 725,303	$1,128,325	$ 710,653
10	$50,000	$ 660,339	$ 847,972	$1,294,597	$ 833,347
11	0	$ 693,356	$ 927,027	$1,392,184	$ 915,327
12	0	$ 728,024	$1,012,956	$1,495,725	$1,003,856
13	0	$ 764,425	$1,106,422	$1,605,873	$1,099,597
14	0	$ 802,646	$1,208,189	$1,723,362	$1,203,314
15	0	$ 842,779	$1,319,072	$1,848,914	$1,315,822
16	0	$ 884,917	$1,440,291	$1,983,961	$1,438,341
17	0	$ 929,163	$1,572,654	$2,129,310	$1,571,679
18	0	$ 975,621	$1,716,904	$2,285,832	$1,716,579
19	0	$1,024,402	$1,874,359	$2,455,148	$1,874,359
20	0	$1,075,622	$2,046,089	$2,638,513	$2,046,089
21	0	$1,129,404	$2,233,615	$2,837,987	$2,233,615
22	0	$1,185,874	$2,438,788	$3,055,485	$2,438,788
23	0	$1,245,167	$2,663,698	$3,292,917	$2,663,698
24	0	$1,307,426	$2,908,163	$3,549,267	$2,908,163
25	0	$1,372,797	$3,175,181	$3,827,522	$3,175,181

This illustration is not authorized for use unless accompanied by illustrations, assuming current and maximum VLI mortality charges, of Death Benefits, Investment Base, Cash Surrender Values and Accumulated Premiums showing values for hypothetical gross annual rates of return of 0.00%, 6.00% and 12.00%. The hypothetical net annual rate of return shown above is assumed to be a constant rate. The values would be different from those shown if the actual gross annual rate of return averaged 12.00% over a period of years but fluctuated above or below that average for individual policy years. Comparable illustrations at other hypothetical net annual rates of return are available upon request.

Illustrated values may vary slightly from actual values due to rounding.

This illustration is invalid and incomplete unless accompanied by "Illustration Notes," at the end of this table and dated 01/01/1980 which explains any numbered references on this page.

Policy Year	Payments (1)	Total Payments Made Plus Interest at 5%	End-of-Year Investment Base (2) (3)	End-of-Year Death Benefit (2) (3)	End-of-Year Cash Surrender Value (2) (3)
26	$ 0	$1,441,437	$3,466,379	$4,128,977	$3,466,379
27	0	$1,513,508	$3,782,948	$4,454,762	$3,782,948
28	0	$1,589,184	$4,125,168	$4,805,160	$4.125,168
29	0	$1,668,643	$4,492,937	$5,180,446	$4,492,937
30	0	$1,752,075	$4,887,010	$5,581,650	$4,887,010

Table 7-2 (cont.)

| | *Beginning of Year* | | | | | *End-of-Year* | | |
| | Payments (1) | Loan or Loan Repayment (6) | Cash Outlay | Loan Interest (7) | Policy Debt (3) | Investment Base (3) (8) | Net Death Benefit (3) (8) | Net Cash Surrender Value (3) (8) |
Pol. Yr.								
1	$50,000	$ 0	$ 50,000	$ 0	$ 0	$ 54,737	$ 99,347	$ 51,587
2	$50,000	$ 0	$ 50,000	$ 0	$ 0	$ 113,981	$ 203,195	$ 108,256
3	$50,000	$ 0	$ 50,000	$ 0	$ 0	$ 178,992	$ 312,993	$ 171,017
4	$50,000	$ 0	$ 50,000	$ 0	$ 0	$ 250,372	$ 429,325	$ 240,472
5	$50,000	$ 0	$ 50,000	$ 0	$ 0	$ 328,745	$ 552,733	$ 317,245
6	$50,000	$ 0	$ 50,000	$ 0	$ 0	$ 414,819	$ 683,872	$ 402,044
7	$50,000	$ 0	$ 50,000	$ 0	$ 0	$ 509,154	$ 823,136	$ 495,429
8	$50,000	$ 0	$ 50,000	$ 0	$ 0	$ 612,425	$ 971,106	$ 598,075
9	$50,000	$ 0	$ 50,000	$ 0	$ 0	$ 725,303	$1,128,325	$ 710,653
10	$50,000	$ 0	$ 50,000	$ 0	$ 0	$ 847,973	$1,294,597	$ 833,348
11	$ 0	$25,000	$−25,000	$ 1,188	$ 26,188	$ 899,145	$1,363,421	$ 887,445
12	$ 0	$25,000	$−25,000	$ 2,431	$ 53,619	$ 954,015	$1,434,176	$ 944,915
13	$ 0	$25,000	$−25,000	$ 3,734	$ 82,353	$1,012,921	$1,507,240	$1,006,096
14	$ 0	$25,000	$−25,000	$ 5,099	$112,453	$1,076,278	$1,583,042	$1,071,403
15	$ 0	$25,000	$−25,000	$ 6,529	$143,982	$1,144,518	$1,661,974	$1,141,268
16	$ 0	$25,000	$−25,000	$ 8,027	$177,008	$1,218,436	$1,745,095	$1,216,486
17	$ 0	$25,000	$ 25,000	$ 9,595	$211,604	$1,298,383	$1,832,805	$1,297,408
18	$ 0	$25,000	$−25,000	$11,239	$247,842	$1,384,614	$1,925,536	$1,384,289
19	$ 0	$25,000	$−25,000	$12,960	$285,802	$1,477,889	$2,024,387	$1,477,889
20	$ 0	$25,000	$−25,000	$14,763	$325,565	$1,578,690	$2,130,049	$1,578,690
21	$ 0	$25,000	$−25,000	$16,652	$367,217	$1,687,849	$2,243,909	$1,687,849
22	$ 0	$25,000	$−25,000	$18,630	$410,848	$1,806,455	$2,367,145	$1,806,455
23	$ 0	$25,000	$−25,000	$20,703	$456,550	$1,935,745	$2,500,853	$1,935,745
24	$ 0	$25,000	$−25,000	$22,874	$504,424	$2,074,848	$2,643,449	$2,074,848
25	$ 0	$25,000	$−25,000	$25,148	$554,572	$2,225,703	$2,796,911	$2,225,703
26	$ 0	$25,000	$−25,000	$27,530	$607,101	$2,388,945	$2,961,639	$2,388,945
27	$ 0	$25,000	$−25,000	$30,025	$662,126	$2,564,778	$3,137,843	$2,564,778
28	$ 0	$25,000	$−25,000	$32,638	$719,764	$2,752,590	$3,324,973	$2,752,590
29	$ 0	$25,000	$−25,000	$35,376	$780,141	$2,951,440	$3,522,447	$2,951,440
30	$ 0	$25,000	$−25,000	$38,244	$843,385	$3,161,096	$3,730,292	$3,161,096

(1) All payments are illustrated as if made at the beginning of the policy year.

(2) Assumes no policy loan has been made.

(3) Additional payments will be required to prevent a policy termination for any year in which an asterick appears.

(4) Corresponds to an assumed hypothetical gross annual rate of return of 12.00%.

(5) Positive numbers represent loans. Negative numbers represent loan repayments.

(6) Calculated based on 4.75% Loan Interest Rate for all years, 4% Loan Credit Rate for years 1-10 and 4.15% Loan Credit Rate beginning in year 11. Assumes interest is not paid.

(7) Investment Base, Net Cash Surrender Value, and Net Death Benefit are computed based upon the hypothetical net annual rate of return applied to separate account investment base and the Loan Credit Rate applied to collateral for loan in general account.

In the second example (Table 7-3), a 55-year-old male contributes $50,000 a year for 10 years into a nonqualified plan that earns 7.97%. Beginning at age 65, the individual begins drawing $25,000 a year out of the plan, using the policy loan provision. Despite the policy loans, the policy's cash value and death benefit continue to grow.

Chapter Seven

Table 7-3 Monarch Life Insurance Company Variable Life Insurance (VLI).

*Illustration of Death Benefits, Investment Base, Cash Surrender Values
and Accumulated Premiums Assuming Current VLI Mortality Charges*

For: Applicant
Age Sex: 55/Male
Underwriting: Simplified

Prime Plan V

	Single Premium	Face Amount	Initial Investment Base
Class: Nonsmoker	$50,000	$91,927	$50,000

Guarantee
Period: For Life

Policy Year	Payments (1)	Total Payments Made Plus Interest at 5%	End-of-Year Death Benefit (2) (3) Assuming Hypothetical Gross Annual Rate of Return of		
			0.00%	6.00%	12.00%
1	$50,000	$ 52,500	$ 91,927	$ 93,636	$ 99,347
2	$50,000	$ 107,625	$171,665	$ 187,147	$ 203,195
3	$50,000	$ 165,506	$249,847	$ 280,249	$ 312,993
4	$50,000	$ 226,282	$322,846	$ 373,093	$ 429,325
5	$50,000	$ 290,096	$390,976	$ 465,751	$ 552,733
6	$50,000	$ 357,100	$454,576	$ 558,348	$ 683,872
7	$50,000	$ 427,455	$513,756	$ 650,753	$ 823,136
8	$50,000	$ 501,328	$568,742	$ 742,968	$ 971,106
9	$50,000	$ 578,895	$619,706	$ 834,937	$1,128,325
10 Age 65	$50,000	$ 660,339	$666,417	$ 926,051	$1,294,597
15	$ 0	$ 842,779	$561,965	$1,000,915	$1,848,914
20 Age 75	$ 0	$1,075,622	$526,041	$1,082,221	$2,638,513
25	$ 0	$1,372,797	$554,030	$1,189,469	$3,827,522
30	$ 0	$1,752,075	$621,015	$1,314,102	$5,581,650

Policy Year	End-of-Year Investment Base (2) (3) Assuming Hypothetical Gross Annual Rate of Return of			End-of-Year Cash Surrender Value (2) (3) Assuming Hypothetical Gross Annual Rate of Return of		
	0.00%	6.00%	12.00%	0.00%	6.00%	12.00%
1	$ 48,794	$ 51,771	$ 54,737	$ 45,644	$ 48,621	$ 51,587
2	$ 97,183	$ 105,431	$ 113,981	$ 91,458	$ 99,706	$ 108,256
3	$144,489	$ 161,100	$ 178,992	$136,514	$ 153,125	$ 171,017
4	$190,732	$ 218,876	$ 250,372	$180,832	$ 208,976	$ 240,472
5	$235,904	$ 278,821	$ 328,745	$224,404	$ 267,321	$ 317,245
6	$280,017	$ 341,024	$ 414,819	$267,242	$ 328,249	$ 402,044
7	$322,945	$ 405,400	$ 509,154	$309,220	$ 391,675	$ 495,429
8	$364,621	$ 471,921	$ 612,425	$350,271	$ 457,571	$ 598,075
9	$404,959	$ 540,519	$ 725,303	$390,309	$ 525,869	$ 710,653
10 Age 65	$443,605	$ 610,735	$ 847,972	$428,980	$ 596,110	$ 833,347
15	$403,185	$ 715,574	$1,319,072	$399,935	$ 712,324	$1,315,822
20 Age 75	$407,929	$ 839,230	$2,046,089	$407,929	$ 839,230	$2,046,089
25	$459,604	$ 986,743	$3,175,181	$459,604	$ 986,743	$3,175,181
30	$543,729	$1,150,561	$4,887,010	$543,729	$1,150,561	$4,887,010

Hypothetical rates of return are illustrative only and should not be deemed a representation of past or future rates of return. Actual rates of return may be more or less than those shown and will depend on a number of factors, including the investment allocations made by an owner, prevailing interest rates and rates of inflation. The Death Benefit, Investment Base and Cash Surrender Value for a policy would be different from those shown if the actual gross annual rates of return averaged 0.00%, 6.00% and 12.00% over a period of years, but also fluctuated above or below those averages for individual policy years. No representations can be made by Monarch or the Series Fund or the Trusts that these hypothetical rates of return can be achieved for any one year or sustained over the period of time.

Illustrated values may vary slightly from actual values due to rounding.

This illustration is invalid and incomplete unless accompanied by ''Illustration Notes,'' at the end of the table and dated 01-01-1980 which explains any numbered references on this page.

Policy Year	Payments (1)	Total Payments Made Plus Interest at 5%	End-of-Year Death Benefit (2) (3) Assuming Hypothetical Gross Annual Rate of Return of		
			0.00%	6.00%	12.00%
1	$50,000	$ 52,500	$ 91,927	$ 93,141	$ 98,831
2	$50,000	$ 107,625	$170,339	$ 185,605	$ 201,519
3	$50,000	$ 165,506	$247,209	$ 276,875	$ 309,189
4	$50,000	$ 226,282	$318,488	$ 366,996	$ 422,189
5	$50,000	$ 290,096	$384,642	$ 456,011	$ 540,892
6	$50,000	$ 357,100	$446,123	$ 543,961	$ 665,696
7	$50,000	$ 427,455	$503,379	$ 630,888	$ 797,030
8	$50,000	$ 501,328	$556,863	$ 716,835	$ 935,355
9	$50,000	$ 578,895	$607,026	$ 801,851	$1,081,175
10 Age 65	$50,000	$ 660,339	$654,328	$ 885,987	$1,235,027
15	$50,000	$ 842,779	$554,294	$ 932,766	$2,380,957
20 Age 75	$ 0	$1,075,622	$521,755	$ 978,783	$2,380,957
25	$ 0	$1,372,797	$552,108	$1,026,644	$3,297,813
30	$ 0	$1,752,075	$620,400	$1,076,875	$4,568,707

Policy Year	End of Year Investment Base (2) (3) Assuming Hypothetical Gross Annual Rate of Return of			End of Year Cash Surrender Value (2) (3) Assuming Hypothetical Gross Annual Rate of Return of		
	0.00%	6.00%	12.00%	0.00%	6.00%	12.00%
1	$ 48,549	$ 51,514	$ 54,469	$ 45,399	$ 48,364	$ 51,319
2	$ 96,476	$104,609	$ 113,088	$ 90,751	$ 98,884	$ 107,363
3	$143,048	$159,257	$ 176,913	$135,073	$151,282	$ 168,938
4	$188,291	$215,461	$ 246,375	$178,391	$205,561	$ 236,475
5	$232,268	$273,231	$ 321,949	$220,768	$261,731	$ 310,449
6	$275,047	$332,566	$ 404,133	$262,272	$319,791	$ 391,358
7	$316,699	$393,444	$ 493,442	$302,974	$379,719	$ 479,717
8	$357,305	$455,827	$ 590,407	$342,955	$441,477	$ 576,057
9	$396,973	$519,680	$ 695,606	$382,323	$505,030	$ 680,956
10 Age 65	$435,824	$584,945	$ 809,626	$421,199	$570,320	$ 795,001
15	$397,726	$667,075	$1,226,375	$394,476	$663,825	$1,846,361
20 Age 75	$404,606	$759,017	$1,846,361	$404,606	$759,017	$1,846,361
25	$458,010	$851,669	$2,735,753	$458,010	$851,669	$2,735,753
30	$543,191	$942,857	$4,000,128	$543,191	$942,857	$4,000,128

Table 7-3 (cont.)

Policy Year	Payments (1)	Total Payments Made Plus Interest at 5%	End-of-Year Investment Base (2) (3)	End-of-Year Death Benefit (2) (3)	End-of-Year Cash Surrender Value (2) (3)
1	$50,000	$ 52,500	$ 53,254	$ 96,492	$ 50,104
2	$50,000	$ 107,625	$ 109,666	$ 195,095	$ 103,941
3	$50,000	$ 165,506	$ 169,880	$ 296,317	$ 161,905
4	$50,000	$ 226,282	$ 234,184	$ 400,423	$ 224,284
5	$50,000	$ 290,096	$ 302,847	$ 507,612	$ 291,347
6	$50,000	$ 357,100	$ 376,180	$ 618,148	$ 363,405
7	$50,000	$ 427,455	$ 454,319	$ 732,030	$ 440,594
8	$50,000	$ 501,328	$ 537,469	$ 849,399	$ 523,119
9	$50,000	$ 578,895	$ 625,795	$ 970,334	$ 611,145
10	$50,000	$ 660,339	$ 719,015	$1,094,263	$ 704,390
11	$ 0	$ 693,356	$ 764,371	$1,144,790	$ 752,671
12	$ 0	$ 728,024	$ 812,212	$1,196,621	$ 803,112
13	$ 0	$ 764,425	$ 862,750	$1,250,011	$ 855,925
14	$ 0	$ 802,646	$ 916,239	$1,305,237	$ 911,364
15	$ 0	$ 842,779	$ 972,926	$1,362,531	$ 969,676
16	$ 0	$ 884,917	$1,033,313	$1,422,600	$1,031,363
17	$ 0	$ 929,163	$1,097,538	$1,485,624	$1,096,563
18	$ 0	$ 975,621	$1,165,664	$1,551,789	$1,165,339
19	$ 0	$1,024,402	$1,238,106	$1,621,746	$1,238,106
20	$ 0	$1,075,622	$1,315,058	$1,695,819	$1,315,058
21	$ 0	$1,129,404	$1,396,831	$1,774,786	$1,396,831
22	$ 0	$1,185,874	$1,483,971	$1,859,223	$1,483,971
23	$ 0	$1,245,167	$1,577,079	$1,949,616	$1,577,079
24	$ 0	$1,307,426	$1,675,340	$2,044,669	$1,675,340
25	$ 0	$1,372,797	$1,779,790	$2,145,447	$1,779,790
26	$ 0	$1,441,437	$1,890,567	$2,251,949	$1,890,567
27	$ 0	$1,513,508	$2,007,527	$2,364,044	$2,007,527
28	$ 0	$1,589,184	$2,130,028	$2,481,142	$2,130,028
29	$ 0	$1,668,643	$2,257,268	$2,602,676	$2,257,268
30	$ 0	$1,752,075	$2,388,919	$2,728,480	$2,388,919

	Beginning of Year					End-of-Year		
Pol. Yr.	Payments (1)	Loan or Loan Repayment (6)	Cash Outlay	Loan Interest (7)	Policy Debt (3)	Investment Base (3) (8)	Net Death Benefit (3) (8)	Net Cash Surrender Value (3) (8)
1	$50,000	$ 0	$ 50,000	$ 0	$ 0	$ 53,254	$ 96,492	$ 50,104
2	$50,000	$ 0	$ 50,000	$ 0	$ 0	$ 109,666	$ 195,095	$ 103,941
3	$50,000	$ 0	$ 50,000	$ 0	$ 0	$ 169,880	$ 296,317	$ 161,905
4	$50,000	$ 0	$ 50,000	$ 0	$ 0	$ 234,184	$ 400,423	$ 224,284
5	$50,000	$ 0	$ 50,000	$ 0	$ 0	$ 302,847	$ 507,612	$ 291,347

Table 7-3 (cont.)

	Beginning of Year					End-of-Year		
Pol. Yr.	Payments (1)	Loan or Loan Repayment (6)	Cash Outlay	Loan Interest (7)	Policy Debt (3)	Investment Base (3) (8)	Net Death Benefit (3) (8)	Net Cash Surrender Value (3) (8)
6	$50,000	$ 0	$ 50,000	$ 0	$ 0	$ 376,180	$ 618,148	$ 363,405
7	$50,000	$ 0	$ 50,000	$ 0	$ 0	$ 454,319	$ 732,030	$ 440,594
8	$50,000	$ 0	$ 50,000	$ 0	$ 0	$ 537,469	$ 849,399	$ 523,119
9	$50,000	$ 0	$ 50,000	$ 0	$ 0	$ 625,795	$ 970,334	$ 611,145
10	$50,000	$ 0	$ 50,000	$ 0	$ 0	$ 719,015	$1,094,263	$ 704,390
11	$ 0	$ 25,000	$−25,000	$ 1,188	$ 26,188	$ 737,232	$1,117,156	$ 725,532
12	$ 0	$ 25,000	$−25,000	$ 2,431	$ 53,619	$ 755,631	$1,138,589	$ 746,531
13	$ 0	$ 25,000	$−25,000	$ 3,734	$ 82,353	$ 774,253	$1,158,684	$ 767,428
14	$ 0	$ 25,000	$−25,000	$ 5,099	$112,453	$ 793,165	$1,177,572	$ 788,290
15	$ 0	$ 25,000	$−25,000	$ 6,529	$143,982	$ 812,421	$1,195,331	$ 809,171
16	$ 0	$ 25,000	$−25,000	$ 8,027	$177,008	$ 832,310	$1,212,495	$ 830,360
17	$ 0	$ 25,000	$−25,000	$ 9,595	$211,604	$ 852,746	$1,229,056	$ 851,771
18	$ 0	$ 25,000	$−25,000	$ 11,239	$247,842	$873,560	$1,245,006	$ 873,235
19	$ 0	$ 25,000	$−25,000	$12,960	$285,802	$ 894,908	$1,260,763	$ 894,908
20	$ 0	$ 25,000	$−25,000	$14,763	$325,565	$ 916,715	$1,276,406	$ 916,715
21	$ 0	$ 25,000	$−25,000	$16,652	$367,217	$ 938,987	$1,292,420	$ 938,987
22	$ 0	$ 25,000	$−25,000	$18,630	$$410,848	$ 961,934	$1,309,070	$ 961,934
23	$ 0	$ 25,000	$−25,000	$20,703	$456,550	$ 985,793	$1,326,503	$ 985,793
24	$ 0	$ 25,000	$−25,000	$22,874	$504,424	$1,009,481	$1,343,222	$1,009,481
25	$ 0	$ 25,000	$−25,000	$25,148	$554,572	$1,033,594	$1,359,883	$1,033,594
26	$ 0	$ 25,000	$−25,000	$27,530	$607,101	$1,057,885	$1,376,147	$1,057,885
27	$ 0	$ 25,000	$−25,000	$30,025	$662,126	$1,081,840	$1,391,551	$1,081,840
28	$ 0	$ 25,000	$−25,000	$32,638	$719,764	$1,104,512	$1,405,226	$1,104,512
29	$ 0	$ 25,000	$−25,000	$35,376	$780,141	$1,124,826	$1,416,324	$1,124,826
30	$ 0	$ 25,000	$−25,000	$38,244	$843,385	$1,142,123	$1,424,343	$1,142,123

(1) All payments are illustrated as if made at the beginning of the policy year.

(2) Assumes no policy loan has been made.

(3) Additional payments will be required to prevent a policy termination for any year in which an asterick appears.

(5) Corresponds to an assumed hypothetical gross annual rate of return of 9.00%.

(6) Positive number represent loans. Negative numbers represent loan repayments.

(7) Calculated based on 4.75% Loan Interest Rate for all years, 4% Loan Credit Rate for years 1-10 and 4.15% Loan Credit Rate beginning in year 11. Assumes interest is not paid.

(8) Investment Base, Net Cash Surrender Value, and Net Death Benefit are computed based upon the hypothetical net annual rate of return applied to separate account investment base and the Loan Credit Rate applied to collateral for loan in general account.

In the third example (Table 7-4), a 40-year-old female contributes $10,000 a year for 25 years into a nonqualified plan that earns 10.96%. Beginning at age 65, the individual begins drawing $25,000 a year out of the plan, using the policy loan provision. Despite the policy loans, the policy's cash value and death benefit continue to grow.

Table 7-4 Monarch Life Insurance Company Variable Life Insurance (VLI).

*Illustration of Death Benefits, Invesment Base, Cash Surrender Values
and Accumulated Premiums Assuming Current VLI Mortality Charges*

For: Applicant
Age/Sex: 40/Female
Underwriting: Simplified

Prime Plan V

Class: Standard
Guarantee
Period: For Life

	Single Premium $10,000	Face Amount $33,217	Initial Investment Base $10,000

Policy Year	Payments (1)	Total Payments Made Plus Interest at 5%	End-of-Year Death Benefit (2) (3) Assuming Hypothetical Gross Annual Rateof Return of 0.00%	6.00%	12.00%
1	$10,000	$ 10,500	$ 33,217	$ 33,699	$ 35,754
2	$10,000	$ 21,525	$ 61,392	$ 66,928	$ 72,671
3	$10,000	$ 33,101	$ 88,793	$ 99,606	$ 111,257
4	$10,000	$ 45,256	$114,023	$131,787	$ 151,672
5	$10,000	$ 58,019	$137,201	$163,467	$ 194,029
6	$10,000	$714,420	$158,487	$194,700	$ 238,514
7	$10,000	$ 85,491	$177,992	$225,492	$ 285,273
8	$10,000	$100,266	$195,828	$255,856	$ 334,473
9	$10,000	$115,779	$212,117	$285,827	$ 386,322
10	$10,000	$132,068	$226,954	$315,421	$ 441,015
15	$10,000	$226,575	$283,022	$458,831	$ 766,269
20	$10,000	$347,192	$317,798	$593,828	$1,200,431
25 Age 65	$10,000	$501,134	$341,270	$718,517	$1,779,301
35 Age 75	$ 0	$816,294	$283,739	$798,644	$3,444,138

Policy Year	End-of-Year Investment Base (2) (3) Assuming Hypothetical Gross Annual Rate of Return of 0.00%	6.00%	12.00%	End-of-Year Cash Surrender Value (2) (3) Assuming Hypothetical Gross Annual Rate of Return of 0.00%	6.00%	12.00%
1	$ 9,769	$ 10,365	$ 10,958	$ 9,139	$ 9,735	$ 10,328
2	$ 19,436	$ 21,086	$ 22,797	$ 18,291	$ 19,941	$ 21,652
3	$ 28,874	$ 32,196	$ 35,775	$ 27,279	$ 30,601	$ 34,180
4	$ 38,088	$ 43,713	$ 50,010	$ 36,108	$ 41,733	$ 48,030
5	$ 47,076	$ 55,647	$ 65,621	$ 44,776	$ 53,347	$ 63,321
6	$ 55,845	$ 68,021	$ 82,753	$ 53,290	$ 65,466	$ 80,198
7	$ 64,395	$ 80,847	$ 101,553	$ 61,650	$ 78,102	$ 98,808
8	$ 72,727	$ 94,140	$ 122,185	$ 69,857	$ 91,270	$ 119,315
9	$ 80,846	$107,922	$ 144,836	$ 77,916	$104,992	$ 141,906
10	$ 88,750	$122,204	$ 169,699	$ 85,825	$119,279	$ 166,774
15	$126,231	$202,827	$ 336,770	$123,306	$199,902	$ 333,845
20	$161,613	$299,445	$ 602,343	$158,688	$296,520	$ 599,418
25 Age 65	$197,540	$412,670	$1,017,599	$194,615	$409,745	$1,014,674
35 Age 75	$204,695	$576,160	$2,484,679	$204,695	$576,160	$2,484,679

Hypothetical rates of return are illustrative only and should not be deemed a representation of past or future rates of return. Actual rates of return may be more or less than those shown and will depend on a number of factors, including the investment allocations made by an owner, prevailing interest rates and rates of inflation. The Death Benefit, Investment Base and Cash Surrender Value for a policy would be different from those shown if the actual gross annual rates of return averaged 0.00%, 6.00% and 12.00% over a period of years, but also fluctuated above or below those averages for individual policy years. No representations can be made by Monarch or the Series Fund or the Trusts that these hypothetical rates of return can be achieved for any one year or sustained over the period of time.

Illustrated values may vary slightly from actual values due to rounding.

This illustration is invalid and incomplete unless accompanied by "Illustration Notes," at the end of the table and dated 01-01-1980 which explains any numbered references on this page.

Policy Year	Total Payments Payments (1)	Assuming Hypothetical Made Plus Interest at 5%	End-of-Year Death Benefit (2) (3) Gross Annual Rate of Return of 0.00%	6.00%	12.00%
1	$10,000	$ 10,500	$ 33,217	$ 33,655	$ 35,708
2	$10,000	$ 21,525	$ 61,336	$ 66,853	$ 72,585
3	$10,000	$ 33,101	$ 88,700	$ 99,452	$ 111,069
4	$10,000	$ 45,256	$113,847	$131,472	$ 151,276
5	$10,000	$ 58,019	$136,930	$162,930	$ 193,331
6	$10,000	$ 71,420	$158,091	$193,842	$ 237,366
7	$10,000	$ 85,491	$177,465	$224,224	$ 283,521
8	$10,000	$100,266	$195,179	$254,090	$ 331,947
9	$10,000	$115,779	$211,353	$283,456	$ 382,807
10	$10,000	$132,068	$226,104	$312,333	$ 436,270
15	$10,000	$226,575	$282,192	$450,085	$ 750,006
20	$10,000	$347,192	$317,183	$578,657	$1,165,113
25 Age 65	$10,000	$501,134	$340,824	$699,998	$1,723,380
35 Age 75	$ 0	$816,294	$283,537	$770,870	$3,303,883

Policy Year	End-of-Year Investment Base (2) (3) Assuming Hypothetical Gross Annual Rate of Return of 0.00%	6.00%	12.00%	End-of-Year Cash Surrender Value (2) (3) Assuming Hypothetical Gross Annual Rate of Return of 0.00%	6.00%	12.00%
1	$ 9,758	$ 10,352	$ 10,945	$ 9,128	$ 9,722	$ 10,315
2	$ 19,420	$ 21,063	$ 22,771	$ 18,275	$ 19,918	$ 21,626
3	$ 28,845	$ 32,148	$ 35,717	$ 27,250	$ 30,553	$ 34,122
4	$ 38,032	$ 43,613	$ 49,885	$ 36,052	$ 41,633	$ 47,905
5	$ 46,987	$ 55,472	$ 65,394	$ 44,687	$ 53,172	$ 63,094
6	$ 55,712	$ 67,733	$ 82,367	$ 53,157	$ 65,178	$ 79,812
7	$ 64,212	$ 80,407	$ 100,946	$ 61,467	$ 77,662	$ 98,201
8	$ 72,495	$ 93,511	$ 121,284	$ 69,625	$ 90,641	$ 118,414
9	$ 80,566	$107,051	$ 143,545	$ 77,636	$104,121	$ 140,615
10	$ 88,428	$121,037	$ 167,904	$ 85,503	$118,112	$ 164,979
15	$125,870	$199,016	$ 329,685	$122,945	$196,091	$ 326,760
20	$161,306	$291,869	$ 584,708	$158,381	$288,944	$ 581,783
25 Age 65	$197,285	$402,110	$ 985,709	$194,360	$399,185	$ 982,784
35 Age 75	$204,550	$556,123	$2,383,496	$204,550	$556,123	$2,383,496

Table 7-4 (cont.)

Policy Year	Payments (1)	Total Payments Made Plus Interest at 5%	End-of-Year Investment Base (2) (3)	End-of-Year Death Benefit (2) (3)	End-of-Year Cash Surrender Value (2) (3)
1	$10,000	$ 10,500	$ 10,958	$ 35,754	$ 10,328
2	$10,000	$ 21,525	$ 22,797	$ 72,671	$ 21,652
3	$10,000	$ 33,101	$ 35,775	$ 111,257	$ 34,180
4	$10,000	$ 45,256	$ 50,010	$ 151,672	$ 48,030
5	$10,000	$ 58,019	$ 65,621	$ 194,029	$ 63,321
6	$10,000	$ 71,420	$ 82,753	$ 238,514	$ 80,198
7	$10,000	$ 85,491	$ 101,553	$ 285,273	$ 98,808
8	$10,000	$100,266	$ 122,185	$ 334,473	$ 119,315
9	$10,000	$115,779	$ 144,836	$ 386,322	$ 141,906
10	$10,000	$132,068	$ 169,699	$ 441,015	$ 166,774
11	$10,000	$149,171	$ 197,089	$ 498,861	$ 194,164
12	$10,000	$167,130	$ 227,224	$ 560,025	$ 224,299
13	$10,000	$185,986	$ 260,365	$ 624,802	$ 257,440
14	$10,000	$205,786	$ 296,799	$ 693,511	$ 293,874
15	$10,000	$226,575	$ 336,770	$ 766,269	$ 333,845
16	$10,000	$248,404	$ 380,622	$ 843,402	$ 377,697
17	$10,000	$271,324	$ 428,735	$ 925,230	$ 425,810
18	$10,000	$295,390	$ 481,468	$1,011,903	$ 478,543
19	$10,000	$320,659	$ 539,228	$1,103,605	$ 536,418
20	$10,000	$347,192	$ 602,343	$1,200,431	$ 599,418
21	$10,000	$375,052	$ 671,301	$1,302,692	$ 668,376
22	$10,000	$404,304	$ 746,806	$1,411,253	$ 743,881
23	$10,000	$435,020	$ 829,373	$1,526,556	$ 826,448
24	$10,000	$467,271	$ 919,319	$1,648,859	$ 916,394
25	$10,000	$501,134	$1,017,599	$1,779,301	$1,014,674
26	$ 0	$526,191	$1,114,316	$1,901,401	$1,111,976
27	$ 0	$552,500	$1,219,922	$2,031,976	$1,333,684
28	$ 0	$580,125	$1,335,049	$2,171,250	$1,333,684
29	$ 0	$609,132	$1,460,249	$2,319,092	$1,459,274
30	$ 0	$639,588	$1,596,840	$2,476,728	$1,596,190
31	$ 0	$671,568	$1,746,100	$2,645,413	$1,745,710
32	$ 0	$705,146	$1,908,636	$2,825,428	$1,908,441
33	$ 0	$740,403	$2,085,103	$3,017,530	$2,085,038
34	$ 0	$777,423	$2,276,588	$3,223,079	$2,276,588
35	$ 0	$816,294	$2,484,679	$3,444,138	$2,484,679

This illustration is not authorized for use unless accompanied by illustrations, assuming current and maximum VLI mortality charges of Death Benefits, Investment Base, Cash Surrender Values and Accumulated Premiums showing values for hypothetical gross annual rates of return of 0.00%, 6.00% and 12.00%. The hypothetical net annual rate of return shown above is assumed to be a constant rate. The values would be different from those shown if the actual gross annual rate of return averaged 12.00% over a period of years but fluctuated above or below that average for individual policy years. Comparable illustrations at other hypothetical net annual rates of return are available upon request.

Illustrated values may vary slightly from actual values due to rounding.

This illustration is invalid and incomplete unless accompanied by "Illustration Notes," at the end of the table and dated 01-01-1980 which explains any numbered referenes on this page.

Table 7-4 (cont.)

	Beginning of Year					End-of-Year		
Pol. Yr.	Payments (1)	Loan or Loan Repayment (6)	Cash Outlay	Loan Interest (7)	Policy Debt(3)	Investment Base (3) (8)	Net Death Benefit (3) (8)	Net Cash Surrender Value (3) (8)
1	$10,000	$ 0	$10,000	$ 0	$ 0	$ 10,661	$ 34,726	$ 10,031
2	$10,000	$ 0	$10,000	$ 0	$ 0	$ 21,933	$ 20,788	
3	$10,000	$ 0	$10,000	$ 0	$ 0	$ 33,952	$ 105,323	$ 32,357
4	$10,000	$ 0	$10,000	$ 0	$ 0	$ 46,774	$ 141,451	$ 44,794
5	$10,000	$ 0	$10,000	$ 0	$ 0	$ 60,447	$ 178,174	$ 58,147
6	$10,000	$ 0	$10,000	$ 0	$ 0	$ 75,040	$ 215,573	$ 72,485
7	$10,000	$ 0	$10,000	$ 0	$ 0	$ 90,609	$ 253,677	$ 87,864
8	$10,000	$ 0	$10,000	$ 0	$ 0	$107,224	$ 292,531	$104,354
9	$10,000	$ 0	$10,000	$ 0	$ 0	$124,957	$ 332,204	$122,027
10	$10,000	$ 0	$10,000	$ 0	$ 0	$143,881	$ 372,743	$140,956
11	$10,000	$ 0	$10,000	$ 0	$ 0	$164,169	$ 414,280	$161,244
12	$10,000	$ 0	$10,000	$ 0	$ 0	$185,886	$ 456,814	$182,961
13	$10,000	$ 0	$10,000	$ 0	$ 0	$209,122	$ 500,437	$206,197
14	$10,000	$ 0	$10,000	$ 0	$ 0	$233,974	$ 545,249	$231,049
15	$10,000	$ 0	$10,000	$ 0	$ 0	$260,488	$ 591,180	$257,563
16	$10,000	$ 0	$10,000	$ 0	$ 0	$288,779	$ 638,315	$285,854
17	$10,000	$ 0	$10,000	$ 0	$ 0	$318,968	$ 686,721	$316,043
18	$10,000	$ 0	$10,000	$ 0	$ 0	$351,144	$ 736,326	$348,219
19	$10,000	$ 0	$10,000	$ 0	$ 0	$385,413	$ 787,084	$382,488
20	$10,000	$ 0	$10,000	$ 0	$ 0	$421,806	$ 838,875	$418,881
21	$10,000	$ 0	$10,000	$ 0	$ 0	$460,452	$ 891,738	$457,527
22	$10,000	$ 0	$10,000	$ 0	$ 0	$501,602	$ 946,066	$498,677
23	$10,000	$ 0	$10,000	$ 0	$ 0	$545,353	$1,001,934	$542,428
24	$10,000	$ 0	$10,000	$ 0	$ 0	$591,648	$1,059,283	$588,723
25	$10,000	$ 0	$10,000	$ 0	$ 0	$640,826	$1,118,605	$637,901

This illustration is not authorized for use unless accompanied by illustrations, assuming current and maximum VLI mortality charges, of Death Benefits, Investment Base, Cash Surrender Values and Accumulated Premiums showing values for hypothetical gross annual rates of return of 0.00%, 6.00% and 12.00%. The hypothetical net annual rate of return shown above is assumed to be a constant rate. The values would be different from those shown if the actual gross annual rate of return averaged 9.00% over a period of years but fluctuated above or below that average for individual policy years. Comparable illustrations at other hypothetical net annual rates of return are available upon request.

Illustrated values may vary slightly from actual values due to rounding.

This illustration is invalid and incomplete unless accompanied by "Illustration Notes," at the end of the table and dated 01-01-1980 which explains any numbered references on this page.

26	$ 0	$25,000	$−25,000	$ 1,188	$ 26,188	$655,450	$1,135,365	$653,110
27	$ 0	$25,000	$−25,000	$ 2,431	$ 53,619	$670,339	$1,151,016	$668,519
28	$ 0	$25,000	$−25,000	$ 3,734	$ 82,353	$685,375	$1,165,294	$684,010
29	$ 0	$25,000	$−25,000	$ 5,099	$112,453	$700,364	$1,177,734	$699,389
30	$ 0	$25,000	$−50,000	$ 7,716	$170,169	$688,369	$1,160,973	$687,719

Table 7-4 (cont.)

31	$ 0	$25,000	$−25,000	$ 9,271	$204,440	$701,468	$1,167,764	$701,078
32	$ 0	$25,000	$−25,000	$10,898	$240,338	$714,350	$1,172,780	$714,155
33	$ 0	$25,000	$−25,000	$12,604	$277,942	$726,707	$1,175,922	$726,642
34	$ 0	$25,000	$−25,000	$14,390	$317,331	$738,415	$1,177,342	$738,415
35	$ 0	$25,000	$−25,000	$16,261	$358,592	$749,533	$1,177,435	$749,533

(1) All payments are illustrated as if made at the beginning of the policy year.
(2) Assumes no policy loan has been made.
(3) Additional payments will be required to prevent a policy termination for any year in which an asterick appears.
(5) Corresponds to an assumed hypothetical gross annual rate of return of 9.00%.
(6) Positive numbers represent loans. Negative numbers represent loan repayments.
(7) Calculated based on 4.75% Loan Interest Rate for all years, 4% Loan Credit Rate for years 1-10 and 4.15% Loan Credit Rate beginning in year 11. Assumes interest is not paid.
(8) Investment Base, Net Cash Surrender Value, and Net Death Benefit are computed based upon the hypothetical net annual rate of return applied to separate account investment base and the Loan Credit Rate applied to collateral for loan in general account.

> In the fourth example (Table 7-5), a 40-year-old female contributes $10,000 a year for 25 years into a nonqualified plan that earns 7.97%. Beginning at age 65, the individual begins drawing $25,000 a year out of the plan, using the policy loan provision. Despite the policy loans, the policy's cash value and death benefit continue to grow.

Table 7-5. Monarch Life Insurance Company Variable Life Insurance (VLI).

*Illustration of Death Benefits, Investment Base, Cash Surrender Values
and Accumulated Premiums Assuming Current VLI Mortality Charges*

For: Applicant
Age/Sex: 40/Female   Prime Plan V
Underwriting: Simplified

	Single Premium	Face Amount	Initial Investment Base
Class: Standard	$10,000	$33,217	$10,000

Guarantee
Period: For Life

Policy Year	Payments (1)	Total Payments Made Plus Interest at 5%	End-of-Year Death Benefit (2) (3) Assuming Hypothetical Gross Annual Rate of Return of 0.00%	6.00%	12.00%
1	$10,000	$ 10,500	$ 33,217	$ 33,699	$ 35,754
2	$10,000	$ 21,525	$ 61,392	$ 66,928	$ 72,671
3	$10,000	$ 33,101	$ 88,793	$ 99,606	$ 111,257
4	$10,000	$ 45,256	$114,023	$131,787	$ 151,672
5	$10,000	$ 58,019	$137,201	$163,467	$ 194,029
6	$10,000	$ 71,420	$158,487	$194,700	$ 238,514
7	$10,000	$ 85,491	$177,992	$225,492	$ 285,273
8	$10,000	$100,266	$195,828	$255,856	$ 334,473
9	$10,000	$115,779	$212,117	$285,827	$ 386,322
10	$10,000	$132,068	$226,954	$315,421	$ 441,015

Table 7-5 (cont.)

Policy Year	Payments (1)	Total Payments Made Plus Interest at 5%	End-of-Year Death Benefit (2) (3) Assuming Hypothetical Gross Annual Rate of Return of		
			0.00%	6.00%	12.00%
15	$10,000	$226,575	$283,022	$458,831	$ 766,269
20	$10,000	$347,192	$317,798	$593,828	$1,200,431
25 Age 65	$10,000	$501,134	$341,270	$718,517	$1,779,301
35 Age 75	$10,000	$816,294	$283,739	$798,644	$3,444,138

Policy Year	End-of-Year Investment Base (2) (3) Assuming Hypothetical Gross Annual Rate of Return of			End-of-Year Cash Surrender Value (2) (3) Assuming Hypothetical Gross Annual Rate of Return of		
	0.00%	6.00%	12.00%	0.00%	6.00%	12.00%
1	$ 9,769	$ 10,365	$ 10,958	$ 9,139	$ 9,735	$ 10,328
2	$ 19,436	$ 21,086	$ 22,797	$ 18,291	$ 19,941	$ 21,652
3	$ 28,874	$ 32,196	$ 35,775	$ 27,279	$ 30,601	$ 34,180
4	$ 38,088	$ 43,713	$ 50,010	$ 36,108	$ 41,733	$ 48,030
5	$ 47,076	$ 55,647	$ 65,621	$ 44,776	$ 53,347	$ 63,321
6	$ 55,845	$ 68,021	$ 82,753	$ 53,290	$ 65,466	$ 80,198
7	$ 64,395	$ 80,847	$ 101,553	$ 61,650	$ 78,102	$ 98,808
8	$ 72,727	$ 94,140	$ 122,185	$ 69,857	$ 91,270	$ 119,315
9	$ 80,846	$107,922	$ 144,836	$ 77,916	$104,992	$ 141,906
10	$ 88,750	$122,204	$ 169,699	$ 85,825	$119,279	$ 166,774
15	$126,231	$202,827	$ 336,770	$123,306	$199,902	$ 333,845
20	$161,613	$299,445	$ 602,343	$158,688	$296,520	$ 599,418
25 Age 65	$197,540	$412,670	$1,017,599	$194,615	$409,745	$1,014,674
35 Age 75	$204,695	$576,160	$2,484,679	$204,695	$576,160	$2,484,679

Hypothetical rates of return are illustrative only and should not be deemed a representation of past or future rates of return. Actual rates of return may be more or less than those shown and will depend on a number of factors, including the investment allocations made by an owner, prevailing interest rates and rates of inflation. The Death Benefit, Investment Base and Cash Surrender Value for a policy would be different from those shown if the actual gross annual rates of return averaged 0.00%, 6.00% and 12.00% over a period of years, but also fluctuated above or below those averages for individual policy years. No representations can be made by Monarch or the Series Fund or the Trusts that these hypothetical rates of return can be achieved for any one year or sustained over the period of time.

Illustrated values may vary slightly from actual values due to rounding.

This illustration is invalid and incomplete unless accompanied by "Illustration Notes," at the end of the table and dated 01-01-1980 which explains any numbered references on this page.

Policy Year	Payments (1)	Total Payments Made Plus Interest at 5%	End-of-Year Death Benefit (2) (3) Assuming Hypothetical Gross Annual Rate of Return of		
			0.00%	6.00%	12.00%
1	$10,000	$ 10,500	$ 33,217	$ 33,655	$ 35,708
2	$10,000	$ 21,525	$ 61,336	$ 66,853	$ 72,585
3	$10,000	$ 33,101	$ 88,700	$ 99,452	$ 111,069
4	$10,000	$ 45,256	$113,847	$131,472	$ 151,276
5	$10,000	$ 58,019	$136,930	$162,930	$ 193,331
6	$10,000	$ 71,420	$158,091	$193,842	$ 237,366
7	$10,000	$ 85,491	$177,465	$224,224	$ 283,521
8	$10,000	$100,266	$195,179	$254,090	$ 331,947

Table 7-5 (cont.)

Policy Year	Payments (1)	Total Payments Made Plus Interest at 5%	End-of-Year Death Benefit (2) (3) Assuming Hypothetical Gross Annual Rate of Return of		
			0.00%	6.00%	12.00%
9	$10,000	$115,779	$211,353	$283,456	$ 382,807
10	$10,000	$132,068	$226,104	$312,333	$ 436,270
15	$10,000	$226,575	$282,192	$450,085	$ 750,006
20	$10,000	$347,192	$317,183	$578,657	$1,165,113
25 Age 65	$10,000	$501,134	$340,824	$699,998	$1,723,380
35 Age 75	$ 0	$816,294	$283,537	$770,870	$3,303,883

Policy Year	End-of-Year Investment Base (2) (3) Assuming Hypothetical Gross Annual Rate of Return of			End-of-Year Cash Surrender Value (2) (3) Assuming Hypothetical Gross Annual Rate of Return of		
	0.00%	6.00%	12.00%	0.00%	6.00%	12.00%
1	$ 9,758	$ 10,352	$ 10,945	$ 9,128	$ 9,722	$ 10,315
2	$ 19,420	$ 21,063	$ 22,771	$ 18,275	$ 19,918	$ 21,626
3	$ 28,845	$ 32,148	$ 35,717	$ 27,250	$ 30,553	$ 34,122
4	$ 38,032	$ 43,613	$ 49,885	$ 36,052	$ 41,633	$ 47,905
5	$ 46,987	$ 55,472	$ 65,394	$ 44,687	$ 53,172	$ 63,094
6	$ 55,712	$ 67,733	$ 82,367	$ 53,157	$ 65,178	$ 79,812
7	$ 64,212	$ 80,407	$ 100,946	$ 61,467	$ 77,662	$ 98,201
8	$ 72,495	$ 93,511	$ 121,284	$ 69,625	$ 90,641	$ 118,414
9	$ 80,566	$107,051	$ 143,545	$ 77,636	$104,121	$ 140,615
10	$ 88,428	$121,037	$ 167,904	$ 85,503	$118,112	$ 164,979
15	$125,870	$199,016	$ 329,685	$122,945	$196,091	$ 326,760
20	$161,306	$291,869	$ 584,708	$158,381	$288,944	$ 581,783
25 Age 65	$197,285	$402,110	$ 985,709	$194,360	$399,185	$ 982,784
35 Age 75	$204,550	$556,123	$2,383,496	$204,550	$556,123	$2,383,496

Policy Year	Payments(1)	Total Payments Made Plus Interest at 5%	End-of-Year Investment Base (2) (3)	End-of-Year Death Benefit (2) (3)	End-of-Year Cash Surrender Value (2) (3)
1	$10,000	$ 10,500	$ 10,661	$ 34,726	$ 10,031
2	$10,000	$ 21,525	$ 21,933	$ 69,773	$ 20,788
3	$10,000	$ 33,101	$ 33,952	$ 105,323	$ 32,357
4	$10,000	$ 45,256	$ 46,774	$ 141,451	$ 44,794
5	$10,000	$ 58,019	$ 60,447	$ 178,174	$ 58,147
6	$10,000	$ 71,420	$ 75,040	$ 215,573	$ 724,485
7	$10,000	$ 85,491	$ 90,609	$ 253,677	$ 87,864
8	$10,000	$100,266	$ 107,224	$ 292,531	$ 104,354
9	$10,000	$115,779	$ 124,957	$ 332,204	$ 122,027
10	$10,000	$132,068	$ 143,881	$ 372,743	$ 140,956
11	$10,000	$149,171	$ 164,169	$ 414,280	$ 161,244
12	$10,000	$167,130	$ 185,886	$ 456,814	$ 182,961
13	$10,000	$185,986	$ 209,122	$ 500,437	$ 206,197
14	$10,000	$205,786	$ 233,974	$ 545,249	$ 231,049
15	$10,000	$226,575	$ 260,488	$ 591,180	$ 257,563

Table 7-5 (cont.)

Policy Year	Payments(1)	Total Payments Made Plus Interest at 5%	End-of-Year Investment Base (2) (3)	End-of-Year Death Benefit (2) (3)	End-of-Year Cash Surrender Value (2) (3)
16	$10,000	$248,404	$ 288,779	$ 638,315	$ 285,854
17	$10,000	$271,324	$ 318,968	$ 686,721	$ 316,043
18	$10,000	$295,390	$ 351,144	$ 736,326	$ 348,219
19	$10,000	$320,659	$ 385,413	$ 787,083	$ 382,488
20	$10,000	$347,192	$ 421,805	$ 838,875	$ 418,880
21	$10,000	$375,052	$ 460,451	$ 891,737	$ 457,526
22	$10,000	$404,304	$ 501,602	$ 946,065	$ 498,677
23	$10,000	$435,020	$ 545,353	$1,001,934	$ 542,428
24	$10,000	$467,271	$ 591,648	$1,059,283	$ 588,723
25	$10,000	$501,134	$ 640,826	$1,118,604	$ 637,901
26	$ 0	$526,191	$ 682,589	$1,163,178	$ 680,249
27	$ 0	$552,500	$ 726,919	$1,209,574	$ 725,099
28	$ 0	$580,125	$ 773,874	$1,257,652	$ 772,509
29	$ 0	$609,132	$ 823,442	$1,307,073	$ 822,467
30	$ 0	$639,588	$ 876,024	$1,358,274	$ 875,374
31	$ 0	$671,568	$ 931,938	$1,411,649	$ 931,548
32	$ 0	$705,146	$ 991,101	$1,467,027	$ 990,906
33	$ 0	$740,403	$1,053,444	$1,524,482	$1,053,379
34	$ 0	$777,423	$1,119,101	$1,584,368	$1,119,101
35	$ 0	$816,294	$1,188,414	$1,647,320	$1,188,414

	Beginning of Year					End-of-Year		
Pol. Yr.	Payments (1)	Loan or Loan Repayment (6)	Cash Outlay	Loan Interest (7)	Policy Debt (3)	Investment Base (3) (8)	Net Death Benefit (3) (8)	Net Cash Surrender Value (3) (8)
1	$10,000	$ 0	$10,000	$ 0	$ 0	$ 10,661	$ 34,726	$ 10,031
2	$10,000	$ 0	$10,000	$ 0	$ 0	$ 21,933	69,773	$ 20,788
3	$10,000	$ 0	$10,000	$ 0	$ 0	$ 33,952	$ 105,323	$ 32,357
4	$10,000	$ 0	$10,000	$ 0	$ 0	$ 46,774	$ 141,451	$ 44,794
5	$10,000	$ 0	$10,000	$ 0	$ 0	$ 60,447	$ 178,174	$ 58,147
6	$10,000	$ 0	$10,000	$ 0	$ 0	$ 75,040	$ 215,573	$ 72,485
7	$10,000	$ 0	$10,000	$ 0	$ 0	$ 90,609	$ 253,677	$ 87,864
8	$10,000	$ 0	$10,000	$ 0	$ 0	$107,224	$ 292,531	$104,354
9	$10,000	$ 0	$10,000	$ 0	$ 0	$124,957	$ 332,204	$122,027
10	$10,000	$ 0	$10,000	$ 0	$ 0	$143,881	$ 372,743	$140,956
11	$10,000	$ 0	$10,000	$ 0	$ 0	$164,169	$ 414,280	$161,244
12	$10,000	$ 0	$10,000	$ 0	$ 0	$185,886	$ 456,814	$182,961
13	$10,000	$ 0	$10,000	$ 0	$ 0	$209,122	$ 500,437	$206,197
14	$10,000	$ 0	$10,000	$ 0	$ 0	$233,974	$ 545,249	$231,049
15	$10,000	$ 0	$10,000	$ 0	$ 0	$260,488	$ 591,180	$257,563
16	$10,000	$ 0	$10,000	$ 0	$ 0	$288,779	$ 638,315	$285,854
17	$10,000	$ 0	$10,000	$ 0	$ 0	$318,968	$ 686,721	$316,043
18	$10,000	$ 0	$10,000	$ 0	$ 0	$351,144	$ 736,326	$348,219

Table 7-5 (cont.)

	Beginning of Year					End-of-Year		
Pol. Yr.	Payments (1)	Loan or Loan Repayment (6)	Cash Outlay	Loan Interest (7)	Policy Debt (3)	Investment Base (3) (8)	Net Death Benefit (3) (8)	Net Cash Surrender Value (3) (8)
19	$10,000	$ 0	$10,000	$ 0	$ 0	$385,413	$ 787,084	$382,488
20	$10,000	$ 0	$10,000	$ 0	$ 0	$421,806	$ 838,875	$418,881
21	$10,000	$ 0	$10,000	$ 0	$ 0	$460,452	$ 891,738	$457,527
22	$10,000	$ 0	$10,000	$ 0	$ 0	$501,602	$ 946,066	$498,677
23	$10,000	$ 0	$10,000	$ 0	$ 0	$545,353	$1,001,934	$542,428
24	$10,000	$ 0	$10,000	$ 0	$ 0	$591,648	$1,059,283	$588,723
25	$10,000	$ 0	$10,000	$ 0	$ 0	$640,826	$1,118,605	$637,901

This illustration is not authorized for use unless accompanied by illustrations, assuming current and maximum VLI mortality charges, of Death Benefits, Investment Base, Cash Surrender Values and Accumulated Premiums showing values for hypothetical gross annual rates of return of 0.00%, 6.00% and 12.00%. The hypothetical net annual rate of return shown above is assumed to be a constant rate. The values would be different from those shown if the actual gross annual rate of return averaged 9.00% over a period of years but fluctuated above or below that average for individual policy years. Comparable illustrations at other hypothetical net annual rates of return are available upon request.

Illustrated values may vary slightly from actual values due to rounding.

This illustration is invalid and incomplete unless accompanied by "Illustration Notes," at the end of the table and dated 01-01-1980 which explains any numbered references on this page.

26	$ 0	$25,000	$ −25,000	$ 1,188	$ 26,188	$655,450	$1,135,365	$653,110
27	$ 0	$25,000	$ −25,000	$ 2,431	$ 53,619	$670,339	$1,151,016	$668,519
28	$ 0	$25,000	$ −25,000	$ 3,734	$ 82,353	$685,375	$1,165,294	$684,010
29	$ 0	$25,000	$ −25,000	$ 5,099	$112,453	$700,364	$1,177,734	$699,389
30	$ 0	$25,000	$ −50,000	$ 7,716	$170,169	$688,369	$1,160,973	$687,719
31	$ 0	$25,000	$ −25,000	$ 9,271	$204,440	$701,468	$1,167,764	$701,078
32	$ 0	$25,000	$ −25,000	$10,898	$240,338	$714,350	$1,172,780	$714,155
33	$ 0	$25,000	$ −25,000	$12,604	$277,942	$726,707	$1,175,922	$726,642
34	$ 0	$25,000	$ −25,000	$14,390	$317,331	$738,415	$1,177,342	$738,415
35	$ 0	$25,000	$ −25,000	$16,261	$358,592	$749,533	$1,177,435	$749,533

(1) All payments are illustrated as if made at the beginning of the policy year.

(2) Assumes no policy loan has been made.

(3) Additional payments will be required to prevent a policy termination for any year in which an asterick appears.

(5) Corresponds to an assumed hypothetical gross annual rate of return of 9.00%.

(6) Positive numbers represent loans. Negative numbers represent loan repayments.

(7) Calculated based on 4.75% Loan Interest Rate for all years, 4% Loan Credit Rate for years 1-10 and 4.15% Loan Credit Rate beginning in year 11. Assumes interest is not paid.

(8) Investment Base, Net Cash Surrender Value, and Net Death Benefit are computed based upon the hypothetical net annual rate of return applied to separate account investment base and the Loan Credit Rate applied to collateral for loan in general account.

Chapter 8   *Corporate Finance*

Corporate finance is just what the term implies: arranging for the funds necessary to finance a new or existing business. Every business requires financing of some sort to exist. A paperboy may need a new bicycle and may borrow the purchase price from his parents, using the profits of the route to repay the loan. A steel company may need a new, more efficient plant in order to remain competitive. To finance it, the company's management may decide to float a bond offering and use the cash flow generated by the new plant to service the bonds. An inventor with a new product may need money to develop and manufacture a product and so may sell an interest in the product to a third party in exchange for the necessary funds.

There is a tremendous variety of ways in which a company's financing needs can be met. In fact, the business and financial news of late has been full of stories about creative new financing vehicles and strategies. Deciding what combination of investment vehicles and strategies works best for a given company at a given time with a given set of objectives is as much an art as it is a science. Some of the many sources of financing and financing vehicles that may be available to a company seeking financing include the following:

1. Owner's personal savings
2. Loans from the owner's friends and relatives
3. Trade credits from suppliers and/or customers
4. Banks/finance companies
   a. Mortgage loans
   b. Installment loans
   c. Receivables financing
   d. Asset financing
   e. Equipment leasing

    f. Secured and unsecured lines of credit

  5. Government programs

    a. Federal programs

      1. Small Business Administration

        a. Guaranteed loans

        b. Direct loans

      2. Small business investment companies

      3. Federal Farm Credit programs

      4. Other programs

    b. State programs

    c. City programs

  6. Venture capital

  7. Private placements

    a. Debt

    b. Equity

      1. Stock

      2. Participation interests

  8. Public offerings

    a. Debt

    b. Equity

    c. Warrants

    d. Convertibles and other hybrids

  9. Foreign sources

    a. Direct investment

      1. Debt

      2. Equity

    b. Swaps

  The structure of a business's financing can range from the very simple (e.g., a five-year installment loan) to the very complex (e.g., Ted Turner's proposed financing for the takeover of CBS ran several hundred pages).

  By now you are probably wondering, "So what?" After all, the competition in the corporate finance arena is fierce. Almost all the larger and many of the smaller investment banking firms have entire departments dedicated to assisting clients to design, structure, and obtain financing on the best terms possible.

  Fortunately, these departments are set up to deal only with larger companies, leaving the small business community's corporate financing needs for you to service. Although most of the larger firms would undoubtedly terminate an account executive who took it upon himself to call on IBM to suggest a refinancing plan, many firms do give their retail representatives the freedom to assist the owners of the local machine shop or processing plant with their financing. Assisting small business owners in structuring and obtaining financing for their businesses can be very lucrative.

  Owners of both small and large businesses are willing to pay high fees to those companies and individuals that are able to assist them in obtaining financing for their companies on favorable terms. The corporate finance department is often one of the most profitable departments in an investment banking firm. The successful professionals employed in the corporate finance department are always some of the highest paid professionals in the firm.

The reason business owners are willing to pay top fees for financing assistance is that financing is the lifeblood of any business. A company that can obtain financing on better terms than its competitors can have a significant and perhaps overwhelming advantage over those same competitors in the marketplace. This is especially true for small businesses because the market for small business financing is relatively inefficient. Large companies need only to read the tombstone ads in the *Wall Street Journal* or *Institutional Investor* or read their competitors' annual reports in order to accurately determine their competitors' cost of capital. Small businesses, on the other hand, often have great difficulty finding any accurate information regarding their competitors' financing costs, and thus they find it difficult to evaluate their own financing programs.

Also, whereas a large business's creditworthiness is often readily and objectively determinable, evaluating a small business's creditworthiness is far more subjective. It is this subjectivity that often results in small business owners' paying higher financing rates for capital than is justified on a risk reward basis. This inefficiency and subjectivity allow you to be of tremendous service to small business owners who are evaluating their existing financing, considering refinancing, or seeking additional financing. If you are concentrating your marketing effort on the small business owner, then situations are bound to arise in which you can be of material service to your clients and also earned substantial compensation.

I should point out that this is not a type of business you should actively chase or prospect. The lead time is too long, and without an already existing client relationship, it's difficult to "close" on this type of business. However, if an existing client who trusts and respects you gives you any indication that he may need financing, you should actively pursue the business.

Finding those businesses that desire to obtain new financing or that could benefit from refinancing is often simply a matter of paying careful attention to everything your clients say. For example:

- If, when you are completing the business profile form mentioned in Chapter 3, you discover that the company is paying what appears to be very high interest rates on its short-term debt, the client immediately becomes a prospect for your corporate finance services.

- A business owner who mentions that business has been especially good recently may be a candidate to have his company refinanced on more favorable terms, either from his current funding source or if necessary, from a different source.

- A business owner who mentions that he's considering expanding his business is a potential corporate finance candidate.

Once you have a client interested in either financing or refinancing his business, the first step *before you do any work of a substantial nature for the client* is to reach an agreement with the client about how you are to be compensated for your services. There are numerous ways in which you can be compensated, including the methods in the following list (either separately or in combination with one another):

- Finder's fees or referral fees paid to you by the financing source for sending them a client.

- Consulting fees paid by the business owner for the privilege of picking your brain about possible financing vehicles and sources.

- Hourly fees for assisting a business owner in preparing the documentation necessary to apply for financing.

- A small equity interest in the new company if the financing is for a new company.

- A percentage of any funds you raise for the client.

- Reciprocal leads or referrals. If, for example, you refer a business owner who is interested in arranging a line of credit to a bank loan officer, you should expect to receive a reciprocal lead from the banker. His lead to you could be a business owner he knows who is interested in establishing a retirement plan or revamping his employee benefit program. Because a lead from a business owner's banker can be a very high quality lead, this may be all the compensation you require, especially if all you had to do to get the lead was place a quick phone call to the banker.

- If your firm has a policy prohibiting its retail representatives from charging fees, you may be able to be compensated in "soft dollars" (see the section, "Compensation" in Chapter 5). You may receive soft dollars either from the business owner or from the funding source. For example, a bank may sell some Ginnie Mae certificates through you for its own account in order to compensate you for sending business the bank's way.

- You may also receive soft dollars in the form of expense reimbursements as opposed to commission dollars. For example, a bank may agree to pick up 100% of the costs you incur at a seminar in exchange for leads and referrals. Although being compensated in this manner is not as attractive as being paid in cash or commissions, a penny saved is a penny earned.

Analyzing and Defining a Financing Program

Once you have a *written* compensation agreement drawn up by competent legal counsel, you can begin the process of analyzing your client's finances, designing a better finance structure, and approaching potential funding sources. If the client's financing needs are relatively simple, you may be able to design the financing plan entirely on your own. If, however, the client's business needs are complex and, like most retail brokers, you are not well versed in the fine points of corporate finance, then your role becomes that of a "pointman." Rather than personally designing financing plans and raising capital for your client, instead pass the client's name on to the corporate finance specialists in your own firm or in an independent firm.

If you are going to design a financing program for a client yourself, then some of the factors you must take into account include the following:

1. The appropriate leverage.
2. The cost of capital.
3. Liquidity.
4. Flexibility.
5. Protection.

The Appropriate Leverage

A company that's highly leveraged will, of course, have a higher return on equity when business is good, but it will also be more vulnerable to business downturns. Decisions as to the degree of leverage a company should have are based on its stability and the predictability of its cash flow. In addition to basing this decision on purely business factors, you also need to consider the owner's relative preference for debt as opposed to equity. Many small business owners are oblivious of the concept of return on equity and are principally concerned with building up equity. Owners who think this way often quote financial gems such as "Businesses that don't owe money can't go broke" (only out of business!).

The Cost of Capital

A recent study by the American Stock Exchange quantified one of the basic economic facts of life of doing business in the United States: Equity is more expensive than debt. Because interest expense is tax deductible, Uncle Sam picks up part of the cost of debt financing. With equity financing, however, Uncle Sam not only does not provide a tax deduction but instead imposes double taxation. Corporate profits are taxed when they are earned and then again when they are distributed as dividends. This difference in tax treatment results in debt financing's almost always having a lower "cost" than does equity financing.

Liquidity

Make sure than any financing plan will provide a company with sufficient working capital to meet business expenses as they arise and to provide a reserve fund for emergencies. One of the leading reasons for small business failures is that they are either undercapitalized or improperly capitalized.

Flexibility

Any financing plan you design must provide your client with as much flexibility as possible. This flexibility can include the option to prepay any loans without prepayment penalties, the ability to draw on a credit facility only as it's needed, the ability to issue additional shares or participating interests or to bring in additional partners if necessary, and so on.

Protection

Make sure your client has as much protection against as many risks as possible. For example, if your client has any bank debt, it should be noncallable. If your client has any debt with a floating rate, it should have a reasonable maximum. And so forth. Remember, when you design a financing program, plan for the worst set of conditions and not for ideal conditions.

Qualifying for Financing

Once you have your financing plan designed, you can begin approaching potential financing sources. The first things a financing source will want to know are the following:

- How much are the business and its principals worth? What is the market value of the business?
- What is the company's cash flow?
- What is the company's growth potential?
- How competent and experienced is the business's owner or management?

Because these are the factors that your financing sources will take into consideration when they consider your requests and proposals, you should learn to evaluate these criteria the way your sources will. In this way, you will not approach a source looking for a $5 million commitment at prime plus two when the company's net worth, cash flow, and business prospects justify financing of only $2 million at prime plus four. If you approach a financing source with a ridiculous proposal, you will not only embarrass yourself but also your firm and your client (and you may also alienate your client).

Determining the Market Value of the Business

It is important to be aware that valuing a business is always an inexact science. Valuing a small business is in many ways more difficult than valuing a large business because much of the value of a small business rests with the owner himself, his expertise, his skills, and his contacts. Also, because small businesses generally lack depth in their management ranks, diversity in their customer base, and diversity among their key suppliers, they are much less stable than large businesses and are more vulnerable to unpleasant surprises.

A number of methods are commonly used to value businesses, although no one method is completely satisfactory. The first method is to determine a business's "breakup value"—that is, the value of all its assets if sold at fair market value, minus any outstanding liabilities. This method is popular with "takeover artists" who attempt to buy businesses below their breakup value and then sell off the assets to realize a profit. This method's principal shortcoming is that it doesn't place any value on the business as an ongoing enterprise. It ignores the goodwill, the customer base, and the expertise that the business has developed over the years.

A second valuation method is simply to compute the company's book value. However, because of our rather complex tax structure, assets may be carried on a company's books at a value that is either far below or far above the asset's fair market value. This is especially true of older assets that the company may have already fully depreciated on its books. The difference between the asset's market value and its book value is one of the major drawbacks of using this method. The other major drawback is that this method also fails to assign any value to the business as an ongoing enterprise.

A third valuation method is to try to determine the business's replacement cost. *Replacement cost* is defined as the amount of money that would be required to build the same business (in similiar condition) from scratch. Again, the drawback of this method is that it fails to assign any value to the business as an ongoing enterprise. Any valuation method that concentrates solely on a business's assets will tend to undervalue the business (at least from the seller's point of view).

A better valuation method is to start with the number of after-tax dollars a business generates and work backward to determine a value. For example:

> Quickie-Clean, a dry cleaning retailer, is up for sale. It generates its absentee owner an after-tax return of $50,000 a year. It has few risks and little potential for significant growth although net profits should keep rising at about the same pace as inflation and the CPI. Buying this business for $500,000 compares favorably with investing in high quality municipal bonds (when these bonds are yielding 10%). Although there is always the risk that business will decline, this risk is offset by the potential for increasing profits and an eventual sale at a slightly higher price (in inflation-adjusted dollars).

Several of the foregoing methods should be used in combination with a little common sense when trying to value a business. Before you approach a financing source about a given business, you should have an approximate idea of what the business is worth and be ready to defend your valuation.

In the final analysis, a business is worth what someone is willing to sell it for and what someone else is willing to pay for it.

Cash Flow

The second thing a financing source will examine is whether or not the company generates enough cash flow to service the proposed debt. The source will be concerned not only about the company's immediate ability to service the debt but also its future ability in the event of a recession or depression. Because of our screwy accounting system, a company's stated earnings often give a misleading impression about a business's strength. Many companies with rapidly rising earnings have gone bankrupt. For this reason, many financing sources are more interested in cash flow than in earnings.

Growth Potential

One of the more subjective areas both you and the financing source will have to evaluate is the business' growth potential. This analysis is often simplified by first examining the growth prospects for the company's industry and then examining how competitive your client's company is likely to be within the industry. It is difficult to justify a projected growth rate that's much different from the company's historical growth rate unless the company is new or has a revolutionary product or service.

Quality of Management

The first questions to ask yourself are: Would I trust the owner of this business with *my* money? and, Do I think this owner really knows what he's doing? If the answer is no to either of these questions, then don't even try to arrange financing for the owner. If you think the owner is disreputable or incompetent, the chances are that any financing source you approach will come to the same conclusion. If, however, you are successful in getting the owner financed and then the deal does go sour, you will have lost a valuable source of financing and damaged your reputation. No one deal is worth jeopardizing your reputation.

Sources of Financing

Various sources of financing place varying degrees of emphasis on the criteria discussed in the preceding section. For example, a finance company may be interested primarily in cash flow whereas a venture capitalist may be more interested in the company's management and in its growth prospects. So that you can meet a variety of potential financing needs, you should build a file of potential sources of financing, noting their requirements and preferences for later reference. Try to contact and establish rapport with one new potential financing souce each week. At the end of a year, you will have an impressive array of financing options and alternatives to bring to bear on solving a client's financing problems.

Banks and Finance Companies

In many communities that are served by multiple financial institutions, there is usually one institution that has a reputation for being more aggressive than the others. This is the first institution with which you should establish a working relationship. Smaller financial institutions are generally more aggressive and approachable than larger institutions. It's a lot easier to deal with the senior loan officer of a small bank than to deal with the calling officer of a money center bank.

Generally, smaller institutions have limited marketing staffs and are thus more appreciative of any business you send their way. They are also more flexible when it comes to participating in seminars and other marketing activities. One other benefit of dealing with smaller institutions is that they generally offer a more limited range of services than a large institution, and thus there is less potential for "territorial" overlaps.

While we are on the subject, carefully reach a gentlemen's agreement with any bank you're involved with over "territory" as early in the relationship as possible. For example, you don't want to get a pension referral from a banker and then immediately turn around and open a central assets account to handle the client's checking. Doing something this stupid will almost always permanently alienate the banker who initially referred the company to you. (A very high price indeed for the $50 commission you earned for opening the account!)

Always work with the client's banker, and do not compete with him. Most small business owners are far more concerned with access to credit then they are about the interest rate they get on their company's checking account. Therefore, if you get into a battle for control of *all* your client's business with his banker, you will probably lose. Let the bank have the client's checking account if the bank referred the company to you. Send it some additional checking accounts. Be satisfied with serving only a portion of your client's financial needs, *the lucrative portion!*

After you get to know the loan officers and calling officers at your local financial institutions, they will usually give you their parameters and requirements for the various types of financing they offer. For example, some institutions may want the company to have been in business for a certain time or want it to have a certain current ratio (current assets divided by current liabilities) before they will consider extending credit. Naturally, different institutions have different policies, so it's important to have a contact in all the leading local institutions in your area.

Finance companies are generally more liberal in regard to the type of company they will lend money to (and this policy is reflected in the interest rates they charge). Even among different banks, there is often a wide variation in loan policies. For example, some banks may finance receivables at a factor of 80% (i.e., they will lend $0.80 against $1.00 in receivables) whereas other institutions may only lend 60% against receivables. Naturally, the bank that lends the higher percentage will usually charge a higher interest rate. If you have a client who needs to borrow a lot of money, you would refer him to the more aggressive bank. If your client needed to borrow only a small sum, however, you would refer him to the bank with the lower interest rate.

As another example, some institutions may always require specific collateral against a loan, whereas others will make unsecured loans. Also, try to find an institution that does not always require that the owner personally guarantee his company's debt. Small business owners really tend to resent having to guarantee their company's debt if they feel their company's financials and business history justify independent credit. (They also don't want to be held personally liable if their business should go down the drain.)

Venture Capital

Most companies are initially financed with venture (i.e., risk) capital. For very small companies, venture capital is often either money that the new owner has saved from his or her job or money that the new owner has raised from family and/or friends. When money is raised from family or friends, the loan arrangements are often very informal.

To finance the start-up phase of larger companies, however, often requires a substantial amount of capital—more than the owner can save on his own or borrow from friends and family. The new owner must turn to outside sources if the new company is going to get the influx of capital it needs. (That is, of course, unless the new owner is fortunate enough to have friends and family that are wealthy.)

There are several sources of venture capital that someone with a sound idea can tap, including the following:

- Wealthy individuals who are seeking high risk/high reward investment opportunites.
- The Small Business Administration (SBA) and the Small Business Investment Companies (SBIC), which provide loans to businesses that ordinarily would not qualify for conventional financing.
- Professional venture capitalists who make both equity investments and high interest loans to new companies.

Regardless of which of these sources is used, the negtiation and arrangement of investments from these sources are always handled in a formal and businesslike manner.

Venture capital can also be used to finance other activities besides business start-ups, including the following:

- Leveraged buy-outs.
- Turnaround and bankruptcy situations.
- New product development.
- Rapid growth and expansion.

Regardless of the source of the outside venture financing or the purpose for which it is needed, the steps in securing the funding remain relatively unchanged.

The first step, assuming that the purpose for the funding is both sound and potentially profitable, is to prepare a detailed business plan. Although the preparation of such a plan is beyond the scope of this book the topics the plan must cover generally remain the same. They are as follows:

- The company's industry.
- The company's history.
- The new product or service.
- The potential market.
- The marketing plan.
- The history and experience of the key employees.
- The use of the funds raised.
- The financial proforma and projections.

Notice that not every project is suitable to be funded by a venture capitalist. As a rule, venture capitalists are interested in backing only companies and products that have a chance of being hugely successful and profitable. No venture capitalist is interested in a 20% annualized rate of return because a return that low can be obtained in ways that are much less risky (e.g., by buying stocks listed on the New York Stock Exchange). The return offered to a venture capitalist must be commensurate with the risk incurred. For a similiar reason, no venture capitalist wants to back the development of a new milling machine if the potential market is only 20 machines at $50,000 each. Again, the potential payoff would not be large enough to justify the risk.

Also, venture capitalists have a strong preference for funding new or improved products as opposed to services. They prefer to back companies in which the assets are tangible as opposed to companies whose assets "go home at night." Contrary to the myth, venture capitalists do not back only high tech deals. Although the high tech deals are the ones that often make the financial news, many venture capitalists (especially the smaller firms and wealthy individuals) prefer low tech deals for which the required investment is lower, in which there is less chance of a product's becoming obsolete before it even gets to market, and for which the potential market can be estimated accurately. Another criterion to consider before you decide to seek venture capital is whether the product under consideration is truly new. Chances are, if you've heard of it—it's not. No venture capitalist wants to back a project that will immediately have heavy competition.

After you are confident that the project is suitable for venture financing, the next step is to approach potential sources of funding with your proposal. To increase your chances of obtaining funding and to save a lot of your valuable time prepare ahead of time.

1. Concentrate your efforts, if possible, on those indivduals or companies that specialize in funding projects of the type you want funded. Most venture capital firms list their areas of special interest in the various venture capital directories available at any library.

2. Prepare a two- or three-page summary of your offering to mail to possible funding sources to determine if they have an interest.

3. Prepare your client for the negotiation process. The venture capital firm will want a high percentage of the equity, a high interest rate (if debt is involved), and onerous restrictions. Having your client decide in advance how much he is willing to give up or pay for financing will make the negotiation process much shorter and increase the likelihood of a successful outcome. Doing some research to determine on what terms similar deals have been consummated is essential before you start negotiating.

Most venture capitalists will promise to provide "value added" in the form of managerial and marketing assistance. Although these services may or may not materialize, and may or may not be of any real value, remember that the venture capitalist's primary function is to provide your client with capital, not advice. If you're fortunate enough to get more than one capitalist interested in funding your client's project, don't let your client pass up the deal with the best terms in exchange for some nebulous promises of value added. If you read the propaganda that some of the venture capital firms send out, you quickly see that they are not opposed to taking complete credit for a product's success. I've never heard one yet accept the responsibility for a product's failure, however.

As a broker, you can assist your prospects and clients with each of these three steps. First, you can assist them in preparing the written business plan. Many venture capitalists complain about the quality and completeness of the business plans they receive. A business owner is often too close to the product to judge accurately what a third party would want to know before he could consider providing financial support. If you're the type of person who enjoys writing (and are competent at it), writing business plans can be a very satisfying and lucrative sideline. Charging a fee of $100 an hour is reasonable for this type of work. Naturally, having a computer with the appropriate software (word processing and a spread sheet) will make this work *much* easier.

You can also be of assistance during the second step: presenting the idea to appropriate potential sources of funding. First, your firm may have a venture capital subsidiary or division that might be interested in funding your client's project. Many firms will pay their brokers a referral or finder's fee for bringing fundable projects to them.

If your firm does not have a venture capital subsidiary or if they elect not to finance your client's proposal, then you can shop the deal around to outside venture capital firms and/or individuals. Call or send a summary of your proposal to the most likely professional sources and approach your wealthier aggressive clients.

Your fee for "shopping" your client's project should depend on a number of variables. If you are working for a percentage of the money raised, then the general rule is the larger the project, the smaller your percentage. For example, you might charge 7% for projects requiring less than $500,000, 4% for projects needing between $500,000 and $5 million and 2% for larger projects. You may also want to adjust your fee based on what you think the level of difficulty will be to sell the deal and what the available supply of capital is. (That is, is money loose or is it tight?)

Regardless of the project's merits or how well you and the owner present it, it may not get financed. Therefore, you should always insist on a small, up-front nonrefundable fee for your services (i.e., $1,500 to $2,000) so that your time is not completely wasted if the project is never funded. Proper business ethics require that you never accept a fee for a proposal that you do not think has a good chance of being funded.

Always try to get an exclusive contract for 90 to 120 days so that you do not end up tripping over another consultant who is trying to obtain funding for the same project. If you haven't been able to get anyone interested in funding the project in 120 days, then give the project back to the client with detailed notes regarding the efforts you made, the sources you approached, and any comments you received in trying to obtain financing. This way, should the client hire someone else to try to get funding, the new consultant will not waste his time or the client's time by retracing the same steps. Naturally, you should have the fee agreement drawn up by competent legal counsel.

Make sure your prospect is prepared to answer any and all questions that the venture capitalist may ask by staging a detailed and grueling dry run of the personal interview that is an inevitable part of the funding process. Remember, it is at this interview that the venture capitalist is going to form his opinion about your client's integrity, dedication, and management skills.

The last step, negotiating terms, will primarily have to be left to your prospect although you can do the research on similar deals to give your client the bargaining chips he'll need.

Besides the potentially lucrative fees you can earn by pursuing this business, there are other rewards. For example, if you help the client with his initial financing, you should get first crack at any subsequent financings or offerings.

Government Programs

That small businesses create more new jobs than large businesses is a fact that has not been ignored by our politicians. Uncle Sam has a number of programs that are designed to assist small businesses in obtaining financing. Most are administered by the Small Business Administration (SBA). Despite numerous attempts by the Reagan administration to kill the SBA, as well as numerous attempts by previous administrations, the SBA is still alive and well.

The SBA provides financial assistance to those companies that are unable to obtain financing on reasonable terms from the more traditional sources. Any business that meets the government's very broad definition of "small" (e.g., Uncle Sam considers manufacturing businesses with up to 1,500 employees to be small) and is creditworthy may apply for one or more of the SBA's numerous financing programs. The SBA's programs are administered either directly or through licensed finance companies. Among the SBA programs are the regular guarantee program, the direct loan program, and the Small Business Investment Company program.

The *regular guarantee program* guarantees between 85% and 90% of a loan (depending on size) that is issued by a participating bank. Maturity can be up to 25 years, and the loan can be either fixed or variable at rates averaging 2 ½% over prime.

The *direct loan program* provides loans directly from the SBA of up to $150,000 for terms of up to 25 years and at rates that are based on the federal government's average cost of funds. Businesses are eligable for this program only after they have been rejected for the regular guarantee program. It is difficult to obtain financing under the direct loan program because of the limited amount of funding available. In addition, the SBA offers special loan programs for handicapped individuals, for seasonal credit needs, and for small businesses trying to tap the export market.

The Small Business Investment Company (SBIC) program licenses financial institutions to make term loans of at least five years' duration. The principals of SBICs consider themselves to be venture capitalists and evaluate financing proposals in a manner very similiar to the way described earlier in the section, "Venture Capital." An offshoot of this program is the Minority Enterprise Small Business Investment Company (MESBIC) program, which specializes in funding minority business ventures. Although terms vary from institution to institution, companies seeking financing from an SBIC should expect to pay a relatively high rate of interest and/or give up a portion of the company's equity in order to obtain financing.

The SBA also guarantees 80% to 90% (depending on the size of the guarantee) of surety bonds for those small businesses that are not able to obtain them independently because of their small size or short business history.

The SBA through its Certified Development Company Loan program (Section 503 Debenture Program) will finance the acquisition and development of fixed assets, including the acquisition, development, and expansion of a company's plant, as well as the purchase of machinery and equipment. The limits on this program are that no one company can borrow more than $500,000 and that the government portion of the financing cannot be more than 50% of the project's or equipment's total cost. Loans made under this program must be fully secured.

Make it a point to get to know the SBA officials in your area. Add several SIBCs to your funding file. Become familiar with the requirements and application procedures for SBA loans. Almost every community has a company that does nothing but assist small business owners to complete the paperwork for SBA programs. Get to know the principals of this company, and start swapping leads. Remember, just like you, these people are dealing with a large number of business owners on a daily basis.

In addition to its financing programs, the SBA also offers a wide range of educational programs designed exclusively for small business owners. These include the Small Business Development Centers, Small Business Institutes, and the Business Development Training Program.

Small Business Development Centers (SBDCs) are located around the country in the major population centers. They sponsor seminars and offer one-on-one counseling at a minimal cost. They also act as resource centers and often coordinate their programs with a local university's business department.

Small Business Institutes (SBIs) are located at more than 500 of the nation's leading business schools. They offer in-depth personalized management counseling to small business owners.

The *Business Development Training Progrm* (BDTP) sponsors or cosponsors management training programs in conjunction with local Chambers of Commerce, trade associations, and other governmental agencies.

For a broker who wants to meet small business owners, there are few forums that are as attractive as these programs. Contact the head of your local SBDC, SBI, and BDTP, and offer your services as a lecturer or as a resource person. Get to know the directors of these programs; they can be tremendous sources of referrals. Attend all the seminars offered in your area. Listen to the questions that are asked. If someone has a problem you may be able to solve, introduce yourself after the seminar. Remember: These people already recognize that they have a problem and are interested enough in getting it solved to take the time to attend a seminar. Thus they are prequalified prospects. The drawback of these programs is that the attendees are often owners of very small businesses and are not particularly wealthy. Every now and then, however, an excellent prospect shows up. Additionally, these programs offer you a good way to get your name known in your local small business community.

Private Placements

Most securities offerings must be registered with the Securities and Exchange Commission. However, if a company wants to offer securities to only a few investors who are financially sophisticated, then the offering may be exempt from the normal registration requirements.

One advantage of private placements is that the expenses involved in preparing a prospectus are often so high and the time delay in getting an offering approved is often so long that they effectively prevent smaller companies from accessing the public securities market. For example, with legal fees alone starting at $30,000 for a public offering, a company that wants to borrow only $500,000 will find the costs associated with making a public offering prohibitive.

This is not to say that only small companies find private placements attractive. Even very large companies often find private placements to be a more attractive alternative than a public offering. For example, when Unocal was trying to avoid a takeover, it used a massive private placement of debt securities with insurance companies as a defense. Had it been necessary for Unocal to wait for the Securities and Exchange Commission to clear the offering, the company may very well have been taken over.

The second advantage of accessing the private market is to secure debt financings for longer terms. Many times a company will want to borrow money for a period of five to 20 years so that it has a stable capital base. Unfortunately, most banks are unwilling to make loans with terms longer than five years—even to their biggest customers. Small businesses often find themselves in the unenviable position of trying to do their long-term planning around a balance sheet of short-term debt. Private placements, on the other hand, can frequently be made with terms as long as 15 years.

Your role in a private placement is to collect the relevant data from the company and present it to your firm's private placement department to see if it can be placed. Unless you are familiar with the private placement market, do not attempt to do this type of business outside your own firm. Your compensation is generally a portion of your firm's fee (usually half of 1% net to you).

Public Offerings

You may be able to refer larger companies that are seeking financing to your firm's corporate finance department for a public offering of the company's debt or equity securities. An opportunity to participate in a public securities offering is something that usually comes along only a few times in a broker's career, but it is often a thrilling event. In addition to a share in the underwriting fee (5% to 10%), you should also try to negotiate (in writing) a compensation package with your company that includes the following:

- A share in the underwriting fee of any subsequent underwritings (2.5% to 5%).
- A guarantee that you will have the exclusive right to solicit orders from the company's employees.
- A guarantee that you will have a block of the stock reserved for you to sell.

I strongly recommend that you attempt to do a public offering only through your own firm unless you have a very strong corporate finance background. The process of offering securities to the public is extremely complex; overlooking even the slightest detail can derail a deal. Even experienced corporate finance specialists sometimes overlook some detail that delays an offering. When you consider the number of steps involved in taking a company public or offering securities, it's not difficult to understand such oversights.

I have known only one retail broker who was able to prospect successfully for this type of business. He got his start by coming across a deal in his usual course of business and then making sure he was personally involved in every subsequent step of the offering process. By leveraging this knowledge, he was able to develop a profitable sideline. It should be noted that his firm was one of the more progressive and liberal on the street. Before you approach any company about a public offering, check with your firm to determine its policies about retail reps soliciting corporate finance business.

A Hypothetical Financing

In the course of your prospecting, you encounter H.L. Jones, who is the principal owner of ABC Windows, Inc. The company is a sales and marketing organization that buys replacement windows from a national manufacturer and then markets and installs them on a local basis.

The company is only six years old. It was started by Jones when a reorganization of the Fortune 500 company he had previously worked for left him without a job. Because Jones started the company on a shoe-string, he was initially not in a position to negotiate attractive financing and eventually ended by borrowing $150,000 from a local finance company at prime plus 5% in the form of a five-year amortizing loan. Additionally, he took out a second mortgage on his house ($100,000 at prime plus 3%). Finally, he was able to arrange for another local finance company to provide his homeowner customers with financing at prime plus 5%, with a 1% up-front fee.

After only one year in business, the company started breaking even. By the end of the second year, the company was bringing a solid 10% of its $600,000 sales down to the bottom line as after-tax profits. Unfortunately, sales could not be increased because this sales volume represented the market saturation point.

To keep his company growing, Jones decided to "clone" his company in a second community and promoted his sales manager to run the second location for him. The second location was organized as a second company, 80% of its stock being owned by the first company and 20% being owned by the erstwhile sales manager. The second company borrowed money from the same finance company although at a slightly better rate—prime plus 3%. Additionally, Jones was able to borrow the entire $250,000 from the finance company and thus did not have to put a further mortgage on his home. This second company also became profitable. The original company was cloned again and again, using similiar structural and financing techniques. At the end of eight years, ABC Window had sales of $4,800,000.

Despite the fact that ABC Windows was rapidly becoming one of the window manufacturer's largest customers, Mr. Jones was unable to negotiate better pricing. In fact, he received several sharp price increases over the last few years. Thus he made the decision to go into manufacturing. He knew the assistant manager at the national window manufacturing company and discreetly approached him about managing the new company.

The manager agreed and a new company was born. Based on the pro-forma and business plan that the two principals developed, the new company was going to need approximately $700,000 in start-up capital. The partners agreed that they did not want to invest their own money in the venture and so would seek outside financing for the entire amount. (Thus they followed the first rule of business, "Never spend your own money unless you absolutely have to.")

Because you already manage the company's pension plan and you are the consultant for the company's employee benefit program, you meet with Mr. Jones on a regular basis. At lunch one day Mr. Jones informs you of his plans for the new company and for the type of financing he desires. However, being very busy running his other businesses and starting this one, he does not have the time (or really the expertise) to arrange a financing package. You offer to help Mr. Jones arrange the financing and agree to be compensated in the following manner:

1. $1,000 nonrefundable retainer to being work.
2. 3% of debt money raised if you can raise money at prime plus three or less, 1% if the cost of money is higher.
3. 8% of equity raised.
4. Client pays all legal costs and other expenses.

Because of a contact you developed at a regional bank (with an aggressive reputation), you are able to arrange a $700,000 7-year term loan at prime plus 1%, the loan being secured by a cross collateral agreement with the window sales companies. Because the cost of money to the client was less than prime plus 3%, your fee is 3% of the amount borrowed or $21,000, a nice fee indeed. (Note, however, that this fee, although rich, is still only half of what many small business loan brokers would charge for the same service.)

Employee Stock Programs

Employee Stock Ownership Plan

An *employee stock ownership plan (ESOP)* is a qualified plan designed to invest primarily or exclusively in the employer's securities. Since an ESOP is a "qualified" plan, it must meet many of the same requirements that other types of qualified plans (see Chapter 5) must meet, including:

1. It must be a written plan.
2. It must meet one of the two participation tests.
3. It must keep all its assets in a trust whose provisions require that all assets be used solely for the benefit of plan participants.
4. It must have a vesting schedule that is at least as favorable to the participants as one of the three alternatives provided by ERISA.
5. It must allocate employer contributions and forfeitures in a nondiscriminatory manner.

However, due to the nature and purpose of ESOPs, they are exempt from other rules that are applicable to other types of qualified plans.

1. ESOPs are appropriate only for incorporated businesses, not sole proprietorships or partnerships. The requirement that the employer's stock contributed to the ESOP be held in trust makes them inappropriate for Subchapters Corporations. Also, because most states prevent nonprofessionals from owning stock in professional corporations, it is often impossible for a professional corporation to establish an ESOP. To meet the participation requirements under ERISA, an ESOP would have to include nonprofessionals which would violate the state laws pertaining to professional corporations.

2. ESOPs established after 1977 cannot be integrated with Social Security. All employee compensation must be used in calculating employer contributions.

3. Because ESOPs are designed to invest primarily in employer securities, there is no "diversification" requirement. However, any percentage of an ESOP's assets that are invested in securities other than the employer's securities must still meet the diversification requirements.

4. An ESOP is exempt from the "fair return" provisions. Thus the fiduciary of an ESOP is not bound to get a fair return on the investments. However, the plan fiduciary is bound to do the best job possible for the plan's participants in buying the employer's securities (timing purchases and the like) and is bound to get a "fair return" for any securities other than the employer's securities that are purchased by the ESOP.

Any employer securities purchased by the ESOP must be purchased at their "fair value." If a public market for the securities exists, the securities must be purchased at or below their current market price. If no public market exists for the securities, as in the case of a closely held company, it is up to the fiduciary to determine the fair value of the securities and not to pay more than that value.

If the fiduciary overpays for the securities, he may be liable for a 5% excise tax. If, following notification from the IRS, the problem is not promptly corrected the fiduciary may be liable for an additional 100% excise tax and the plan may be disqualified.

5. Because an ESOP is either a stock bonus plan, or a combination

stock bonus plan and money purchase plan, the company does not need any profits (current or retained) to establish and/or contribute to an ESOP. The same carry-over rules for eligible but unfundable contributions apply to ESOPs as apply to other stock bonus and profit sharing plans. (See Chapter 5 for a complete discussion.)

If a company wants to make larger contributions than are allowed under a single stock bonus plan (limited to 15% of payroll), it can establish a combination stock bonus and money purchase ESOP. In a combination ESOP a company can increase its contribution to 25% of employees' compensation although the $30,000 limit still applies. However, if a company establishes an ESOP where no more than one-third of the contributions are allocated to officers, highly compensated employees, and employees who own more than 10% of stock, then the contribution can be as large as $60,000 for an individual participant. The 25% compensation limit still cannot be exceeded. So in order to be eligible for a $60,000 contribution, an employee must draw a salary of at least $240,000.

6. Unlike any other qualified plan, ESOPs can borrow money either directly from the employer or other related parties, or indirectly on the strength of the employer's credit. Companies can deduct any interest expense (without limit) incurred in paying off the loan (see below).

7. ESOPs can deal with "parties in interest" as long as the interests of the plan participants are protected. Since one of an ESOP's principal functions is to acquire employer securities from the company owners, an ESOP would have to be exempt from the usual rules barring transactions between qualified plans and parties in interest. This exception is also available to any regular profit sharing or stock bonus plan, but not to any type of pension plan.

ESOPs are also bound to some rules that are applicable only to ESOPs and not to qualified plans in general.

When an ESOP makes a distribution, the employee may be given the right to choose whether he wants the distribution to be in cash or in the form of employer stock.

If the distribution is in the form of employer stock, the employee has the right to put back the stock in two 60-day windows. If the employee exercises his put, the ESOP can repurchase the shares in lieu of the company. (Of course, if the company's stock is publicly traded, then the company is not required to provide the put feature since the employee will already have liquidity.)

If the employee elects to take his distribution in the form of employer stock, the employer can require that it have the right of first refusal for any subsequent sale. This means that, if the employee receives a bona fide offer to sell the securities, he must first give the company 14 days to buy the stock for the same price. The employee can also exchange his securities for other qualified securities without triggering a taxable event. This way, an employee can exchange the employer's securities for a well diversified portfolio. (For example, shares distributed from an ESOP that are publicly traded can often be exchanged for shares in a mutual fund.)

If the employee takes the distribution in the form of "cash" the distribution is taxable as ordinary income. If, however, the employee elects to take the distribution in the form of stock, then that portion of the sale proceeds representing the difference between the stock's sale price and the stock's value when it was purchased by or contributed to the ESOP is eligible for long-term capital gains treatment. Under the 1986 Tax Reform Act, this distinction between income and capital gains may be rendered "moot."

If the employee exchanges the employer stock for a diversified portfolio, the distribution is taxed when the dversified securities are sold. The delaying of taxation and the favorable capital gains treatment of distributions are two of the most important advantages of establishing ESOPs. (Note that under the tax Reform Act of 1986 distributions from ESOPs may be subject to alternative minimum tax provisions.)

Employees who participate in ESOPs must be given certain voting rights. If the securities are registered, then the plan participants must be allowed to vote on all matters that customarily require shareholder participation (including all proxies). If the securities are the type that do not require registration (securities of a closely held company), then the employees only have to be given the right to vote their shares on "important" corporate matters such as mergers, acquisitions, and the like. Plan participants have voting rights only on shares that are actually allocated to their accounts. Thus employees have no voting rights for shares held in a suspense account (see below).

The shares that are contributed to or purchased by the ESOP must have voting rights at least as liberal as the most liberal form offered by the company or a company in the same control group. This is to present management from funding the plan with shares that have one vote per share while retaining shares for themselves that have ten votes per share. The voting rights of both preferred stocks and convertible bonds must be included in this "voting rights" analysis.

Leveraged Employee Stock Ownership Plans

As already mentioned, an ESOP can borrow money with which to buy employer securities. An ESOP that borrows money is called a *leveraged ESOP*. The basic steps in this process are:

1. The company forms an ESOP.
2. The company borrows money, usually from a bank, on the strength of the company's guarantee, with appropriate collateral if necessary. The company, in turn, lends the money to the ESOP.
3. The ESOP buys the employer securities.
4. The ESOP uses the annual contributions from the employer to pay off the debt.

By using "leverage" an ESOP is able to buy larger blocks of employer securities than would be possible if the ESOP had to pay "cash" for all its purchases. As we shall see, this ability to "borrow" is instrumental in an ESOP's ability to achieve its goals.

A leveraged ESOP has its own special rules that it must follow.

First, the interest rate charged on the debt must be reasonable.

Second, the purchased shares must be held in a suspense account (an unallocated account within the ESOP) and allocated only as the loan is paid down. (Set formulas define the schedules by which the securities must be released from the suspense account as the loan is retired.)

Third, the bank (or lender) cannot have any recourse to any part of the ESOP or any securities therein that are not specifically purchased by the loan proceeds. Because the value of the securities in an ESOP can decline, potentially leaving the bank unsecured, most banks require that the employer guarantee any loan to a company's ESOP. If the employer securities held in a leveraged ESOP generate any income (dividends), the income can be either allocated to the participants or used to retire debt, whichever is specified in the plan document. (Note that dividends paid on stock held in an ESOP are tax-deductible for the company if they are paid out to the plan participants under the terms of the ESOP.)

To encourage banks to make ESOP loans, the federal government allows banks to exclude 50% of their interest earnings on ESOP loans. Thus banks are encouraged not only to make ESOP loans but also to make ESOP loans on favorable terms.

Any company establishing an ESOP must make sure that the contributions required to retire the loan do not exceed the plan's contribution limits. If, to retire the loan, the company would have to contribute more than it legally can, it will be faced with the unpleasant decision of refinancing the loan or defaulting.

When a company is determining how large a loan it can service, it needs to make allowances for forfeitures and voluntary employee contributions under the ESOP and any other qualified plan maintained in addition to the ESOP. Because both forfeitures and voluntary contributions reduce the maximum employer contribution, they both also reduce the size of the loan the ESOP can service. Finally, any loan to an ESOP cannot be callable except in the event of a default, although a bank can require certain reasonable prepayment penalties.

Uses of ESOPs

ESOPs can be used to solve a wide variety of problems and to meet a wide variety of objectives, particularly in small business situations.

First, an ESOP can be a excellent tool with which to recruit employees. Small businesses compete with large businesses to recruit quality employees and must often offer an extra enticement to be competitive. Offering employees a share of the business via an ESOP can provide such an attraction. This extra enticement is designed to compensate for the extra risk of working for a new or financially less stable concern, as opposed to a large stable one. Naturally, equity in a company that has a high probability of being acquired at an attractive multiple or going public is more attractive to prospective employees than equity in a publicly held company.

The second reason for installing an ESOP is to retain employees and encourage the workforce to be more productive. Giving a large percentage of the workforce an equity interest in the company can go a long way towards alleviating the adversarial relationship that often exists between employers and employees in U.S. companies. Employees who are stockholders are likely to be more productive, require less supervision, focus on longer-term goals, and be more likely to contribute new ideas than are employees who have no interest in the company's success other than a paycheck.

Also, an ESOP can function as a type of "golden handcuff" contract. Employees who are partially vested in a company-sponsored ESOP will be less likely to leave.

Sometimes, to provide employees with a large enough equity position in a company to make it attractive to either a new or a key employee, the employer may need to form a new company or at least a division. A company interested in increasing employee productivity can create a subsidiary and give or sell a portion of the subsidiary's stock to the subsidiary's employees.

Once divided into smaller groups, the employees may also feel more personally involved in the company and may be able to relate their performance more directly to the company's performance. Consider the case of an assembly lineworker at General Motors. Just how much can the employee's performance affect GM's bottom line? However, if a large company is broken up into a number of smaller companies, then each employee's actions and contributions will have a greater effect on his or her company's bottom line. The theory is that, if an employee feels his actions have a direct effect on the company's bottom line, he will be more productive.

Still another use of an ESOP is to raise capital. Capital raised via an ESOP can be used for any corporate purpose, but most frequently it is used to finance a merger or an acquisition.

The steps in this process are as follows:

1. The company establishes an ESOP.
2. The ESOP borrows the necessary funds.
3. The ESOP then buys the stock of the company that's being acquired or the ESOP buys the stock of a newly formed subsidiary and the new subsidiary purchases the stock of the acquired company.

The advantage of the company's using an ESOP to finance an acquisition (as opposed to just borrowing the money directly) is that ESOP financing offers the company a lower up-front net cost. Because contributions to an ESOP are tax-deductible and these contributions can pay off the cost of the acquisition, the company, in effect, can deduct both the principal and the interest payments it makes to pay off the loan. If the company instead elected to finance the acquisition directly, it would be able to deduct only the interest payments. Also, a bank will often make a loan to an ESOP at a lower rate than it will to the sponsoring company because of the 50% interest exclusion applicable to ESOP loans. This exclusion also reduces the cost of ESOP financing. The deductions for principal payouts in the ESOP's early years are later "balanced" by the company's nondeductible payouts to retired employees who cash in their stock by putting it back to the company.

An ESOP can also be a defense against a hostile takeover. If a company is threatened by an unwelcome suitor, it can establish an ESOP and have the ESOP acquire either any stock available on the open market or shares newly issued by the company. In either case the percentage of stock owned by the unwelcome suitor is reduced. The plan's fiduciary can vote the shares until they are allocated to the employees and presumably will side with management (since the fiduciaries usually are management).

Finally, one of the best reasons for a small business to establish an ESOP is to give a retiring owner of a closely held company a ready market for his interest in the company. In addition to providing liquidity, by selling the shares to an ESOP the owner helps to determine the value of the shares for income and estate tax purposes. An owner's estate can also sell shares of stock to an ESOP and the ESOP can pay the owner's estate taxes. Further, under the 1986 Tax Reform Act, the owner's estate can take a 50% deduction for proceeds from the sale of stock to an ESOP.

To insure that it has sufficient liquidity, the ESOP can buy life insurance contracts on the participants as long as the cost of the insurance can be justified as a prudent use of the ESOP's liquid assets.

Regardless of whether the shares are purchased from a living owner or a deceased owner's estate, they are subject to capital gains treatment (when applicable), and the ESOP contributions used to pay for the securities are tax-deductible by the company. When this is compared to an owner's selling his interest directly to the company (in which case the company must buy the shares with after-tax dollars and the owner may be taxed at ordinary income rates), the advantages of the ESOP method are obvious.

Companies with retained earnings problems may also use an ESOP to siphon off some of the company's earnings and thus alleviate the retained earnings problem.

Compensation

As a broker you can be compensated either by commissions or fees. You can earn commissions if the company's stock is publicly traded by purchasing stock on the open market for the ESOP. Note that any commissions must be charged to the company and not to the ESOP.

You can charge the client consultation fees for explaining how an

ESOP can be used to solve particular objectives. You can also charge fees for preparing a written proposal and for explaining the plan to employees. If your firm has an administration service, you might also be able to share in the fees the company is charged for administration services.

Of course, you should also get referrals from the attorney you recommend the company use to draft the plan.

Incentive Stock Options

Another way a company can retain key people, recruit employees, and increase productivity is to grant the employees "stock options." Stock options fall into two categories: statutory and nonstatutory, that is, options which meet the IRS statutes on options and those that don't meet the statutes.

An option that meets the statute requirements is often referred to as an *incentive stock option (ISO)*. ISOs are different from an ESOP in that the company is not required to make any cash contribution to an ISO plan when it is established. Instead, it only has to be prepared to sell to the employee the number of shares of employer stock the option called for at the exercise price. Thus, at least initially, an ISO plan is less expensive to establish than an ESOP.

If a company's ISO plan meets the rules as will be outlined, the employee is not taxed neither when he receives the options nor when he exercises them, but only when he sells the stock. Even then, he is taxed at "capital gains" rates. Thus the incentive for employers to adopt option plans that meet the statute rules is the very favorable federal income tax treatment that employees paticipating in such programs receive. The major statute rules are as follows:

1. The company must have a written plan that specifies:
a. Who is eligible to grant the options (Board of Directors, Chairman, President).
b. The total number of shares that may be issued under the plan.
c. Which employees or classes of employees are eligible (Senior Management, Middle Management, Key Employees, and so on).
2. The plan must be approved by the shareholders within 12 months before or after it is adopted. Any significant change in the plan regarding eligibility, the maximum amount of stock involved, and other key aspects, will require that the plan be reapproved by the shareholders.
3. The plan can include or exclude anyone, regardless of title, at the pleasure of whoever is empowered to grant the options. The plan can even cover only one person. This lack of any participation requirement is a major advantage of ISOs over ESOPs.
4. Any options granted under the plan must be granted within 10 years of the plan's adoption. The options themselves must not have a duration of longer than ten years or an exercise price that is below the fair

value of the stock on the date the option is granted. If, however, the employee to whom the options are granted owns 10% or more of the voting stock in the company, its parent company, or a subsidiary company, the option exercise price must equal or exceed 110% of the stock's fair market value on the day the option is granted. Additionally, the duration of the option(s) for such a person must not exceed five years.

5. The total amount of stock options granted to a single employee for a single year usually cannot exceed the right to purchase $100,000 worth of stock, using the value of the employer's stock as of the day the option is granted. For example, if ABC Manufacturing's stock was valued at $20 on the day the options were granted, no employee could receive options for more than 5,000 shares in that year. (Note that there are some "carry-over" provisions which may allow a company to exceed this $100,000 ceiling under certain circumstances.)

6. Options must be exercised in the order they were granted, starting with the first ones issued, even if they were issued at a higher exercise price. This rule prevents companies from, in effect, converting worthless options into valuable ones by reissuing them at a later date and at a lower exercise price. For example, let's assume ABC Manufacturing originally issued Joe Employee a stock option exercisable at $20 a share and the stock price never exceeded $20 again, but instead fell to $10. If the company issued Joe additional options at $10 a share, Joe would either have to exercise the $20 options (or wait until they expired) before he could exercise the $10 ones.

7. To qualify for the favorable tax treatment the employee must not sell or disperse the stock obtained via an option withinn two years of the date the option is granted or within one year of the date the employee receives the shares (by exercising the options) or disposes of the options. Thus an employee who exercises an option six months after receiving it would have to hold the stock at least 18 months in order for the sale to qualify as a capital gain. An employee who exercised an option two years after receiving it would only have to hold the stock for one year. If an employee should die, his or her beneficiary is exempt from these holding period requirements.

8. A *disposition* of an option is defined as a sale of the options, a gift of the options, or a transfer of legal title except when the transfer is between a deceased employee and the estate or beneficiary.

9. Also to qualify for the favorable tax treatment of ISOs, an employee must be employed continuously by the employer from the date the option is granted until at least three months before it is exercised. The only exceptions are for generally recognized leaves of absence: sickness, military service, and the like.

Options that fail to meet one or more of these rules are *nonstatutory*. Whereas statutory options are subject to taxation at capital gains rates, options that do not meet the statutes are subject to taxation at ordinary income rates. This is the principal difference between the two types of options.

Nonstatutory options are further divided into two categories: those that have a determinable fair market value and those that do not. The difference between these two classes is *when* they are taxed. Those with a determinable value are taxed when they are granted (as ordinary income), while those without a readily determinable value are taxed when they are exercised (also as ordinary income).

Of course, regardless of category (statutory, nonstatutory, with or without a determinable market value), once the option is exercised, the employee will be liable for capital gains tax on any subsequent rise in the value of the stock before it is sold.

Because of the many requirements that an option must meet to have a "determinable fair market value," almost all options fall into the second category and thus are taxable when they are exercised. This, of course, is favorable for the IRS since the tax liability to the employee is usually much greater when the options are exercised than if they were taxed when the options were granted.

Which type of options are preferable—statutory or nonstatutory? Either type can be better, depending on the objectives and the circumstances of the specific situation. With a statutory option the employee receives more favorable tax treatment at the employer's expense (the employer is not entitled to a corresponding tax deduction). With a nonstatutory option the tax treatment is less favorable to the employee, but the employer can receive a corresponding tax deduction when the employee reports the income, usually upon exercising the option. Under the 1986 Tax Reform Act, capital gains treatment has been eliminated. It remains to be seen what effect this may have on stock option plans.

One final note on stock options. Instead of "real" stock, an employer can grant an employee a "phantom" stock option, otherwise known as a *stock appreciation right (SAR)*. With an SAR an employee receives the difference between the value of the employer's stock when the option is granted and the value of the employer's stock when the option is exercised. The employee can receive this increase in value in either cash or employer stock. If the SAR is statutory the gain will be taxed at capital gains rates. If the SAR is nonstatutory this gain is taxable as ordinary income.

The difference between phantom stock options and actual stock options is that the employee does not need to come up with any cash to exercise the options, nor does the employee actually have to receive any stock. This makes SARs particularly well suited to a number of different situations.

First, they are very appropriate when the employer does not want to transfer stock to the employee, that is, where the employer wants to retain 100% control of the company.

Second, SARs can be used in conjunction with other regular options so that the employee will have sufficient liquidity to exercise the options and pay the taxes.

Chapter 9   *Life Insurance*

Retail brokers do not sell enough life insurance. There are several reasons for this.

First, brokers generally do not find selling insurance to be a very "sexy" pursuit. We have a wide variety of products and services that we can sell, and most of them offer more "sizzle" than insurance. After all, "day trading" futures and options, arranging bond swaps, and restructuring portfolios are all more "glamorous" than selling life insurance.

Second, insurance salespeople in general suffer a "poor press" as the butt of incessant bad jokes. As a result, most brokers feel that the brokerage profession has more prestige and view selling life insurance as a step down.

Third, the level of knowledge required to become a broker is much greater then the level of knowledge required to sell insurance. The Series 7 exam is much tougher than any state's insurance exams. Brokers thus sometimes feel that, if they concentrate on selling insurance, they are wasting their extra training and expertise.

Fourth, most brokerage firms do not actively encourage their retail sales force to sell insurance. While most investment banking firms have an insurance department, a quick review of the volume of sales literature generated by the mutual funds department as opposed to the volume of sales literature generated by the insurance department, will clearly illustrate most firms' priorities. Also, most firms have very few sales meetings on insurance and ways to sell it.

· Fifth, many brokers, although insurance-licensed, are not really familiar with the various insurance products that are available and thus are uncomfortable talking about them to their prospects and clients. This is especially true now that the insurance industry has started to create a wide variety of new and innovative products.

If these reasons were ever valid ones for brokers' ignoring life insurance, they are no longer. The artificial walls between the insurance business and the brokerage business are rapidly disappearing. Insurance agents are now calling on your clients with mutual funds and limited partnerships. And account executives who don't add insurance products to their product portfolios will find themselves getting "squeezed out" of the most lucrative portions of the financial services business.

The need to deal in insurance is especially great if you are going to concentrate your marketing effort on small business owners. A business owner typically spends more than 50% of his financial service dollars on insurance products, many of which we will touch on in this chapter.

In addition to protecting your own business from the onslaught of the huge (and very persistent) insurance salesforces, there are other reasons to sell insurance.

Often It's an Essential Purchase

The first reason to sell insurance is that many types of insurance, particularly life insurance, are "essential purchases." The question is not whether the client is going to buy insurance, but only where he is going to buy it. Often insurance is purchased from one salesperson instead of another simply because the owner likes or trusts one vendor more than another. If you have a good rapport with a prospect or client, he might as well buy his insurance from you!

Insurance sales lend themselves to the "oh-by-the-way approach. When you're about to hang up on a client, simply say, "Oh, by the way, when was the last time you had your life/health/disability insurance reviewed?" The reason this approach is so effective is that people's insurance needs change over time—especially a business owner's insurance needs. Also, insurance products have been dramatically improved over the last few years. Any insurance program that's more than a few years old is probability insufficient, inappropriate, or obsolete.

Very Versatile Tool

Insurance is a very versatile tool that can be used to solve many problems and meet many objectives. Often insurance is not just one way of solving a problem or the best way of solving a problem, but is in fact the only way to solve a problem, as we will see.

Very Tax-Advantaged

Many of the favorable tax treatments associated with insurance products are a result of the strong lobbying effort by the insurance industry. (The insurance lobby is regarded as one of the most powerful lobbies in the nation.) In fact, under the 1986 tax act, life insurance products have emerged relatively unscathed, thus improving the attractiveness of insurance products relative to other investment vehicles.

Life insurance products can offer the purchaser one or more of the following tax advantages:

1. They can sometimes be purchased with pre-income tax dollars.
2. They almost always offer tax-deferred compounding of the earnings on the policy's cash value.
3. They offer income-tax-free loans and policy swaps.
4. They offer income-tax-free death proceeds to named beneficiaries.
5. They offer various estate tax and gift tax advantages.

In fact insurance products may just be the best tax shelters of the late 1980s and 1990s.

Great Commissions

Another very important reason to sell insurance is that the commission rates are very high. The commission levels are highly regulated (like brokerage commissions prior to "May Day"). The commission levels are set so that even the inefficient salesperson can make a living selling insurance. If you can develop efficient ways to sell insurance, you can get a tremendous leveraged return on your time and effort.

For brokers who are used to working for a 2–3% commission, receiving 85% of the client's first year contribution to an insurance policy as your commission can come as a very pleasant shock.

There is currently a legal challenge to the high fixed commission rates on insurance products in Florida. If this challenge is successful, then this battle to deregulate the commission rates for insurance products will no doubt move to other states. For this reason I suggest you consider selling insurance now, while it's still attractive and available.

Steady Income

Since insurance sales are not dependent on the market's "being hot," you can sell insurance anytime regardless of what's happening in the market. Also, many insurance products pay "residuals" (ongoing commissions for servicing the client), that can quickly become an annuity for you. Imagine starting each year with $200,000 gross before you even make your first phone call.

Support for Your Sales Effort

No organizations provide better sales and marketing support for their sales staff than the support provided by insurance companies. This support takes many forms.

Brochures and Literature. Insurance companies create marvelous brochures and literature. The larger ones have their own printing companies and some of the most talented graphic artists around. Some of their more creative publications have to cost at least a couple of dollars each to produce; yet you can get all the copies you need free of charge.

Proposal Illustrations. A picture is worth a thousand words and that is certainly true of insurance proposals. While it's important to talk to small business owners about wealth accumulation, protection for their businesses and loved ones, and tax-deferred growth and tax savings, talking until you're blue in the face will never have the power of showing a prospect a custom-prepared illustration and proposal. In a proposal you can illustrate the policy particulars using as your starting point whatever factors the client wants: the premiums the client wants to contribute, the rate of interest the client expects the cash value to earn, the withdrawals the client expects to make. You can also start with the client's ultimate objective and work backwards until you work out a realistic premium contribution schedule.

Either these illustrations can be done on your own personal computer, or the insurance company can prepare them for you (with a few days turnaround time).

Seminar Scripts. Many insurance companies offer top-quality slide slows, films, seminar scripts, seminar advertisements, and invitations— in short, everything you need to put on a successful seminar.

Wholesalers. Insurance companies often make available to their salespeople the services of regional wholesalers and other service personnel to answer any technical questions you may have or to help you close tough prospects.

Multimillion Dollar Advertising Budgets. When an insurance company comes out with a new product, it spends millions to advertise it. Frequently this advertising includes a program to generate leads, which are then distributed to those representatives and agents who have been marketing the company's products.

Expense Allowances. After you have started to produce insurance business for a given insurance company, you can expect to receive additional sales and marketing support in the form of an expense allowance for entertaining, seminars, and computer hardware.

As I said, quite a bit of support on top of the generous commissions!

Uses of Insurance

Key Man Insurance

One risk that small business owners often overlook is the risk if a key employee was to die suddenly. Since small businesses generally only have a few key people, the loss of the expertise of even one can be devastating. Losing one sales representative will not cripple IBM, but it can be very costly to a business whose entire sales force is composed of two individuals.

There can be many costs to a small business when a key employee dies:

- The cost of hiring a headhunter to replace the lost employee (up to 30% of one year's salary).
- Lost business.
- Lost time—the owner or another key employee will have to spend time training the replacement.
- Lower productivity until the new employee gets up to the productivity of the replaced employee.
- Lost customers or clients if deadlines are missed as a result.
- Loss of rapport with key customers or suppliers.
- Loss of specialized technical or manufacturing knowledge.
- Other business and personnel disruptions.

Every business owner needs to decide how much of these risks he wants to assume and how much to insure against each of them. For example:

1. Company XYZ is a small manufacturer of specialized electronic measuring devices. The company was started thirty years ago and is owned by Mr. Brown and his wife. For the first twenty years, Mr. Brown did most of the selling personally, but over the last ten years he has delegated increasing amounts of that responsibility to Mr. Smith, who is the firm's one and only full-time representative. Annual sales for Mr. Brown's Company are $18 million with about $10 million of that coming from the company's catalog and $8 million coming in from Mr. Smith's direct sales efforts. The company's profit margin is 15%.

If Mr. Smith were to die or become incapacitated, the company would risk losing a percentage of that $8 million in sales revenue. A new sales representative would have to be hired and trained while at the same time the company's competitors would be losing no time trying to take business away. The loss of Mr. Smith (who earns $120,000.00 a year) could potentially cost the XYZ company the following amounts of money:

- $40,000 in headhunter fees to find a sales rep with detailed knowledge about electronic measuring devices.

- $50,000 worth of Mr. Brown's time to train the new sales rep about the specifics of XYZ's product line.
- $600,000 of lost profits the first year, assuming that XYZ loses 50% of its direct sales. The loss in the second and other years is unknown, determined largely on how the new sales representative performs.

Certainly insuring Mr. Smith for $1 million is not unreasonable.

The preceding scenario assumes that the new sales rep works out. If he does not, the company will have to recruit and train another sales rep, and will probably lose more of its direct sales business in the process. Depending on how hard it is to find and retain good salespeople in the XYZ's industry, insuring Mr. Smith for an amount greater than $1,000,000 may be called for.

2. A mid-size company on the West Coast develops customized software applications packages on a individual contract basis. Ms. Jones is the company's best project manager and programmer, and so she is always given the most important projects for the company's most important accounts. If Ms. Jones were to die or become disabled, the company would probably fall behind on its promised delivery dates, and thus risk losing its best clients.

The specialty software business is very competitive and finding people who possess both programming and managerial skills is difficult, time-consuming, and expensive. Finding someone with the skills necessary to step into an ongoing project is especially difficult. Since it would be pressed for time the company would probably end up overpaying Ms. Jones's replacement just to fill the position quickly.

Thus the cost to the company of losing Ms. Jones is both the lost business and the higher compensation paid to her replacement.

Most major insurance companies offer software programs that will assist brokers in determining the "value" of a given employee to a given company. The illustrations these programs generate can be used to help you close key employee insurance sales.

Frequently, such insurance can be combined with a split dollar program (which will be explained) or a funded nonqualified deferred compensation program (see the chapter on nonqualified compensation).

Business Continuation
And Buy/Sell Agreements

Another problem that confronts small business owners is the potentially disastrous results stemming from the death of one of the business's *principals*. This is true regardless of whether the business is organized as a sole proprietorship, a partnership, or a corporation. However, the solution to the problem will vary depending on how the company is organized.

Sole Proprietorships. In the case of a sole proprietorship, one owner owns and operates the business. The business has no separate legal identity and thus the assets of the business are considered to be part of the personal assets of the owner.

The problem is that much of the value of any sole proprietorship is derived from the knowledge, skill, contacts, expertise, and goodwil developed by the proprietor. The minute a business owner dies, this value is lost and the value of the business drops accordingly. Thus many small businesses are worth much more "alive than dead" (that is, worth more as an ongoing operation than the liquidation value of the business's assets). This is in sharp contrast to many large publicly held corporations, which are worth more dead than alive.

Immediately upon the owner's death his beneficiaries suffer a financial loss from the decline in the value of the business, from the loss of the income that the owner previously generated, and from the imposition of death and estate taxes (the so-called "triple whammy").

The best solution for a business owner to get full value for his business is, of course, to sell it intact when he's alive.This way he can oversee the transition to the new owner with the business's suppliers, creditors, and customers and thus demand top dollar for the business. This approach assumes, of course, that the owner lives until he wants to sell the business (usually retirement age), that the business is of a type that would appeal to potential buyers, that a buyer can be found, and that financing can be arranged. All in all, those are a lot of "if's."

If the owner dies before retiring and has made no other provision for the business, then a court-appointed personal representative will have to dispose of the business. The representative will first try to find a buyer for the business as a whole. Failing that, the representative will be forced to auction off the business's assets separately and often at a fraction of their true value.

Thus the only way an owner can be sure that his family will receive the true value of his business upon death is to be insured for the value of the business. The owner can own the policy personally and name his family as beneficiaries, in which case the insurance proceeds will be included in his taxable estate (although they will be exempt from income tax).

If he wants to sell the business to another family member or an employee, he can enter into a purchase contract with that person and have them purchase the insurance on his life. Thus, when he dies, they will have the funds available to buy the business from the owner's beneficiaries (more on this in the chapter on estate planning). The one situation an owner should avoid is naming his estate as the beneficiary of his policy since this will subject the death proceeds of the policy to income taxes.

Partnerships. A business that's organized as a partnership has only two choices when one of the partners dies. It can liquidate or it can reorganize. It cannot continue as a viable entity because the remaining partners are prohibited from entering into many types of transactions (such as contracts or loans) after one of the partners dies.

Since liquidation of a partnership has the same drawbacks as liquidating a sole partnership, the preferable option is to reorganize the partnership, either as a sole proprietorship, as another partnership, or as a corporation. A liquidation is called for only when the deceased partner's knowledge or expertise is not replaceable, when the remaining partner(s) are no longer able to continue the business (for age or health reasons), or when the business is not worth saving.

Assuming none of these conditions is applicable, the problem becomes how to reorganize the partnership. The remaining partners can reorganize as a sole proprietorship or as another partnership. The remaining partners might elect to seek a new partner with the same expertise as the deceased partner, or they may incorporate. Regardless of what the remaining partners want to do, they must first deal with the deceased partner's beneficiary, who now owns a piece of the partnership.

Unless the beneficiary has the same skills as the deceased and can step in and fill the vacated position at the company (a rare occurrence), it's generally better for all concerned if the deceased employee's beneficiary is bought out by the remaining partners. In such a case, the remaining partners will not have the beneficiary, who's probably unfamiliar with the business, interfering with the day-to-day operation of the business.

Being bought out is also often beneficial to the beneficiary. By keeping the interest in the business, the value of a beneficiary's inheritance becomes dependent on how well the remaining partners manage the company. By selling out, the beneficiary locks in the value of the interest and is not disturbed by business worries immediately after the death of a loved one.

When a partner dies, the company or the remaining partners must have the ready cash with which to buy out the beneficiary. The company might be able to borrow the money but a loan could hamper the business's growth. Also, lenders may be less willing to lend funds to a company that has just lost a key partner. The remaining partners might be able to borrow the money personally, but at the time it's needed they may either be unable or unwilling to come up with a sufficient amount of cash to buy back the beneficiary's interest. Where does the buyout money come from?

The answer, of course, is for the partners to enter into a buy/sell agreement and to fund that agreement with life insurance. A funded buy/sell agreement guarantees that the deceased's interest will be sold to the remaining partners and that the remaining partners will have the cash to buy out the beneficiary. As a provision of the agreement, neither partner is allowed to use the proceeds for any other purpose than buying back the other's interest.

Most buy/sell agreements specify the sale price for a partner's interest based on a formula of sales, book value, or some other criterion. This prevents endless negotiations on the part of the remaining partners and the beneficiary over how much the deceased partner's interest is worth. The value is predetermined by those who should know best: the partners themselves. Prevaluing the partner's interest with a buy/sell agreement will also help the beneficiary justify the value of the deceased's interest for estate tax purposes.

Both bank and trade creditors look very favorably upon partnerships that have funded buy/sell agreements because they know that one partner's death will not bring the business to a standstill. The cash value that builds up in the policies over time can strengthen the company's balance sheet and can be used as collateral for loans.

Generally companies use whole life insurance to fund their buy/sell agreements so that the premiums are predictable and budgetable. However, a company with a sufficient cash flow might also elect to use a declining face amount term policy coupled with an in-house sinking fund. In any event a company should not use an endowment policy because these policies are often included in retained earnings calculations made by the IRS (see Chapter 2).

The premiums for insurance to fund a buy/sell agreement are not tax-deductible because they cover the key employees, but the death proceeds are income-tax-free to a named beneficiary (either the company or the other partners).

The actual buy/sell agreement should be drawn up by a competent attorney because the exact wording of such an agreement is very important and can vary from state to state. Under no circumstances should you allow a client to rely solely on a "prototype" agreement.

Corporate Buy/Sell Agreements. If the company is organized as a closely held corporation, then the problems of a deceased shareholder's interest in the company can be solved in one of two ways. The shareholders can agree to buy each other out as with a partnership (usually referred to as a *cross purchase plan*). As an alternative, the corporation itself can buy back the deceased owner's shares (usually referred to as a *stock redemption plan*) and either retire the shares or hold them as treasury stock.

Each of these methods has its advantages and drawbacks. In a stock redemption plan the company owns the insurance and is the beneficiary of the policy. This exposes the cash value and the insurance proceeds to the claims of corporate credits. There is no such exposure with a cross purchase plan. However, in a company where there are multiple owners it is often easier to have one master policy as opposed to each shareholder's owning an insurance policy on all the other shareholders, which would be required by a cross purchase plan.

Another factor that needs to be considered when deciding between these plans is the relative tax bracket of the shareholders as opposed to the corporation. If the corporation's tax bracket is higher than the shareholders', it is cheaper for the company to pay the shareholders enough extra salary to cover the cost of the insurance premium. Using this method the shareholders pay income tax on the extra salary at their lower rate and the corporation takes a tax deduction for the salary payments at its higher tax rate. If, however, the shareholders' overall tax bracket is higher than the company's tax bracket, then the preferred method is for the company to pay the premiums.

Group Insurance

Group life insurance is one of the most popular fringe benefits in America today for a number of reasons. Because it is administratively less expensive for insurance companies to insure multiple lives at one time, via one policy, than it is to sell insurance to the same number of people individually, the "load" for group life is lower. Thus group plans are often a 'better buy" in most cases than individual policies. To keep the costs of providing this benefit low, most companies elect to purchase one-year renewable term policies.

The federal government encourages employers to provide their employees with group life by giving it favorable treatment under the tax laws. A qualified group life plan is tax-deductible to the employer, and the value of the first $50,000 worth of coverage is not included in the employee's compensation for income tax purposes.

For a group life insurance plan to receive the favorable tax treatment afforded group plans it must meet certain requirements. The ten most important of these are as follows:

1. Employees cannot be required to take medical exams although they may be required to answer medical questionnaires to determine if they are insurable. Employees who are uninsurable for age or health reasons are excludable from the plan.

2. The waiting period before an employee becomes eligible to participate in the plan cannot be longer than six months.

3. Part-time employees (defined as employees who normally work fewer than twenty hours a week or fewer than five months full time a year) are excludable.

4. The policy must be carried by the employer and provide coverage in a way that precludes individual selection and discrimination against lower-paid employees. Instead the company must base both benefit levels and participation requirements on age, years of service, compensation level, or position.

If a plan meets one of the following three tests, it will not be considered discriminatory for participation purposes.

a. The plan benefits 70% of nonexcludable employees.

b. 85% of the employees covered by the plan are not key employees.

c. Any other rules approved as nondiscriminatory by the Treasury Department.

5. To prevent discrimination with regard to benefit levels, a plan must offer benefits that either:

a. are based on a percentage of the employee's salary,

b. provide the same benefits for each employee, or

c. provide benefits based on classes of employees.

In this last method employees with different salary levels are grouped into different "classes." No class can be given a benefit more than 2.5 times the class below it, and the top class cannot have more than 10 times the benefits of the bottom class. (Note: Other guidelines must be followed to use this class method, but it's not important for you to know them all.) Whichever insurance company does the illustration and proposal will verify that the proposal is in compliance with the discrimination rules.

6. If the plan is discriminatory either on a participation or benefit basis, the income exclusion for the first $50,000 of benefits for all key employees is lost.

7. Group plans must cover at least 10 lives although insurance companies will frequently combine different employees from different companies to meet this requirement.

8. The cost of insurance benefits in excess of $50,000 is taxable to the employee and must be included on the employee's W-2 or Form 1099. The value of the excess benefit is determined via the appropriate uniform premium table. (The insurance company will provide the client and you with all the necessary tax information.)

9. A group plan can cover only an employer's employees and any independent contractors meeting the service requirement. A plan cannot cover shareholders, customers, or other outsiders.

10. The employer cannot be the beneficiary (either directly or indirectly) of an employee's group coverage.

Retired Life Reserves

In addition to covering employees with group life insurance while they are working, many employers are also electing to cover their employees after they retire. This type of program is called a *retired life reserves (RLR)* plan. In an RLR plan an employer can prefund the costs of providing such coverage during the employee's working years by making contributions to a reserve fund designed to pay the benefits. While all employers may find these plans attractive, they are especially attractive to small businesses and their owners because they represent a way for the owner to provide himself with personal insurance protection in his retirement years with his company's tax-deductible dollars.

An employer's contributions to an RLR plan are deductible in the year they are made. The principal rules affecting RLR plans are as follows:

1. The reserve fund is held solely for the purpose of providing life insurance (no other benefit) to active and/or retired employees and can be used for no other purpose as long as even one participant remains alive.

2. The contributions to the reserve fund cannot be any larger than the amount necessary to actually fund the plan's benefits. The contribution levels must be actuarially determined.

3. The investment earnings on the contributions are allowed to grow and compound—tax deferred—as long as the contributions are held in an insurance contract, by an insurance company, or in an exempt employee trust.

4. The employee cannot have the right to receive the funds in any form other than life insurance protection at any time or for any reason.

5. The employee has no rights to the money set aside for his benefit

while he's working; so he is not taxed on the contributions as the employer makes them to the fund. Instead he's taxed when he receives nonforfeitable rights to the benefits, usually upon retirement.

Bonus Plan

A company can also install a bonus insurance plan for its key employees. A bonus plan can cover whomever the employer wants to cover. It is exempt from the rules that cover qualified retirement plans (see Chapter 5), such as those affecting participation, vesting, and the like. However, an insurance bonus plan *does* need a fiduciary and *does* need to be documented. These requirements are usually met by adopting a corporate resolution authorizing the corporate expenditures for the plan and specifying that a given officer within the company will act as the fiduciary for the plan. These bonus plans have no reporting requirements beyond providing the Secretary of Labor with a copy of all plan documents, if so requested.

A company can either give additional salary directly to the employee so that the employee can purchase the insurance himself or the employer can purchase the policy directly. Regardless of how the company pays for the insurance, the expense is normally tax-deductible to the employer and taxable to the employee. Naturally, the lower the employee's tax bracket, the more attractive a bonus plan becomes. The Tax Reform Bill of 1986 lowered the maximum individual tax bracket and thus made bonus plans more attractive in future years.

Split Dollar Insurance

Split dollar insurance plans are programs in which the employer and employee split the premium payments, cash value, and death proceeds. The insurance policy purchased under a split dollar arrangement is almost always a whole life policy.

Of course, under a whole life policy an insured overpays for the insurance during the early years the policy is in force and underpays during the later years. The problem with whole life is that the payments are too high for many young people to afford, even though they would benefit from the lower payments a whole life policy would cost later in life. For this reason many employees look to their employers for financial assistance in acquiring the whole life insurance protection they desire. Split dollar plans an also be used by small business owners as a way to draw money out of a company.

The rules governing split dollar plans are relatively simple and flexible.

1. They can cover or exclude any employee on a completely discretionary basis.

2. Either the employer or the employee can own the policy. If the employer owns the policy then it files an endorsement with the insurance company about how the cash value and proceeds are to be split so the employee's rights are protected. For this reason this method is often called the *endorsement method*. If, instead, the employee owns the policy he gives his employer a collateral assignment to protect the employer's interest. This method is called the *collateral assignment method*.

3. Under a split dollar plan the employer makes funds available to the employee for the purpose of buying life insurance (in effect the employee receives a loan which he may or may not pay back to the employer depending on the terms of the plan). Thus the employee receives an economic benefit from a split dollar arrangement. The economic benefit the employee receives is called the PS58 cost. The employee incurs an income tax liability for any portion of this PS58 cost that his employer pays. If, however, the actual benefit an employee derives is less than the official PS58 table, then the employee incurs a tax liability only on the lower amount. This situation can occur when the cost of a given insurer's original issue policy is lower than the PS58 cost.

4. Because split dollar plans are discriminatory and the employer receives part of the benefits tax-free, the employer receives no tax deduction for its portion of the premium payments.

Employees often buy out their employer's interest in the policy after their income increases. If the employer is not bought out, then the employer is paid back when the policy is cancelled or when the employee dies.

Either the employer or the employee can borrow against the portion of the cash value to which each is entitled. For example, an employer may elect to borrow out the cash value that represents its interest as a way of recouping its expense.

Depending on the objective of the split dollar plan, the employer and employee can split the premium payments, cash value, and death proceeds.

Premium Payments

Premium payments can be split several ways including:

1. Employer pays the entire premium.

2. Employer pays an amount each year equal to the increase in the cash value of the policy, the increase in the surrender value of the policy, or the net premium, whichever is lower. The employee pays the balance of the premium payment. This is often referred to as the *standard method*.

3. In the "leveled" standard method plan, the employer overpays the preceding costs in the early years and underpays them in later years so as to even out the employee's payments. Because the increase in cash

value is minimal in the first few years, many employees would not be able to afford even their portion of the split dollar premium without this "leveling."

4. In the PS58 method, the employee pays an amount of the premium equal to his IRS-determined benefit and the employer pays the balance.

Naturally, a small business owner looking to take money out of his company would opt for the first method, while a company looking to recover its costs and to protect its interests would favor one of the other choices.

Cash Value

The cash value can also be split in a number of ways:

1. The employer recovers the amount of the premiums it pays on the employee's behalf.
2. The employer recovers the amount of the premiums it pays on the employee's behalf *plus* what the company would have earned on those funds if it did not have them tied up in the employee's policy.
3. The employer receives all the cash value regardless of how much it contributes to the policy.
4. The employer is entitled to the greater of the cash value or the premiums paid.

Again the choice depends on the objectives of the split dollar plan.

Death Benefits

Generally, the employee receives the entire death benefit minus any amount necessary to reimburse the employer in accordance with the terms of the agreement.

Chapter 10

Trusts and Custodial Accounts

Retail brokers who become familiar with trusts and custodial accounts and who take the time to develop good working relationships with trust companies enjoy three important benefits: the opportunity to provide a necessary service to business owners, the ability to pursue new business by using an approach that's both innovative and interesting, and the advantage of retaining a greater degree of control over their clients' assets. Unfortunately, few retail brokers are knowledgeable with respect to custodial accounts and trusts and how to work with trust companies.

Although most brokers have used trust companies as custodians of IRAs, profit sharing plans, and pension plans, few brokers use trusts to solve problems and achieve objectives unrelated to retirement plans. Trusts are actually some of the most flexible financial tools that a broker has at his disposal.

Types of Accounts

Trust companies can be used for three types of account: (1) individual accounts held in the name of the individual (individual custodial accounts), (2) pension accounts held in the name of the pension (pension custodian accounts), and (3) individual accounts held in another name (trust accounts).

Type 1

Individual custodial accounts are somewhat misnamed in that they are used not only to house individual accounts but also partnership accounts, joint accounts, corporate accounts, and any other account that is not a pension account and that is held in the same name as that of the creator(s) of the account. If XYZ Inc. creates an account named "XYZ Inc." it is considered an individual account. The same is true if a partnership called International Investment Partners forms an account named "International Investment Partners." Most of the accounts you open will fall into this category.

Traditionally, most brokers have simply held their client's assets at their own firm (in safekeeping) or have delivered the securities to the client by mail or by a DVP (delivery versus payment) settlement. However, more and more brokers are realizing the principal advantage of having their clients' assets held by an independent trust company: control over their clients' assets.

It's no secret that the financial services industry is moving toward complete deregulation. Banks, insurance companies, and brokerage firms are raiding each other's turf and battling for control of their clients' assets as never before. As a result of this battle, most firms have devised a number of ways to gain control over client assets and to tie the client to the firm.

On the surface this may not appear to be a bad thing. After all, if your firm ties your client to the firm, then the chances of another broker's taking the account away are reduced. Unfortunately, everything that your firm does to increase its control over your clients' accounts usually has the side effect of reducing your control over your clients' accounts. Because you never know what the future may bring, it's essential to maintain as much control as you can over your clients' accounts.

Even if you are currently happy with the firm you work for, your feelings may change. Your payout may be cut, you may get a new manager with whom you cannot work, your firm's operations may deteriorate, or your firm may be acquired by another firm with which you do not want to be associated. Also, let's face it, the people who run Wall Street firms are not known for their paternalistic attitudes toward their retail brokers. Most firms would slash their retail payouts if they could, and that desire to slash payouts will only increase during the next economic and business downturn.

The only thing that stops firms from reducing payouts is the leverage that the brokers have—that is, their ability to change firms and take their accounts with them. Many brokers, however, are being short-term selfish instead of long-term greedy by sacrificing control over their clients' accounts for a quick buck. Consider the following examples.

As a way of collecting assets, most firms really push their brokers to put their clients into the new "super" accounts (checking, charge or debit card, money market, and securities account all in one). The pitch used to motivate you to do the extra paperwork is usually that "clients who are in these accounts are more active than other accounts and generate more commissions." Of course, no one mentions that the clients for whom this type of account is most appealing are clients who are active traders, and so it only stands to reason that the clients who like these accounts would on average generate more commissions regardless of the type of account they have.

In exchange for placing your clients into these accounts, you receive a whopping $50 to $100. From that time on, every time your client writes a check or charges a purchase, the relationship between the firm and the client is reinforced. Any broker who has ever changed firms and tried to transfer the assets in these super accounts knows just how difficult this transfer can be.

First, you have to convince the client to turn in his checks and charge cards, sign a broker-to-broker transfer form (Form 412), wait for the account to settle, supply a copy of the client's last statement updated for any changes, and then wait for the transfer to occur—which is a process that (in violation of numerous NYSE regulations) almost invariably takes months to complete.

In the meantime, some broker at your old firm who has offered a higher payout on any account of yours that he can keep is calling on your accounts like crazy while you're powerless. This delay and hassle inevitably result in your losing a number of accounts—not your best accounts, for sure, but a number of accounts that you talk to three or four times a year and that generate $500 to $1,000 per year. Losing them is a heavy price to pay for the $50 to $100 dollars you received for putting the client into the account in the first place.

Another method firms use to tie clients to the firm is by the use of proprietary products. By offering you a higher payout on an "in-house" product, your firm encourages you to collect assets for the firm, often to the detriment of your client. For example, the chances are that your firm's growth fund is probably not the best one available. It probably doesn't have the best track record, the best managers, or the lowest management fee. What it does have is a higher payout. Instead of collecting a 35% payout, it may have 45% payout—so you sell it anyway.

This hurts you in a number of ways. First, your client will start thinking of you not as a professional advisor but merely as a salesman who is paid to push the firm's product out the door. Second, every proprietary product you sell again reinforces your firm's relationship with the client and weakens your relationship with your client. Third, if your clients are fully invested in firm ABC's products and you move to firm XYZ, do you really think the client will follow you?

If your client is in a super account that is full of proprietary products and you ask the client to follow you, you are not asking the client merely to move an account but to turn his financial world completely upside down. Even if the client does want to follow you to firm XYZ, many proprietary products are nontransferable—meaning that your client will have to maintain a relationship with your old firm even if he elects to move with you.

Still another method firms use to tie up clients' assets is the in-house investment manager referral program. Under this program, you collect client assets and refer them to independent money managers that your firm has screened for performance. The idea behind this program is that because the manager makes the day-to-day investment decisions, the broker's time is freed to pursue new accounts while the manager runs trades through the broker's number. These money managers are collecting assets from hundreds of your firm's brokers, so their first loyalty is to your firm and not to you. If you were to change firms, the commission stream generated by the assets you collected would continue to accrue to your old firm and would not follow you. If you either elect to change firms or are forced to change firms, an in-house referral program is just another way to lose control of client assets.

Custodianing your "individual" clients' accounts at a trust company will largely solve your control problem. All that changes if you use a custodian is that after you present an investment idea to a client, you (or your client) notify the trust company of the trade. You then settle the trade with the trust company, usually on a DVP basis (delivery versus payment).

With your clients' assets held outside your firm, your leverage as a broker increases. If your firm ever mistreats you, you can leave without worrying about losing a substantial portion of your business because of the transfer process. The fact that you can take most of your business with you also makes you more valuable to other firms.

Once you are at your new firm, the trust company will simply execute the trades you and your clients agree on through your new firm. (Some trust companies require a letter from the client giving them permission to start using a different firm for executions although this is still much easier than dealing with those 412 forms.)

Type 2

Pension assets (assets in IRAs, profit sharing plans, and pension plans) must, by law, be held in a custodian account at a trust company. The larger brokerage firms usually have their own trust companies. Smaller firms usually use a independent trust company. The problem with using these companies is again one of control. These companies' first loyalty is to the firms and not to the broker. Transferring these accounts can be very difficult, especially if the trust company (or an affiliate of the trust company) is also the administrator of the plan.

Type 3

The third type of account held at a trust company is an individual trust account. This type of account is set up by an individual, partnership, couple, or corporation and creates a separate legal entity. For example, a father can establish a trust for the benefit of his son. In this case, the law recognizes three distinct parties: the father, the son, and the trust for the benefit of the son. Likewise, an individual can set up a trust for his or her own benefit. In this case, the law recognizes two parties: the individual and his or her trust.

Each trust account has the party that establishes that trust, usually called the grantor, and the party who benefits from the trust, usually referred to as the beneficiary. Trust accounts are established for a number of purposes, including the following:

1. Protecting an individual in the event he or she becomes incapacitated.

2. Providing for the smooth transfer of assets from the grantor to his or her beneficiaries without the expense and delay of probate.

3. Reducing an individual's income and estate taxes.

4. Protecting a family member who is either unable or unwilling to manage a large sum of money from the burden of having to do so.

5. Protecting a spendthrift heir or an heir who has a substance-abuse problem from himself by providing him with his inheritance in a series of periodic payments rather than as a lump-sum payment. Further conditions can be placed on the beneficiary such as not abusing drugs or alcohol, holding a job, and so on.

6. Insuring that a business to which an individual has devoted his life will continue to exist after the founder's death instead of being sold by the founder's heirs.

Advantages of Making Use of Trusts

Let's briefly review the advantages and limitations of some of the various types of trusts, it's appropriate to review why brokers interested in the corporate market should become familiar with trusts.

The first reason to become familiar with trusts is that wealthy individuals (a category that includes many business owners) need trusts to meet their financial objectives and solve their financial problems. Like any essential service that your client needs, if you don't offer it, your client will be forced to seek it elsewhere. This means that another financial institution and another professional are going to end up with control of a large portion of your client's assets. You need to become familiar with trusts to defend your existing business from other institutions.

After you become familiar with trusts, you can also use that knowledge as an offensive weapon by prospecting for trust business. Although most wealthy prospects have heard numerous stock stories and have been presented with tax-advantaged investments by the bucketful, the chances are that they have not recently heard an effective presentation of trust services. If you approach a new prospect with a trust service pitch, you just might strike a more responsive chord than if you had led off with a more traditional product or service.

Another reason to learn about trusts is because the prospects most interested in these vehicles are usually senior citizens. Fortunately, senior citizens are both the fastest growing (demographically speaking) and the wealthiest segment of our population, which gives you an almost unlimited supply of suitable prospects to approach with your trust services.

Because each trust must be adopted with the assistance of the client's attorney, working in the trust area gives you the opportunity to work with and develop a rapport with numerous attorneys, each of whom can be a source of future referrals.

You can also develop a marketing plan to pursue prospects who have already established trusts and custodial accounts with other institutions, particularly their local banks. The advantage of pursuing these prospects is that you don't need to educate them about the advantages of establishing trusts and custodial accounts; they already know the advantages. Instead, you market your services from the point of view of lower fees and/or better investment performance. Trust departments of local banks tend to charge high fees, and although generalities can be dangerous, if the trust officers who manage trust accounts at small banks were that good, would they be working for $40,000 to $50,000 a year?

The fact is that many people who have set up trusts with their local banks quickly become disenchanted with the banks' performance and are open to being approached with any idea of how to improve the account's performance, even if that requires that they move the account to a new institution.

Moving the account from one institution to another is usually easy if the person who established the account is still alive. Most trust documents allow the person establishing the account to move it (or even terminate it) any time he or she wishes. If, however, the prospect is the beneficiary of a trust or custodial account established by a deceased relative, transferring the account can be more difficult.

Some beneficiaries have the right to change trustees but are unaware that they have that right (and the bank naturally doesn't go out of its way to inform the beneficiaries of their rights). Even if the trust document doesn't allow the beneficiary to change trustees, your prospect can still petition the probate court to allow the trust to be moved to another institution if the investment performance has been very poor. Pursuing prospects who have already established trusts can be an entire business unto itself.

Concentrating your marketing effort on opening trust and custodial accounts can also be rewarding if you would like to become an independent money manager. If, for example, over a 10-year period you establish five trust accounts a year with an average value of $1 million for each account, then by the end of the tenth year the value of the assets under your control would exceed $75 million (assuming an average annual return of 10% on the accounts).

If you provide the accounts with quality service and investment advice, convincing your clients to allow you to manage their trust and custodial funds (on either a discretionary or nondiscretionary basis) should be fairly easy. If you are able to convert just half of these brokerage accounts into money management accounts, you would be able to start your firm with more than $30 million under management. At a fee of 1% per year, your first year revenues would be $300,000 from this source alone (which certainly beats starting from scratch). The investment results of your trust accounts also give you an auditable track record that you can use when soliciting new clients. Thus, working with trusts can be a lead into becoming a money manager.

The last advantage of using trusts is that you can continue to earn commissions from your clients' accounts even after they're dead (now, that's control!). If you assist your clients in establishing trust accounts and your clients are pleased with the trust company's performance, there is a good chance that they will appoint the trust company to manage their assets upon their death for the benefit of their heirs. You can usually get a clause inserted into the trusts at the time they are drawn up that directs the trustee to run the trades through you even after the clients' death (as long as your executions and commissions remain competitive).

Note, however, that even if you had full discretionary control over a client's account while the client was alive, the instant the client dies you must relinquish control of the account to the trust company. The reason for this is that most firms will not allow their brokers to be fiduciaries on trust accounts because of the liability involved. The only alternative usually available to brokers who do not want to relinquish control over a client's accounts upon the client's death is to form their own investment advisory firm.

Keeping those benefits in mind, let's briefly review some of the different types of trust that you have at your disposal. It's important to note that as a broker you do not need to become an expert on trusts in order to use them effectively. The fine points of any trust document will be explained to your client by either the client's attorney or an officer affiliated with the trust department. What you do need to know is the features, benefits, and limitations of each of the various types of trust so that you can interest appropriate prospects enough to motivate them to meet with their attorney and or a trust company official.

The Living Trust

The first type of trust you should be familiar with is the living trust. A *living trust* is so named because the grantor establishes it during his or her lifetime and usually makes himself or herself the primary beneficiary. (The individual establishing the trust can even act as his or her own trustee.) Thus, rather than opening a brokerage account in the name "John Smith," the account would be opened as "Trust dated 00/00/0000 for the benefit of John Smith." Why would anyone go through the bother of creating a trust for himself? For several reasons.

First, you can specify in the trust document who is to handle your affairs in the event you become ill or incapacitated. In this way you have the peace of mind that comes from knowing that someone whose judgment you respect, whom you trust, and who knows you, will be paying your bills, making decisions regarding your medical and financial affairs, and in short working for your benefit. An added feature is that this arrangement can be kept completely private. If you were to lose your capacity for rational thought, your family would have the embarrassment and delay of a competency hearing in a public courtroom.

The second and perhaps more important benefit of establishing a living trust is that in the event of your death your assets can be distributed to your beneficiaries without first having to pass through probate, as they would if they were passed on to your beneficiaries through your will.

Probate is, for most people, one of the great ripoffs inflicted on us by the legal profession. Probate is the process of collecting and distributing your assets in accordance with the instructions contained in your will. The process is supervised by the probate court and an executor (sometimes called an administrator) who is usually named by the deceased in his or her will. Unless your executor is very familiar with estate matters (not very likely), the executor will have to turn to an attorney for assistance. For providing assistance with the settling of your estate, the attorney will usually take a fee of between 3% and 8% of the estate, depending on the degree of complexity and the size of the estate. Imagine paying an attorney $20,000 (4%) to settle a $500,000 estate (transferring a house, its furnishings, and some securities to your spouse or children)!

With a trust, however, your property is distributed to your secondary beneficiaries as specified in your trust document. It does not go through probate, and thus the transfer is simpler, faster, and less expensive. At the time of your death, your spouse or children will probably not be in a frame of mind to deal with the hassles in which our Byzantine court system can ensnarl them. Setting up a trust will make their burden much easier to bear.

A quick comparison of using a will versus a living trust to settle an estate should be enough to convince you that everyone who needs to have a will (and that means every adult) would be better served with a living trust.

Table 10-1. Comparison Table.

Will	*Living Trust*
Only valid in state it is drawn in.	Valid nationwide.
Propetry passed by will must go through probate.	Property is exempt from probate.
Is no help in the event of disability.	Provides protection in the event of disability.
Becomes a public document upon death.	Remains a private document.
Can be changed or cancelled at any time.	Can be changed or cancelled at any time.
Easier to attack by disgruntled beneficiaries.	More difficult to attack by disgruntled beneficiaries.
Inexpensive and quick to establish.	Inexpensive and quick to establish.

As trusts go, a living trust is a relatively simple document. The person establishing the trust can change it or revoke it entirely right up until the time he or she dies or becomes incapacitated. If the person establishing the trust feels that the beneficiaries would be better off not receiving their inheritance in a lump sun, the trust document can specify that the trust company manage the assets and distribute them on a predetermined schedule.

Provisions can be made for minor children that give the trustee the right to release money from the trust to meet certain expenses (food, shelter, medical attention, education, and so on). In fact, there are so few limitations on what you can accomplish with a living trust that they are really not worth discussing.

Charitable Trusts

A client can often reduce income or estate taxes by setting up a charitable trust. There are many types of charitable trusts, so consultation with a trust expert is essential to select the exact type of trust that is most appropriate for the client's situation. Charitable trusts generally fall into one of two categories: charitable lead trusts and charitable remainder trusts.

In a *charitable lead trust* a client establishes a trust and places in it some income-bearing securities or income-bearing real estate. The income generated by securities and/or real estate is donated to a charity for a predetermined period. After that period, the property or securities then pass on to the client's heirs.

The advantages of establishing a charitable lead trust are that the grantor is not liable for any income tax on the income stream generated by the securities or real estate because that income stream is going to the charity. Furthermore, the value of the property or securities (for gift and estate tax purposes) when they are finally transferred to the grantor's heirs is the same value they had on the day they were first donated to the trust minus any income paid to the charity.

Let's assume a client donates some property with a fair market value of $1 million to a charitable yield trust and that the property generates an income of $100,000 per year. After 10 years, the property's market value may have appreciated to $2 million, but for gift and estate tax purposes its value is zero [$1 million − (10 × $100,000)]. A charitable lead trust is therefore an excellent way to transfer income-producing property to heirs.

If the client needs to retain some of the income generated by the securities or properties, he might elect to establish a charitable remainder trust. In a charitable remainder trust, the grantor establishes and funds a trust but retains a large portion of the income from that trust for a long period. Despite receiving most of the income generated by the trust, the grantor still gets to take a partial tax deduction when the trust is established.

For example, consider the case of a 65-year-old male who establishes such a trust and funds it with $100,000 of tax-free municipal bonds that yield 7%. If the individual elects to receive 6.5% per year on that $100,000 (or $6,500 per year), then the individual also receives an income tax deduction of $55,819.50 (based on IRS tables). (Notice that you can deduct up to only 50% of the individual's annual income per year so that if the deduction is larger than 50%, the excess must be carried forward).

Depending on the client's tax bracket, this tax deduction is like receiving a refund on the charitable contribution even though the individual continues to receive most of the income from the trust. Upon the individual's death, the assets in the trust are passed on to the charity and are not included in the client's estate for estate tax purposes.

Transferring Illiquid Assets

One of the biggest problems a small business owner faces is how to transfer his business to his heir. Small business owners are often asset rich and cash poor. When an owner dies, his estate often has the problem of finding the cash with which to pay the estate taxes without being forced to sell off the assets of the business.

One possible solution to this problem is for the owner to give money each year to his heir, which the heir can then use to buy a life insurance policy on the owner. When the owner dies, his heir will receive the life insurance proceeds, which the heir can then use to buy the business's assets from the estate. Thus, the heir ends up with the business, and the estate has the cash with which to pay the estate taxes. Even more important, however, is the fact that because the heir is both the owner and the beneficiary of the policy, the proceeds are not subject to estate taxes or probate, a significant tax savings.

To ensure that both parties live up to the transaction (for example, that the heir really does use the insurance proceeds to buy the business's assets so that the estate taxes can be paid), it's a good policy for the father to give the money to a trust for the *benefit* of his heir, rather than directly to his heir. This way the father can put the necessary restrictions on the use of the gift proceeds.

Marital and Family Trusts

As of January 1, 1987, any couple with an estate worth $1,200,000 or less can arrange their affairs so as to be completely exempt from paying any estate taxes. For this reason, when tax attorneys speak of estate taxes, they often refer to them as *optional taxes*. The reason the first $1,200,000 can be exempt from estate taxes is that each person is entitled to a unified exemption of $600,000 as of January 1, 1987. When used in conjunction with the unlimited marital deduction, this unified credit becomes a powerful weapon for tax avoidance.

Consider the case of a couple with assets of $1,200,000. Were one spouse to die, all the assets could be transferred to the other spouse free of estate taxes. However, this is not always the best strategy. The reason is that were the second spouse to die, the second spouse's estate would then be liable for estate taxes on all amounts over $600,000, which for the sake of simplicity we'll assume is $1,200,000 minus $600,000 for a taxable estate of $600,000. The tax on this amount is currently $235,000, one heck of a tax burden.

If, instead, when the first spouse died the couples' $1,200,000 were divided evenly among two trusts, a marital trust (Trust No. 1) and a family trust (Trust No. 2), then when the second spouse died there would be no estate tax consequences. How does this work?

Well, in simplest terms, the marital trust can be considered to be the assets that the first spouse leaves to the second spouse. Because interspouse transfers of assets are not taxable, there is no tax consequence of this transfer. The second trust can be considered to be the transfer of assets from the first spouse to a second legal entity (i.e., the trust), which is exempt from estate tax consequences up to the amount of the unified tax credit ($600,000). When the second spouse dies, the only asset in his or her name is the $600,000 in Trust No. 1, which the second spouse's unified tax credit exempts.

Beyond the straight tax planning, your clients can also use these trusts to exercise a large degree of control over how much discretion the second spouse is to have with the marital assets. This becomes especially important in situations in which a business owner remarries but yet wants the children of his or her first marriage to receive the bulk of his or her assets.

Depending upon how the trusts are drafted, the surviving spouse can have either a maximum or minimum amount of discretion, as Table 10-2 illustrates. As the table shows, there can be quite a bit of difference in the results of establishing these trusts, depending upon how they are written.

Table 10-2

Maximum Control	Minimum Control
Marital Trust	
1. Spouse gets all income.	1. Spouse gets all income.
2. Spouse has unlimited access to the principal.	2. Spouse cannot touch the principal.
3. Spouse can leave assets to whomever spouse chooses.	3. Spouse cannot leave assets to anyone except those beneficiaries that the owner specifies.

Family Trust

1. Spouse receives all income.	1. Children receive all income.
2. Spouse receives $5,000 or 5% of trust principal per year, whichever is greater.	2. Spouse has no rights to principal.
3. Spouse can leave assets to select beneficiaries.	3. Spouse has no right to select beneficiaries.

A lot of thought must be given to how the assets of estates that are smaller than $1,200,000 are to be divided between the two trusts. Spouses have certain rights (which vary on a state by state basis) and you cannot allow your clients to attempt to give them nothing. The spouse will quickly take the trust to court and have it overturned.

Likewise, for estates that are larger than $1,200,000 there is a multitude of ways to reduce (yet not completely eliminate) estate taxes. These options are beyond the scope of this text but can be found in any recently published textbook on trusts and estate planning.

The degree of success you have in marketing trust and custodial services will largely depend on the level of service that your trust company provides to both you and your clients. You will therefore want to select the firm you use very carefully. Also, because working with a number of different trust companies can be confusing, it's often best to select one company and then concentrate your efforts on developing a good working relationship with that company. In the trust game, loyalty begets loyalty. Some of the many you should consider as you look for a trust company follow.

1. Is the trust company set up to hold the entire range of assets that your clients may have? One of the key points that you can use to sell your clients on using a custodian is that they can have their financial assets, hard assets (gold, silver, gems, etc.) and collectibles (artwork, antiques, etc.) all in one account. This makes record keeping extraordinarily easy for the client and the client's heirs when the client dies. (I know of one trust company that is storing a three-foot-high jade Buddha in its vault for a client).

2. What type of statement does the company generate? Is it clear, concise, and comprehensive? The company should be able to accurately value thinly traded bonds as well as units of publicly offered limited partnerships. Each statement should have up-to-the-minute tax information to assist you and your client in planning the clients' future investment and tax strategies. An end-of-year statement that provides the client and/or the client's accountant with a summary of the information necessary to complete the client's returns is a big plus, too.

Look for a trust company that allows only one broker of record per account. This will prevent a broker who does an occasional trade with your client from receiving a complete listing of your client's holdings. This policy also serves to prevent your old firm from obtaining a listing of your client's holdings if you should move to another firm.

3. The trust company should also offer a variety of prototype trust

documents for a nominal cost. You can frequently bill the client $250 to $500 for providing a document that his or her attorney will need only to review as opposed to drafting from scratch. (Assuming, of course, that the client is not a referral from an attorney!)

3. The trust company should offer some form of training designed to acquaint you with the many types of trusts and custodial accounts that are available and how they can be used to solve a variety of your clients' financial problems and to achieve your clients' financial objectives. This training program can take the form of a series of seminars, some one-on-one time with a qualified trust officer, or some study material.

4. The adoption agreements and forms should be easy to understand and to complete. Because of time and distance constraints, you may often find yourself doing business through the mails and over the phone. If your clients can't understand how to complete the paperwork on their own, the paperwork is probably not going to get completed.

5. The trust company should offer sales and promotional materials that are both attractive and timely. A well-prepared brochure on the benefits of establishing the various types of trusts can be a great help to you when you are presenting trusts to clients and prospective clients.

6. If you do not want to make the day-to-day investment decisions for your clients yourself, you may want to find a trust company that offers in-house asset management. The key ingredient to look for in a trust manager is consistent performance. Most of the money that clients put into trust accounts is ''serious money,'' meaning that the client is not willing to risk large losses to pursue go-go returns.

Or you might decide to refer clients to independent money managers who would in turn make the day-to-day investment decisions. Operationally, the investment manager would tell the trust company what to buy or sell, and the trust company in turn would place the order through you. However, it's often better to use in-house management if you can find he right company. The reason is that if the assets are managed in-house and the investment performance is successful, the client will be favorably inclined to let the trust company continue to manage the assets after his or her death, keeping your commission stream alive after your client dies.

7. The responsiveness of the staff personnel of the trust company is another important consideration. There are two kinds of people: those who will tell you why something can't be done and those who will find a way to do it. It's not hard to determine how responsive a trust company is going to be. Is the person who answers the phone helpful? When you request literature, does it go out to you the same day? If a company's staff provides lousy service before you even start doing business with them, don't expect any better after you start dealing with them.

Some trust companies have both operational procedures and a corporate culture that facilitates working with brokers whereas others simply do not. Ask if the company has a broker hotline, a problem resolution officer, a broker liaison department, and so on.

8. Select a company that is financially sound. Most trust companies are, but it's always a good idea to review carefully the past 10 years of financials to check for any signs of a weakening financial trend.

9. The company's fee structure is also important. Everyone needs to make a living, but if the company's fees are too high, marketing its services can be difficult. Some trust companies charge a flat fee; others charge a percentage of assets. The fee structure that is better for you and your clients depends largely on the average size of your clients' portfolios.

Find out whether or not the company is willing to share its fee with you (fee splitting). Some companies will split their fees with you so long as the split is fully disclosed to the client.

10. One of the most important considerations is the availability of marketing support from the trust company. Does the company have a preapproved seminar script complete with slides, printed invitations, and the like? Is the staff available for joint seminar programs? Are staff members available on short notice for a one-on-one meeting with a prospective client, and are they willing to meet with you and your prospect at either your location or your prospect's location? Some trust companies insist that both you and your prospect come to their location for a one-on-one meeting. Will the company provide your clients with a monthly or quarterly newsletter to inform them of the latest developments in the area of trusts and tax planning?

11. Do the trust company's officers have that rare combination of in-depth technical knowledge and salesmanship? Nothing will turn off your prospects faster than exposing them to an incompetent backslapper or to someone who can talk only in technical jargon. Does the company have a high rate of employee turnover? Constantly reestablishing rapport with new trust officers is time-consuming.

12. Is the firm willing to fight within its industry? If you are going to try to take business from other trust companies, you are going to need support from the company with which you are working. Do they have the stomach for a fight, or will they back off if they get a hostile phone call from a competitor?

13. Is there any possibility of receiving additional business from the trust company after you generate a significant amount of business for them? Every trust company has accounts that were referred in by lawyers or generated solely by the trust company's in-house sales force. The trades that are generated by these accounts have to be run through someone. What is the trust company's policy concerning running "leverage trades" through brokers that refer business to it?

14. Finally, consider whether the trust company is likely to become your future competitor. If, for example, you elect to work with a bank trust department, there's always a risk that at some point in the future they will try to cut you out, especially if you stop bringing them new business. If you believe in the saying, "better safe than sorry," you might want to stick with trust companies that aren't affiliated with banks and other financial institutions.

As the financial services business becomes more competitive, it's important to exploit fully every potential advantage. Being familiar with trusts, custodial accounts, and trust companies is a big advantage.

Index